Choosing Love

Choosing Love

What LGBTQ+ Christians Can Teach Us All About Relationships, Inclusion, and Justice

DAWNE MOON

AND

THERESA W. TOBIN

Oxford University Press is a department of the University of Oxford.
It furthers the University's objective of excellence in research, scholarship,
and education by publishing worldwide. Oxford is a registered trade mark of
Oxford University Press in the UK and certain other countries.

Published in the United States of America by Oxford University Press
198 Madison Avenue, New York, NY 10016, United States of America.

© Dawne Moon and Theresa W. Tobin 2025

All rights reserved. No part of this publication may be reproduced, stored in a retrieval system, transmitted, used for text and data mining, or used for training artificial intelligence, in any form or by any means, without the prior permission in writing of Oxford University Press, or as expressly permitted by law, by license or under terms agreed with the appropriate reprographics rights organization. Inquiries concerning reproduction outside the scope of the above should be sent to the Rights Department, Oxford University Press, at the address above.

You must not circulate this work in any other form
and you must impose this same condition on any acquirer

CIP data is on file at the Library of Congress

ISBN 978-0-19-777651-3

DOI: 10.1093/oso/9780197776513.001.0001

Printed by Sheridan Books, Inc., United States of America

CONTENTS

Preface vii

Introduction 1

1. Love and Relationships 17
2. The Complementarian Commandment 27
3. A Sacrament of Shame: "I Love You, but Hate Your Sin" 54
4. How Relationships Can Heal Toxic Shame 84
5. Becoming an Ally 111
6. Inside and Outside the Evangelical Bubble: Productive and Destructive Tension 137
7. Love, Shame, Humility, and Justice 161

Acknowledgments 179
Methods 183
Notes 189
References 201
Index 217

PREFACE

This is a book about love, and what it means to say that human beings are relational creatures.

For two years, we participated in The Marin Foundation's biweekly Living in the Tension discussions. The group's mission was to help LGBTQ+ and heterosexual conservative Christians engage in difficult conversations around faith and sexuality in a spirit of empathy. At the Living in the Tension discussions, Christians and a couple of non-Christians, LGBTQ+, and cisgender/heterosexual people listened to each other's perspectives to learn from each other, with no one feeling pressured to convert or convince anyone else. Dawne Moon, now firmly secular, had grown up going to church, but it was among LGBTQ+ conservative Christians and their allies at The Marin Foundation that Christian love first actually felt to her like *love*. This love buoyed her spirits and inspired her to be more gracious, more forgiving, better at sharing what she had, and more mindful of the effects of her actions on others.

Jack, a pastor in a small, fundamentalist denomination, had shared with Dawne a story he had learned about doing missionary work. Some American sheep farmers were visiting similar ranches in Australia and noticed the lack of fences.[1] "How do you keep your sheep from wandering off?" they asked.

"You Americans keep your sheep by building fences," was the reply, "but here, we build wells."

If the church's goal is to draw people in, Jack seemed to be saying, it must provide what they need and not worry about keeping some in and others out.

"The church isn't supposed to be a private club," Dawne often heard people say at these gatherings. "We are supposed to be Christ's ambassadors of love to the world."

That's why she was so shocked as she sat across the table from Margo. They were having lunch at an otherwise empty, touristy fajita restaurant in Atlanta, where five two-tops had been pushed together to form a long table for ten of the participants in The Reformation Project's training conference. Margo was the supportive straight/cisgender mom of a conservative Christian gay man. She was white and carried herself with maternal authority, although she probably wasn't quite old enough to be Dawne's mother. Margo very expertly asked Dawne question after question about herself: "Where are you from?" "Where did you go to school?" "Where do you work?" "Are you married?" It all made her feel a little like a forty-five-year-old child, but also like she might just be interesting. As they talked about raising kids—Margo's are grown while Dawne's was five—Margo said, "It takes a lot of prayer to know how to make the right decisions when it comes to raising kids."

"Well," Dawne replied, "to be honest, my partner and I don't even have that. I left the church in the '80s, right around the time I came out as queer."

Margo's face instantly changed. She leaned across the table, placed her hand on Dawne's paper placemat, and urgently said, "I need you to give Jesus another chance. I am certain that he and God care about you and love you, your partner, and your child."

In that moment, Dawne felt like a *thing* that Margo felt an intense need to collect for God, a soul she badly needed to reap. She knew that Margo had a loving intention; after all, Margo was convinced that God loved Dawne's little queer family just as they all were. Still, as the conversation abruptly shifted, Dawne felt like an *it*. In his book *I and Thou*, the early twentieth-century philosopher Martin Buber distinguished two kinds of interactions: *I–you* intimate *relationships* and *I–it* objectifying *experiences*.

I–it interactions are the means to an end. They are necessary and take up a lot of our lives: asking your mom where your keys are or asking a teacher for help understanding an assignment may be *I–it* experiences, and there's nothing wrong with that. We need those. Ideally, we also engage in what he called *relationship*. In a relationship, Buber says, I am open to being transformed by my connection with you (in German, the intimate *du*). Ego—what he calls the "armor" we wear in everyday life—falls away and I am open to being "touched at the core," transformed by our connection.

Martin Luther King Jr.'s understanding of love was inspired, in part, by Buber. A lot of people have been inspired by Buber. According to Buber, love is about relationships. When *I* approach *you* in the attitude of relating, I listen to you and learn from you. When you tell me your story, I hear you and feel some of what you feel. Rather than as a clearly bounded ego, I approach you with openness to *you*, and in our connection I understand more and better—I grow. As soon as someone starts thinking in terms of a means to an end, what could have been a mutual relationship is transformed into a situation in which one becomes an object to the other, someone not to learn from, but to do something *to* or *with*.[2] Love, a radically equalizing responsibility and connection to another, emerges from relational connection.

Fear is one thing that can disrupt a love relationship and make it harmful. Echoing Buber, Paolo Freire offered in *Pedagogy of the Oppressed* that "Because love is an act of courage, not of fear, love is a commitment to others [and] the cause of liberation."[3] Later on, we'll talk about the connections we've seen between love and liberation. Here, what is striking is the fear. Margo's instant shift gave Dawne the impression that she was *afraid* for what would happen if Dawne didn't "give God another chance."

Doing the research we have done from 2013 to 2023, in the overlap of sociology and philosophy, faith and justice, we have seen the profound potential that comes from real relationships entered into wholeheartedly and with humility. Who would have thought that LGBTQ+ Christians would have something to teach straight/cisgender conservative Christians? Who would have thought that conservative Christians would have something to teach secular LGBTQ+ activists? When we listen to what others have to say, when we hear the wisdom that comes from their perspective, we might not come away agreeing with them 100 percent, but by hearing them, we learn more about the world. Our own tiny perspectives become a little less tiny.

At that downtown restaurant in Atlanta, Dawne felt like Margo had switched from trying to have a little moment of relating to her over their tourist-friendly fajitas to seeing her as an object of conquest, a potential notch on her Bible-case. Margo meant well, but in Buber's words, a *purpose* had intervened. In the moment, Dawne felt like Margo closed off to her and to learning from *her* about what it had been like for her to go to church as a young person and why she stopped. When she mentioned the interaction to a group of people later at the conference, Mike—a young gay man whose Christian friends all stopped talking to him when he came out—replied, "How could someone who is *here* not understand why a queer person would leave the church?"

Talking about the incident later back home at Chicago's Center for Inclusivity,[4] Dawne learned that Margo was enacting a particular conservative Christian style of evangelism. Participants recounted the ways they had been taught to engage with non-Christians: quickly "establishing relationship" with personal questions so that you have a chance to let them know about Christ's love before the moment passes; always thinking of yourself as potentially "the closest that person will ever get to Jesus," being terrified of the huge responsibility non-Christians posed: if you don't save their soul, they—and maybe you!—might spend eternity in Hell. That means of questioning secures control over the conversation, with a clear purpose in mind—to prevent what you most fear, an eternity in Hell for them and maybe even *yourself*. In this version of evangelism, love is conditional. And from the outside, it doesn't seem much like love at all to say that God loves you so much he might just have to torture you forever and ever.

Buber's framework helps us to understand these dynamics. He pointed out that "relationship" isn't established in a barrage of questions. Love is experienced in connection, not in control. If I am trying to control or manipulate you, I am treating you as an object. If we are in what he called "relationship," that means I can learn and grow by virtue of relating to you.

* * *

This is also a book about the radical potential of love in movements for social justice. At the 2016 conference of the Gay Christian Network (GCN), the Reverend Allyson Robinson, possibly the first openly transgender person ordained by a Baptist Church, gave a keynote address that echoed King's and James Baldwin's insistence on the importance of love for ending cycles of oppression and domination. Robinson spoke in the wake of the Supreme Court's 2015 *Obergefell* decision legalizing same-sex marriage, a time when it seemed that if there was any such thing as a "culture war," LGBTQ+ people and their allies were winning. Acknowledging the temptation following this political victory to vilify those who dissented, Robinson ended her talk by entreating her audience to bring humility and love to public disagreements, saying:

> We LGBT people know what it's like to have others read "love your enemies," . . . and to try and put it into practice, and to get it all wrong . . . . Here . . . is our chance to get it right. It begins, I think, with . . . loving the people with whom we disagree, not as our enemies, but as human beings whom God loves and for whom Christ died.
>
> I believe that if we can live together in this way, if we can live out this humbleness, this mercifulness toward our enemies, if we can devote ourselves to a justice that includes freedom of conscience for everyone, and a harmony that does not demand homogeneity, then we ourselves will be blessed. . . . It won't be easy. Especially for us culture warriors. But we must try. And it must begin with us.

It wasn't just keynote speakers at GCN calling for this kind of radical love. In an icebreaker session, Theresa was paired with Aaron, a gay man from a non-affirming church who was sitting next to her. Aaron shared, with a big smile, that he had just successfully helped his church move the first openly gay person into a leadership ministry position. Theresa asked him how he led this transition. He said the work was slow and indirect, getting people to know LGBT church members in small group settings to break down stereotypes and build trust.

Aaron emphasized that it was important to extend grace and mercy to church members who opposed him, recognizing that their "certainty walls" are still up and recalling how hard it was for him to knock down his own certainty walls. He was patient with people because he knows "how scary it is when those walls begin to crumble." Loving your enemies is no guarantee that they will change. Still, at this GCN conference, Theresa was learning about tiny revolutions of love happening slowly in local church communities led by LGBTQ+ people refusing to accept dehumanization and to give up on the possibility that those who exclude and marginalize them can do better.

Witnessing LGBTQ+ person after person in this movement enact the kind of love King and Baldwin were talking about had a profound effect on Theresa. For most of her youth, Theresa had been on the other side of the culture wars, complicit in her church's persecution of LGBTQ+ people. Her Catholic upbringing taught her that God was all-loving and forgiving and planted seeds of compassion and care for those who suffer on the margins of society. But this same Catholic upbringing also taught her, and she internalized, that LGBTQ+ people (or, as they would say, "those who choose a homosexual lifestyle") were uniquely sinful, dangerous even, and that she should avoid them as potentially threatening to her own virtue. LGBTQ+ people were often scapegoated, along with so-called loose women, as being responsible for sinfulness. Theresa did not know any openly LGBTQ+ people or have any LGBTQ+ friends until she was in graduate school in her early twenties. She knew some girls in her high school who later came out, but they likely did not feel safe or comfortable around her or sharing who they were with her. She was taught that loving God and being good meant not loving them; indeed, that they were "the enemy."

In the early 2000s, while in graduate school, Theresa came to her own consciousness about the harms of internalized gender-based shame her church upbringing instilled in her through purity culture, and her complicity in perpetuating this dynamic toward LGBTQ+ people. She was also reeling with anger from experiences of betrayal and hypocrisy by Catholic church leaders who often blamed women and gays for sexual sinfulness while so many in their ranks were sexually abusing children and covering it up. When she started this research with Dawne in 2014, Theresa's faith in God remained strong, but she felt like she no longer had a trustworthy community to nurture her faith. Sitting in that GCN conference surrounded by thousands of LGBTQ+ Christians and their allies, and now counting herself among those striving to be allies, she listened to Robinson and others proclaim their commitment to love those who hated them—to love those who resemble the person Theresa used to be—as the only hope for lasting justice and thriving for all. The message brought Theresa to tears and, over time, learning from this community has renewed her faith and transformed her approach to social justice, including her work to make her own faith community more just and loving. Following their example, she, too, is trying to foster tiny revolutions of love in her family and local communities. The LGBTQ+ people Theresa was taught to hate are teaching her lessons in radical love that she is passing on to her own children to break intergenerational cycles of gender-based religious shaming.

Theresa now finds herself among social justice advocates striving to be in solidarity with LGBTQ+ people. Her church upbringing planted seeds of social justice, but also taught her to shun her enemies and she is still tempted to do that, now seeing "the enemy" as those who actively uphold systems of oppression. Those early church lessons in building fences to keep people out are hard to shake. She is learning from LGBTQ+ people in this movement to build wells, to love others and draw them toward justice. She has realized that to "love your enemies" is not to accept their abuse or to remain complicit in their abuse of others but to being unwilling to give up on their humanity. It is to refuse to dehumanize them so that cycles of abusive power might be broken, and right relationships reimagined and forged.

Introduction

Sandra moved[1] around a lot as a military kid. She got adept at fitting in—by hiding parts of herself. When her family lived in Michigan, she was one of just a few Black kids in the area. She endured demeaning questions from white children—"Why is your butt like that?"—and tried to walk differently to fit in.[2] When she moved to South Carolina and was called "teacher's pet," she asked the teacher not to give her special jobs so that she would fit in.

But she never hid her Christianity. Speaking to the Leadership Development Cohort of The Reformation Project—a Christian group that promotes LGBTQ+ inclusion—she remarked, "When I was a teenager, I was so consistent in hanging out with God on a daily basis that my adult bible study leader asked me to hold *her* accountable. I was *into* it." As a lesbian, speaking to an audience of LGBTQ+ people and allies, most of them Christian, she remarked on the ironies of being told that church is for healing and wholeness, but that her own wholeness wasn't welcome. "Being asked to fit to the image of the white, Western, evangelical world—that minimized my gender, that ignores my Blackness, and rejects my sexuality. That is an act of violence." Speaking hypothetically to the people in the ministries she had been part of, she continued, "You want to experience the gifts that God has given me, but you don't want to see *me*. And that is a problem."

Sandra is hardly alone. In the years that we have been working on this book, we heard these sentiments over and over from LGBTQ+

conservative Protestants: that professing your Christian love for someone while asking them to hide, eliminate, or downplay parts of who they are doesn't feel much *to them* like being loved. What is true for so many LGBTQ+ conservative Christians is more often articulated among Black people, Indigenous people, and people of color (BIPOC) because their experiences make it more visible. Their experiences also make visible how race, gender, sexuality, and the like cannot be separated from peoples' experiences of religious community.

Sandra and many in her audience embrace what might seem to outsiders like a peculiar combination of identities: both LGBTQ+ and conservative Protestant. Some are conservative Christians who are attracted to people of their same sex, or for whom another person's sex is not what determined whether they were attractive or not. Some are conservative Christians who know in their hearts, guts, and minds that their gender identity is not what others see when they look at them. Some leave their churches. Not all of them want to—or think they should have to. As the old LGBTQ+ slogan goes, "We're everywhere"—including in conservative churches.

A lot of people—on both the political left and right—see "gay" and "Christian" as clear opposites. When LGBTQ+ people are open about their gender and sexual identities, or even when people are open about having been born intersex, we often assume they must say goodbye to the religions they grew up with, perhaps especially if they are conservative Christians.[3] There's a reason for this. For many LGBTQ+ people, Christians have been their personal tormenters and the drivers of hostile laws. The news seems to overflow with stories of people claiming that their religious beliefs entitle them to discriminate against LGBTQ+ people. On a more personal level, many LGBTQ+ kids have experienced abuse—physical, mental, emotional—at the hands of their conservative Christian families or have been sent away to be "cured." Often, they have been shunned. Sometimes their parents just put their stuff out on the curb and changed the locks.[4]

Having love withdrawn like that is traumatic, especially so when it is withdrawn by the most important people in your life, all at once. And even more so when the people you love tell you that your capacity to love *anyone* is damaged and dangerous. LGBTQ+ conservative Christians have formed groups like The Reformation Project, the Gay Christian Network (now Q Christian Fellowship), and CenterPeace to both provide refuge for LGBTQ+ conservative Christians and to encourage churches to be less hostile and more loving. Groups like The Marin Foundation, Love Boldly, and Canyonwalkers have been founded by cisgender, heterosexual allies to provide safe havens for LGBTQ+ and straight/cisgender Christians to discuss how they can affirm LGBTQ+ people without turning their backs on everything they know and love. Although these groups all see their mission as supporting LGBTQ+ and allied Christians and improving church environments for LGBTQ+ people, their impact is far broader. From their struggles, they offer lessons that can help us all create more just communities and loving relationships.

* * *

LGBTQ+ conservative Christians defy conventional boundaries, which can make them seem suspect. To a lot of progressives, liberals, and secular LGBTQ+ people, LGBTQ+ evangelical and fundamentalist Protestants are not just delusional to think they could stay in their churches, but in bed with the enemy. Meanwhile, many conservative Christians think it's literally not possible to be LGBTQ+ if you truly love Jesus.

But LGBTQ+ conservative Christians exist, and they do sometimes stay in their communities.[5] Many find that their faith motivates them to work for systemic social justice. They navigate questions of identity that can be quite literally life-or-death. Often, just to be able to exist, they are forced to articulate what Christianity means to them and how their churches and families have failed them, as well as what being LGBTQ+ means to them and how LGBTQ+ communities could be more supportive. In doing so, they have developed insights that can help *all* of us with clearer understandings of the toxic dynamics of shame, as well as the connections among love, pride, humility, and justice.

In our time observing and interviewing the people we met through organizations in this loose network of conservative Christian pro-LGBTQ+ groups, we have learned more than just facts about LGBTQ+ evangelicals.

We've learned about the paradoxical dynamics, particularly for people of color, that make conservative Christian shame about gender and sexuality so toxic. From people who have shared heart-wrenching stories of friends, family, and pastors who turned against them, we have learned how profoundly harmful it is to deny a person mutual connection in which people learn from each other and grow. Their experiences show us what it means to say human beings are social creatures, how profoundly we need connection with others. We learned about humility, and how it can't be separated from healthy pride. We saw how people can disagree without dehumanizing each other. We learned about love, and how crucial it is in movements for justice—a point long emphasized by movements for justice led by Black, Indigenous, and people of color—and why if you love someone you really can't tolerate them being treated unjustly. We've seen just how impossible it is to fully disentangle intimate relationships and systemic oppression, personal emotions and liberation. We have learned how to be better allies to people who are oppressed in ways that we are not.

A lot of people have things to say about shame, pride, humility, love, and justice. There are whole academic disciplines (including our own) dedicated to exploring the idea that human beings are fundamentally social beings. The LGBTQ+ Christians we've learned from affirm some long-standing ideas about these themes, but they also offer new insights precisely because they occupy intersections most people think are impossible. They have a unique vantage point in our society.

* * *

The stories of conservative Protestant LGBTQ+ people aren't the stories of some silent majority.[6] Their numbers are relatively small. But their unusual perspective gives them profound insights that can benefit others in the same position, and the rest of us as well—LGBTQ+ people who aren't conservative Christians, conservative Christians who aren't LGBTQ+, and the many people who are neither. These perspectives and the insights about love and justice that we can learn from listening to LGBTQ+ Christians become visible when we think about the Black feminist concept of *intersectionality*.

Black feminists and other feminists of color have shown in countless ways that where you are in the intersections of power affects what you can see about injustice and how to eliminate it.⁷ Patricia Hill Collins has pointed out that it's easier to see the dynamics of social power from a marginal position than from thoroughly within their midst. Similarly, by coining the term "intersectionality," legal scholar Kimberlé Crenshaw emphasized that each of us is always fully who we are; we aren't our gender on Monday and our race on Tuesday. Men have a gender, and white people have a race. There is no "neutral human." It's been hard for white feminists, male civil rights organizers, and white men to wrap their heads around this insight: Remedies designed with the needs of Black men or white women (or white LGBTQ+ people) in mind fail to help Black women (or Black LGBTQ+ people, or other women and LGBTQ+ people of color) and often reproduce the very injustices they are trying to remedy. This insight remains true for all the intersecting vectors of identity that our society uses to discriminate.

Some feminists and queer theorists of color have argued that centering the experiences of those who are most marginalized is a more effective way to improve conditions for those who are oppressed, including those who are also oppressed in fewer or more straightforward ways.⁸ This is also why we have tried to center the experiences of LGBTQ+ Christians of color in this book. In a country where sexuality and gender have been tied up in understandings of race since before the first colonizers landed in this hemisphere, there's just no way to promote justice on the basis of sexuality while ignoring gender and race.

If it's hard to picture having both a race and a gender at the same time, now picture people who occupy intersections that a lot of us think of as *impossible*, who occupy categories often defined as mutually exclusive.⁹ People who are *both*—Black and white, Jewish and Christian, male and female—occupy particularly active intersections, more like a chemical compound than a crossroads. Being both/and may feel endlessly frustrating. There is so much that is glaringly obvious to you that others just don't see. They constantly demand explanations that fit into their worldview and categories: "What are you?" "Can you even exist?" "Are you really who you say you are?" People who are mixed-race get those questions all the time, and from even more directions. Bi-, ambi-, and pansexuals—people who "fall in love with a person, not a gender"—are constantly told they can't and don't exist, that *everyone's* attractions are *really* structured by a binary conception of gender. Some intersex people, those born with bodies that don't fit into typical categories of male *or* female, have since the 1950s been surgically modified, starting in infancy, just to preserve the myth that a person *can't* be both, or neither. Trans and nonbinary people, too, are told they can't exist and made to prove they are who they say they are again and again. It's hard for us to imagine how someone who is mixed-race, disabled, intersex, bi+, *and* trans can get anything done while constantly being asked to provide proof that they exist.

Think about how impossible it seems to be both LGBTQ+ and a conservative Christian, an evangelical, a fundamentalist. Add to that being a person of color and/or a person with a disability. People who occupy those small but explosive intersections are in positions to distill crucial insights about love and relationships—things that are important not just to LGBTQ+ people, Christians, and people of color, but to pretty much *everyone*. These are things a lot of us can take for granted because they're not as visible in our lives. Because no one makes them a problem. Many of us who don't live on that burning line might take for granted the relationships that allow us to live every day.[10]

And if we take them for granted, our own relationships can suffer. The stories of LGBTQ+ Christians are important in their own right, and they make clear just how terrible are the consequences of severing a relationship with someone just because of who they are. At the same time, the LGBTQ+ and allied conservative Christians we've listened to and observed give us a clearer picture of what it means for human beings to be relational creatures, how to repair or foster connection, and the centrality of love to justice and human thriving. In a time that seems fraught with divisive political discourse, increased racial animus, isolation and disconnection, fear and anger, LGBTQ+ Christians and their allies provide insights about how to create a more just and loving world—a world that is actually *livable* for more people.

It's not that Christians have a monopoly on insights into these matters—most religions and traditions have wisdom to share about the importance of loving others. What we are saying is that LGBTQ+ conservative Christians' unique standpoints give them powerful insights that are relevant beyond their own social group and that are lessons for a way forward. Those closest to the problem are closest to the solutions. Their lives are the terrain on which the US "culture wars" are being fought. The divide between the sides isn't some vast chasm, but a burning, bubbling line where people who are both LGBTQ+ and conservative Christian live in a world that tells them from every direction that they can't exist. That their existence is *wrong*.

* * *

In communities of color, the love of home and church can often provide a refuge from the grinding racism of daily life and offer support in surviving white-dominated culture and institutions.[11] Some BIPOC individuals told us that the existence of LGBTQ+ people in some communities of color can seem like a betrayal, like proof that the stereotype is correct and people of their race really are sexual deviants. To some it seems literally demonic. If you haven't lived it, imagine being part of such a church community and realizing you're LGBTQ+. Its love and refuge would start to feel conditional, and yet leaving might feel like being set adrift. Being fully out might feel like bringing trouble to people you know have suffered enough already, even if they would accept you. Naively mentioning being gay might lead to extreme efforts to cure you or to total rejection. LGBTQ+-affirming churches in these traditions exist, but not everywhere. Liberal, predominantly white churches can be white-centered and racist. A lot of LGBTQ+ Christians of color must just try to find some kind of balance they can live with.

Many predominantly white conservative churches promote the notion that they are God's army in the so-called culture wars. Sociologists have found that roughly 80 percent of white evangelicals are either somewhat or fully immersed in White Christian Nationalism, a worldview that correlates strongly with seeing "homosexuality" and "gender ideology," along with antiracism and immigration, as existential threats and sees defeating them as a sacred mission.[12] Other predominantly white churches aren't so militant, but might still see "homosexuality" as an unforgivable sin, a sign that someone is in league with the Devil.

Now, if you haven't lived it, imagine realizing you're LGBTQ+ in one of these churches. Most LGBTQ+ Christians aren't trying to fight a war at all; they're just trying to go on living while people tell them from all sides that they shouldn't exist. That intersection can be a site of pain and trauma where people who claim to love them often cut them off from not just romantic relationships, but *any* relationship. The fact that loved ones can do this even while they think they're being loving and supportive makes that dynamic even more toxic and confusing. In a 2016 open letter to his church, a white, queer Christian named Brandan Robertson wrote about the "side glares" and hateful email he got once he came out publicly. He found it ironic that being honest about who he was had brought him closer to God than ever before, but the people who had previously called him "anointed of God" now called him "repugnant."[13]

This point of seeming impossibility in which LGBTQ+ Christians live their lives is also a site of resilience, courage, and creativity. Some LGBTQ+ people of all races vulnerably share their stories, over and over, with potentially hostile people who believe cruel and harmful stereotypes. It takes courage and energy to patiently explain how you know you're a woman, or that sex is no more or less important to gay people than it is to heterosexuals, that being gay isn't "white people's disease"— and that work is most effective when it happens in the context of an existing relationship. Some church members have been changed by those stories, or by seeing the goodness in those LGBTQ+ people who stayed with them despite how exhausting it could be. In the United States, politics and much of civic life are shaped by a sizable voting bloc of Christians of all races who see LGBTQ+ people as sick, sinful, and dangerous. When LGBTQ+ Christians get their churches to change their policies or get their loved ones to see LGBTQ+ people as *people*, their work can have far-ranging and unpredictable ripple effects. They help change the minds of people who vote, who sit on school boards, and who decide how they'll treat people in their workplaces and neighborhoods. Their vulnerability and honesty can inspire others to treat LGBTQ+ people as human rather than monstrous in personal interactions and the institutional decisions they make.

To people who aren't conservative Christians, it might seem like LGBTQ+ Christians' lives would be better if they just stopped being part of a religion that oppresses them, and maybe just went out for brunch on Sunday instead. Have a couple of mimosas. Many do leave. But to some, that can sound like being told to stop being who they are or to cut themselves off from God, whom they see as the source of life—which isn't any more loving or less ignorant when it's coming from secular LGBTQ+ people and allies than it is when it's coming from a homophobic and transphobic pastor. In both cases, people are invalidating who they are rather than being in a relationship with them and learning from them about what they can see from their unique perspective. Actually listening to them is a way to treat them justly and to learn from their experience.

* * *

Sandra's audience, The Reformation Project's (TRP) Leadership Development Cohort, had devoted months to rigorous Bible study to debunk claims that the Bible condemns gay people and same-sex marriage. Addressing this group, Sandra affirmed the importance of the work they would do to try to change their churches' harmful teachings and policies about LGBTQ+ people. She appreciated their resistance to toxic church messages, saying, "You're really pushing this notion that Jesus is saying 'Love your neighbor as yourself,' while some communities that don't allow us to exist as who we are, are saying 'Love your neighbor, hate yourself.'" For Sandra, and many involved with TRP and similar groups, when Christians don't accept LGBTQ+ people as they are, they're missing the mark as Christians, they're failing at Christian love, and they can do better.

"Love is the answer" is a cliché because the truth of that statement is overpowered by the many and ubiquitous ways people get it wrong, acting as if love just means to "be nice," or to just say "I love everyone!" To those harmed by systemic oppression, such attempts often don't even feel nice, much less feel like actual love. Listening to the people engaged in this movement, we have seen again and again that love without justice isn't really love. We have also learned that justice without love isn't really justice because you can't promote justice for people you don't see as your equal and aren't open to learning from.

Being open to learning about how our own lives are implicated in others' struggles—and acting to alleviate those struggles—this kind of love has the potential to help us to create a world where everyone can thrive. People who are truly guided by love can steadfastly refuse to accept dehumanization, leading them to remake social institutions and cultural assumptions that produce many of the toxic outcomes we see around us. Some LGBTQ+ Christians articulate, and many enact, a politics based on radical love that just might offer a way to a better future.

* * *

The groups we have observed—The Marin Foundation (TMF), TRP, the Gay Christian Network (GCN; later, Q Christian Fellowship), and the Center for Inclusivity (CFI)—all existed to help LGBTQ+ conservative Christians to navigate life and to help their cisgender, heterosexual friends, family, pastors, and churches better to understand LGBTQ+ people and learn to love them better. We spent more than five hundred hours at these groups' conferences, workshops, and discussion groups, and interviewed numerous participants (see the appendix on methods for more details). We heard a lot of powerful stories that really showed us the transformative power of love, and just how damaging it can be to have that love withdrawn.

The stories of LGBTQ+ conservative Christians and their allies make very clear the destructive power that is unleashed when people fail to relate to others with love and treat them instead as objects or problems. We have heard testimony from many people—including some cisgender heterosexuals—who saw how their church's teachings were harming the people they purported to love, and who decided to look twice at what the Bible really taught about gender, sexuality, and love. We heard from a Tennessee megachurch pastor whose church shrank from two thousand members to a few hundred when he chose to love and accept a six-year-old trans kid who attended his church and to make that church a safe place. And we spoke to a number of other pastors who lost their jobs or their denominational credentials when they chose to follow the path of love to a place of affirming LGBTQ+ people in their families or congregations. We talked to parents and clergy who practiced humility; were open to the possibility that their assumptions were wrong; and who opened themselves to new information about the Bible, God, and the sexual orientations and gender identities they had always assumed were dysfunctional, if not monstrous and evil. We heard from people who believed that their "traditional" approach to "homosexuals" would protect them from hell, until they saw the hell they put their own kids through. And we heard from white, cisgender gay people whose experiences of being asked to "tone down the gay" led them to look twice at what kind of friends they had been to people of color and to embrace social justice as Jesus's central message. When we think of humility, pride, love, and justice as inseparable, we work toward a world in which everyone can thrive.

* * *

A number of people have written about life at the overlap of LGBTQ+ experience and conservative Christianity in the United States, and there are way too many memoirs, studies, and other books out there to do justice to them all here.[14] We highly recommend these books for anyone interested in examples of how people have navigated these questions.

Scholars have written about a number of different aspects to the overlap of religion, gender, and sexuality. Some focus on the history, theological understandings, and everyday teachings of conservative churches, including how Black church communities have often tried to navigate the sexual stigmatization at the heart of racism in ways that compounded the stigmatization of their own LGBTQ+ (and women) members.[15] Others focus on the experiences and struggles of LGBTQ+ people of faith living in these contexts. There have been studies about how LGBTQ+ Christians struggle to reconcile seemingly conflicting religious and sexual/gender identities, including books and documentaries about "ex-gay" conversion therapy, its harmful effects, and its general inability to change people's sexual orientation or gender identity.[16]

Not all LGBTQ+ people of faith experience their religion and sexuality or gender identity as being in conflict.[17] Other scholars highlight the work people are doing to create change, either within their own churches and religious schools, or by creating new, more accepting ones. Jonathan Coley explores how groups of LGBTQ+ and allied students at Christian colleges and universities make the case for more inclusive policies. Jon Burrow-Branine focuses particularly on one of the same groups we do, TRP, exploring how participants cultivate understandings of evangelical faith and LGBTQ+ identities as coherent as they work to change the conservative church from within. Deborah Jian Lee explores the ways that some evangelicals are framing racial and gender justice and LGBTQ+ inclusion as fully coherent with the teachings of Jesus. Examining a progressive, predominantly LGBT church in Toronto, David Seitz finds that religion and sexuality come together particularly fruitfully—sparking all kinds of seeming paradoxes. We also find that, for instance, organizations that don't cut off communication with with "anti-gay" churches can end up helping those churches become more inclusive and welcoming than anyone thought possible, while organizations that strive to be sites of solidarity and radical welcome can end up silencing some of the very people they seek to empower.[18]

Many scholars have studied how people experience human connection and threat through emotions.[19] We look at the substance and effects of emotions not just in the experiences of suffering and salvation, but in everyday life and the relationships that LGBTQ+ Christians say give their life meaning. What many Christians call "the spirit" includes human beings' capacity to connect with the divine and other people, and that is through emotions. Emotions are actually both *personal* and *social* experiences, so they can shape and be shaped by social hierarchies—socially determined rankings of what is closer to God's ideal and what is farther away. They can motivate or inhibit political action as well.

We explore the significance of four emotions in the lives of LGBTQ+ Christians on the front lines of the culture wars: shame, humility, pride, and love. Scholars debate the definition and value of shame.[20] Our book illuminates a particularly toxic dynamic in which churches require LGBTQ+ people to display shame, an emotion that signals unworthiness of relationships, as the requirement for some semblance of a relationship. This paradox is unlivable for most. Through humility, pride, and love, LGBTQ+ Christians creatively navigate their way through this dynamic, revealing new insights about these emotions.

Scholars who think about humility often conceive of it in highly individualistic terms. In these accounts, humility means taking the appropriate attitude toward one's own limitations, flaws, or standing, an admission that "I could be wrong."[21] LGBTQ+ Christians show us how humility can be relational. In their lives, humility is often a stance they take to prioritize relationships over certainty. This opens them to new information and leads them to consider that what the Church has taught them about themselves and other LGBTQ+ people might be wrong. Scholars and non-scholars alike tend to think that humility is the opposite of pride, and conservative Christians define pride as hubris, the deadliest of deadly sins. Our book challenges both ideas. The work LGBTQ+ Christians must do to survive toxic shame and thrive reveals a type of pride that many of us take for granted and that is not the opposite of humility but is its counterpart. Relational pride is basic confidence in one's worthiness and it works with humility to ground love. LGBTQ+ Christians teach us that pride is the opposite of shame, not the opposite of humility.

Our book also extends scholarship and activist work on the power of love in movements for social justice. Love is difficult to define, easily misused and misunderstood, and hotly contested, especially when people say we should love those who harm us, which a lot of Christians say. Many Black feminists, civil rights activists, and queer thinkers of color have argued that love may be necessary for justice, and that justice without love is hollow and incomplete. We draw on the work of thinkers such as Audre Lorde, Patricia Hill Collins, bell hooks, June Jordan, Martin Luther King Jr., James Baldwin, and Grace Lee Boggs to explore the radical potential of love to propel people into political action that can feel spiritual.[22] LGBTQ+ Christians offer a model of political love that is not about being nice to people or accepting their mistreatment of you, but is an active choice not to dehumanize others even when they dehumanize you.

* * *

The stories of LGBTQ+ conservative Christians show just how deeply we depend upon mutual connections to learn and grow. The evidence of the social sciences convinces us that human beings are relational creatures whose lives are structured by institutions and culture, and society works best when institutions and culture grow and change by fostering relationships. In the way we're using the term "relationship," we don't mean every person we interact with, even regularly. A relationship is not the same as being related to someone or even necessarily knowing them really well. When we talk about relationships, we're talking about mutual connections in which people can care for and learn from each other, growing together. Connections that change you and become part of you. The connections that feel like when they end, something in you breaks.

We'll show the damage that can occur when people prioritize belief systems over relationships. Some worldviews demand that individuals conform to them and force others to do the same—and that can break people. What LGBTQ+ Christians and their allies have found, however, is that Jesus's teachings don't break people. Reading and loving the Bible doesn't break people. It's some of the cultural trappings of Christian life that break people—by breaking trust, as when a pastor urges the parents of a teenager to throw them out of the house because they're LGBTQ+. Conditional love can break people. And conservative Protestants aren't the only ones who use conditional love to shame and control people. People of any religion or no religion, conservative, liberal, or progressive, can do it, too. That's why we all have something to learn here.

We'll discuss how a particular construction of gender and sexuality and a belief system based on this construction have come to seem like a moral (even a divine) imperative to some conservative Christians, with the harmful effect of insisting that simply being LGBTQ+ is itself sinful. We'll describe the particularly toxic form of shame that falls upon many conservative Christians who discover themselves to be at odds with the gendered and sexualized demands of their community and its understanding of God. In these communities, putting ideology above relationships ends up making shame—a fear of being unworthy of mutual connection until you "fix" yourself—into the condition for belonging. In other words, "You only belong if you demonstrate the constant fear that you are unworthy of belonging." Pause on that for a moment. Living in that paradox is nearly impossible, and people in this movement show that trying to navigate it often has toxic or even deadly effects. As conservative Christians aren't the only ones who misuse shame in ways that diminish instead of repair relationships, what is highly visible in the experiences of LGBTQ+ conservative Christians can help the rest of us to learn how to avoid toxic shaming dynamics.

We'll explore the emotional antidotes to this toxic shame dynamic—humility and relational pride—both of which are anchored by relationships. We define humility as an openness to realistic information from others about your gifts and room for growth. We have found that humility, defined in this way, actually helps people restore relational pride, the confidence that they're worthy of love and connection. Both humility and relational pride help them to grow better at loving others. We'll explore the humility that it takes LGBTQ+ conservative Christians to recognize that their understanding of God and the Bible may have been wrong, and maybe God can love them just as they are. We'll share stories of how love compels some heterosexual/cisgender friends, pastors, and family to revisit the Bible to see how they have been projecting into it, like the white evangelical dad who resolved to study the Bible with his gay son so his son could see for himself that same-sex marriage was forbidden—and then affirmed his son's desire to one day marry when he realized the Bible didn't really say that at all. We'll meet an Arab American pastor who was shaken to the core when he realized one of his best friends, his church's music director, was terrified to tell him she was gay and had a girlfriend. His church soon publicly announced that it affirmed same-sex marriage and LGBTQ+ identities—and lost a huge number of members. And we'll show how some white LGBTQ+ conservative Christians in this movement have exercised that same humility to learn to be better allies to Black people, Indigenous people, and people of color.

Finding a way to navigate and repair relationships leads some LGBTQ+ and allied Christians to work to change their institutions and culture. In the final chapters of this book, we zoom back out to the level of institutions by exploring tensions in this movement that follow from how often their churches and the broader culture have defined LGBTQ+ as the opposite of both "conservative" and even "Christian." At stake is what it means to be "conservative" in a way conservative Christians will recognize, to hold space where the next ones who realize they're LGBTQ+ can go on living—and whether it's possible to do that without prioritizing some people's survival over that of others. We'll explore how the different groups we have observed have navigated this tension. We'll close by discussing how LGBTQ+ conservative Christians and their allies' insights about love and justice can help us all to make stronger movements and a better future.

1

Love and Relationships

Darren Calhoun was getting ready for the day, taping big poster paper sheets to the wall. He was preparing for The Reformation Project's Racial Justice Academy preconference. Dawne had met Darren—a Black gay man, then in his mid-thirties—back in Chicago through The Marin Foundation, and he was helping us with the research for this book.

Darren had once lived alone in a church building. His Pentecostal pastor had wanted him to exorcise the "demon" of homosexuality. So, Darren took up residence in the sanctuary—praying constantly, sleeping on the altar, fasting two days per week, working in the preschool, and cleaning the church building for $50/week. After *four years*, when he finally said, "I don't think Jesus wants me hiding away from life," his pastor offered to keep him locked in his basement. When Darren declined that hospitality, the pastor instructed the rest of their church community to stop talking to him.[1]

Darren found another church, a predominantly white megachurch that needed some antiracism training and, like his old church, required him to be celibate, but allowed him both to lead worship and to acknowledge the fact that he was gay. He did social justice work all over Chicago, and he was active on the boards of several Christian social justice organizations. He exuded patience when he taught white people about racism, when he taught Christians about LGBTQ+ people, and when he taught progressives about Christians. He exuded love everywhere he went.

When Dawne walked into the room early for the Racial Justice Academy, he looked up from his work and said, "Dawne!" in a way that said, "I'm so happy to see you," and they hugged.

The preconference and main conference were intense, giving people a lot to think about and a lot to feel. Darren helped lead the Academy for Racial Justice all day Thursday, he spoke on the "LGBT 101" panel Thursday night, and he spoke on the "Intersections of Race and LGBT Issues" panel on Saturday. When he wasn't on stage, he was helping with everything from running the soundboard to meeting with people who needed spiritual guidance. It seemed to Dawne that, for Darren, the conference was work. Pastoral work, possibly soul-feeding work, but she was friends with enough clergy to know that facilitating a spiritual experience for others is no vacation. When their paths crossed, the two chatted a few times between speakers or events, but he was always on his way to another meeting or something else he had to do. On the last day, Dawne awkwardly explained to Darren that she had felt awkward (and probably acted that way) when they ran into each other because she was afraid that maybe talking to her was more work for him, and he was already doing so much. He said it wasn't, she smiled, they hugged, and he walked her to a cab stand.

The next afternoon, with the conference over, Dawne sat in her living room unwinding from a tough day with the five-year-old she hadn't seen for four days. Her phone lit up with a Facebook message from Darren that said, "I love you SOOOOOOOOO much."

She was confused. Did he intend this for her, or for someone else? Was this a mistake? Could she even ask him if it was a mistake? *What could he possibly say if it was? How should she reply?*

In that moment of confusion, it occurred to her that as a Christian, he felt called to love others. In that moment, Dawne groggily decided to accept Darren's message as the love she had heard described, in which people who follow the life and teachings of Jesus are called to see the face of Jesus in everyone they meet, called to reach out to others with the kind of love that lifts them up and shows them that they are worthy. She let herself feel uplifted and worthy. It felt good. She felt like she mattered. She felt loved.

By letting her know that she mattered, he let her know that she had a place, a voice. She decided to accept his message as a gift. She didn't want to simply parrot the script that directs us to say, "I love you, too," and she felt starkly aware that, not being Christian, she could not love him with this same love.

And yet she could. Even though she usually didn't say "I love you" to people she hadn't known for a long time, she realized in that confused moment that she did love Darren in the same spirit in which she accepted his message. She thanked him and said she loved him, too, because he's amazing.

"Aw shucks," he replied.

He was modeling a different way to think about love, and as he did, he showed a kind of Christian love that wasn't all about reaping her soul.

* * *

Alicia T. Crosby-Mack was the co-founder, and eventually executive director, of the Center for Inclusivity (CFI),[2] an antiracist, pro-LGBTQ+ organization she founded with another former staff member of the Marin Foundation. When we first met her, before she herself had come out, she told us the story of when a friend came out to her in college. Having been a Black Republican pastor's kid—"a good girl," in her words—Alicia's immediate reflex was to argue: "What about *this*? What about *that*?" She made assertions about bestiality and "Who knows what else." Her friend stopped her and said, "You know me. You know me in a way that most people here don't. Would you really equate me to someone who would abuse an animal?" Alicia continued:

> And I'd taken one of those Bible verses and pelted her with it, and I remember feeling, kind of this pause from the Holy Spirit in that moment to, like, reframe and step back. Because I realized what I was doing was harming her. I was throwing this verse at her, not really having any context for it, but just understanding that that and bestiality was spoken about in the same space, and obviously these things are detestable to God, and so: "Tell me why! Ugh!"

For Alicia, at that moment, her friend brought her back to the reality of their actual friendship rather than the abstract associations Alicia had been taught about the book of Leviticus. Alicia reflected:

> And her saying that, like, it gave me pause, and I stopped, took a step back, and then I asked, I'm like, "Okay. You're right. I do know you. So how do you reconcile your sexuality and your faith?" And that's probably the question I should have asked on the top end of things. But coming from like a very conservative, evangelical-amongst-other-things background, we were taught to throw the Bible verses.

This conversation could have ended their friendship if Alicia had opted to focus on her fear rather than her love for her friend. She reflected:

> This is a relationship that was almost lost, because of the way I chose to approach it, and not doing so really out of love. And her question [made me think], "Maybe we have to step back into love." I wanted to be right. And for her to be right, and for her to be safe and not go to Hell, because I thought that's what would happen. And it was fear. And so, fear is that thing that undergirds like how parents treat folks, how pastors treat people. It's fear of what will happen to someone's soul . . . It's fear of not understanding. It's fear of this person pushing back against your theology.

Fear had nearly overpowered Alicia's capacity to love.

* * *

Christians widely agree that Christianity is about love for God and neighbor[3]—about relationships. They say that human beings' fundamental nature is to love. But for those who see heterosexuality as God's plan for everyone from the beginning of time, that fundamental understanding of love gets twisted. Christians often distinguish among different kinds of love—*eros*, *philia*, *storge*, and *agape*—but for our purposes, that distinction isn't very important. As we'll show later, conservative Christians tend to see LGBTQ+ people as having a disordered capacity for sexual or romantic love, *eros*, which tarnishes their ability to love *anyone*, barring them from ministering to others—from showing *philia* (friendship) and *agape* (love of others because God loves them)—for fear that their "sin" will infect people.[4] Clearly, conservative Christians don't see a clear division between these kinds of love.[5]

Conservative Protestants tend to see marriage as the ideal love relationship and the apex of a person's relationship with God—to the point of being suspicious of people still not married by their thirties.[6] Yet many of them also claim that LGBTQ+ people can have a relationship with the divine while being denied marriage (or often, *any* intimacy at all, even friendship). We have a lot to learn from asexual and aromantic people, but the stories of LGBTQ+ conservative Christians make it clear that for people who see marriage as the apex of love, *prohibiting* a believer from experiencing romantic love also cuts off their ability to experience divine love by declaring them unworthy of connection. In the case of trans people, or anyone who defies conservative Christian gender ideals, even their understanding of *who they are* can make their capacity to love seem suspect.

* * *

Human beings are made for relationships in which each participant is open to learning from others and being transformed by those connections.[7] When we insist on our own and others' humanity and worthiness of connection, we can find ourselves questioning the social dynamics that produce many of the toxic outcomes we see around us. Being open to learning about how our own lives are implicated in others' struggles, and the empathy to want to make it better—this kind of love has the potential to help us to create a world where everyone can thrive. A radical politics based on love—a steadfast refusal to accept dehumanization—just might offer a way to a better future.

We have heard stories from countless people who have been cut off from everyone in their lives, people who were told that, because they were gay, lesbian, bi+, or trans, their capacity to love made them dangerous to the very people they loved. That who they were was fundamentally unacceptable to God, but God—for whom nothing is impossible—would do nothing to change them, no matter how much they begged. We have seen how believing that God loved them after all, that they were worthy to love and serve others as Christians are supposed to, allowed them to heal and help others to heal. We have heard from people whose firmly Christian convictions about loving the outsider, the stranger, and the oppressed, have led them to rebel against churches that taught that racism, sexism, and poverty were not the concerns of true Christians. Their stories have taught us that if we're going to have a society that allows everyone in it to thrive, our actions must be based in the love that compels us to treat other people like they matter. The stories of LGBTQ+ conservative Christians—sometimes pushed to the brink of death, sometimes restored by others' love—make clear just how deeply people depend on love from other people to live.

* * *

People tend to think of love as defying all attempts of language to pin it down, something for poets to explore, not regular folks. But if we want to say that LGBTQ+ conservative Christians have taught us about love, we need to be clear about what that means. Human beings are born into the hands of others, and it takes longer for human beings to be self-sufficient than it takes other animals—think of a foal being born and immediately walking around, while human babies can't do that for a year or so.[8] Our brains are literally formed in relationships with others. When we die, we are mourned and laid to rest by others—when we're lucky, by those who feel that they've lost part of themselves. In between, we speak—and even think—in languages that others have created and use to communicate with us, and we connect to those who give us a sense of who we are and our place in the world.[9] When those people cut off relationships with us, the results can be devastating. Human beings need each other to thrive. We are created to love and be loved.

We define love as a relationship of openness and vulnerability to someone that changes you by virtue of your mutual connection.[10] We are compelled by the definition of love that Jennifer Nash has distilled from

Black feminism, as a "labor of actively reorienting the self, pushing the self to be configured in new ways that might be challenging or difficult," to do the work to allow others and us to thrive.[11] Or as James Baldwin described it, love involves openness to being touched, changed by others, to growing, something crucial to being alive.[12] Love requires humility—openness to the possibility that we ourselves are imperfect and have more to learn. Love in this sense is not just for the people to whom we are related, or even necessarily the people we know well. It does not require affection. Love as we define it is an ethical stance, a way of relating to others that reflects their inherent worthiness of human connection, and of a relationship with us in particular. When you love someone, you treat them in a way that says that they matter.

We have learned that love feels like being loved when it is relational in this way. When you love someone, you are vulnerable and open to being affected by them, never closed off from their perspective. If you are afraid of or put off by some aspect of who they are, when you love them, you are willing to listen anyway, to stay open to learning from them about their experience. You affirm their humanity—even if what they say challenges your values and understanding of the world. You want to know their truth because you want to help them to thrive, because, to an extent, their thriving is your thriving, and their suffering is your suffering. Because you love them.

Love can fail in many ways. Seemingly loving relationships can be superficial, but they can also be abusive, dominating, neglectful. What seems like relational love can easily slip into the one-sided love of an object, the way we love ice cream—for what it does for us, rather than what it teaches us. Love is not controlling. If I try to control others, I'm closing myself off to the possibility of growing by virtue of our connection. I'm closing myself off to learning from them. They have become an object to me, like a token on a gameboard, or a tool to use. We're not in a relationship anymore. That kind of "love" doesn't feel like being loved to the person being controlled.

Love is also not indifferent. If your friend is being harmed and you just want to ignore it, that is neglectful, and your connection may be toxic to that person because you are neglecting their need. That's not love. If you love someone, what hurts them hurts you, too. You might not experience their suffering in the same way or fully understand their experience, but you are affected by their suffering in a way that makes indifference impossible.

Love is radically equalizing even in unequal or fundamentally dependent relationships; relational love is not a hierarchy in which one person's needs and comfort outweigh those of the other person. Yes, a parent must have authority over a two-year-old by virtue of their unequal experience and knowledge, but treating a young child with love involves constant openness to new information about what that child needs at any given moment. That doesn't mean you indulge every tantrum because part of what they need to learn is how to regulate their own emotions. But a loving parent learns from their child's tantrum about how that child experiences the world and makes appropriate changes so their child can learn what they need to learn to flourish. Being a parent is humbling.

Many LGBTQ+ conservative Christians are conservative, not radical. But they and their allies can teach us something about the radical potential of love. In a world structured by dehumanizing systems of discrimination and inequality, love is political. From our years of observing and interviewing, we've developed a perspective on the kind of love that is crucial for justice: the resolute, steadfast, uncompromisingly-sure-of-its-humanity love that Audre Lorde called on feminists to dip deeply into, that Baldwin wrote about in *The Fire Next Time*, that Martin Luther King Jr. called *agape*[13]: the love that says, "Not only am I human, but I must hold out the hope that the people who oppress me are also human, and therefore able—no matter how tiny the chance seems—to learn and grow, be better, and do better."

If you love someone, you can't be indifferent to their oppression. You want to learn how you yourself might contribute to it—even if you consider yourself an ally—so you can stop and then contribute instead to their liberation. When people we love can point to systemic injustices causing their suffering, loving them means learning from them and acting to make that system fairer. If we love them, their crisis is a crisis for us, too.[14] A relationship is not loving if people fail to recognize their different positions in social hierarchies, including institutional inequalities. Injustice causes suffering; it dehumanizes people, and love can't abide those things. How much do you love someone if you ignore that they're being harmed, *particularly* when the harm is coming from institutions that might benefit you? How much do you love someone if you ignore the fact that *you* may be harming them yourself? Love comes through in meaningful solidarity to change personal behavior, institutions, and cultural understandings in ways that the people being harmed recognize as helpful, without centering the perspectives of the helpers. Injustice dehumanizes others, and tolerating their oppression is a failure to love.

Because love is rooted in reality—including the reality of our own and others' humanity—it also includes refusing to allow ourselves to be dehumanized; that is, to be treated as an object, a problem, or a thing. Love is connected to the awareness of ourselves as human and worthy. We call that awareness "relational pride." King says that love upholds self-worth in the face of those who diminish us. Baldwin, too, describes love as a steadfast refusal to allow our humanity to be diminished. And for both these thinkers, loving your "enemies" doesn't mean accepting their dehumanization of you, but holding out the hope that those who dehumanize others can stop—and that when they see those others as human, they'll become more human themselves. Love is a politically necessary commitment to your own humanity and that of those who oppress you, because even dehumanizing your oppressor dehumanizes you by cutting you off from love.[15] Approaching everyone, even your enemies, with a practical attitude of love keeps you from walling yourself off in arrogance and keeps you open to learning and growing. It keeps alive the hope that others can do better and become better, to join in the work of making a future that's better than the present.

That said, we have heard many times from LGBTQ+ Christians that holding love and grace as ideals does not mean that people who have been oppressed, battered, or abused are required to cultivate empathy or compassion for those who harm them or remain indifferent to their suffering.[16] And that *needs* to be said, given that many churches have routinely told battered wives to forgive and stay with their abusers—and their abusers to forgive *them!*—and told sexual assault survivors not to ruin their assailants' reputations by telling people. If someone continually dehumanizes you, no good comes from keeping that dynamic alive and hoping they'll magically be different tomorrow. Forgiving others can help you to thrive, but not if that "forgiveness" means negating yourself and your own worthiness of love, life, and safety.

* * *

Whereas love is a relationship of openness and vulnerability, shame is a feeling of being unworthy of relational connection—of love. Shame is a ubiquitous experience among the LGBTQ+ conservative Christians who shared their stories with us. It comes about because of how conservative Christians understand gender—not as a description of human variation, but as Godly ideals to which people must conform. It comes about because conservative Christians define love in terms of this understanding of gender and elevate it to the level of sacred commandment. In the next two chapters, we will talk about where conservative Christianity gets its understanding of gender, and the toxic effects of treating this particular belief as a commandment from God.

2

The Complementarian Commandment

It seemed as though gender was the currency in the Black spaces. In the white spaces the gender expression wasn't as big of a deal as the sexuality. What I mean by that is, they didn't necessarily care that I was more flamboyant in say, my hand gestures or more eclectic in my style of dress, as long as they knew privately that I was not sexually engaging in anything that would be considered deviant. . . . Whereas, you know, in Black spaces it seemed to be . . . opposite . . . where you needed to have an outward gender expression that was cis[gender], while what you did privately wasn't as much of a concern. I still didn't feel liberated because I knew I couldn't be who I really was. Definitely not openly without being rejected.

—*Aurora, Black trans woman, twenty-six, who grew up attending both predominantly Black and predominantly white churches*

Ask any Christian—conservative, liberal, of any race or nationality—what it means to be Christian, and it probably won't be long before they tell you their faith is all about loving and serving God and other people.[1] Christians see Jesus as the central figure of their faith, and the Gospels (the books of

Matthew, Mark, Luke, and John) are the four books of the New Testament that chronicle his life and teachings. They all tell the story in different ways, but three of the four say that when Jesus was asked to identify the most important commandment, he replied that the commandments all boil down to loving God and neighbor. In a word, relationships.

But that love is not universal. If it were, evangelical Christians wouldn't be declaring "war" on some of their fellow Americans, and there would be no need for an evangelical LGBTQ+ movement.

To a lot of liberals and progressives, the conservative obsession with LGBTQ+ people seems completely irrational: why do they care so much if someone else is gay or not? Why are institutions filled with powerful adults spending their time attacking trans children's access to healthcare and trying to ban drag shows? As we heard the testimonies of LGBTQ+ conservative Christians, questions like these only multiplied.

Conservative Christians treat certain ideas about gender and sexuality—those considered "normal" or "natural" by the dominant culture—as sacred. That "common sense" shapes a lot of non-conservative people's assumptions, too, about what's natural and what has always been true. But that culture has a history, and looking at that history helps us understand today's gendered, sexual, and racial landscape.

Over and over, people talked about a paradox—they heard all the time about Christianity being all about God's universal love, and at the same time, young people in conservative Christian communities learn from the outset that same-sex attractions and nontraditional gender identities make people unlovable to God and the community. Less than human. Most of the people we heard from, ranging in age from college students to people in their seventies, had always known being queer or trans would make them abhorrent to God, putting them outside of God's kingdom. From their earliest memories, many absorb the powerful message that to be LGBTQ+ is to embrace the worst of all sins. That it can get people expelled from the church, from the other relationships that matter, and from God's supposedly universal love. Westboro Baptist's famous "God Hates Fags" signs say explicitly what a lot of conservative Christians seem to be thinking, even if they say otherwise.

While the Supreme Court's legalization of same-sex marriage in 2015 seemed to put a damper on the Religious Right's shrieks about the end of civilization, at least for a while, same-sex marriage is still decried as an outrageous attack on (conservative) Christianity, even by people who recognize that they need to show "grace" to heterosexual members of their churches and families who find themselves, contrary to Jesus's teachings, divorcing and remarrying.

Televangelist John Hagee blamed a "homosexual parade" in New Orleans for Hurricane Katrina, and Jerry Falwell and Pat Robertson blamed gays and lesbians (along with the ACLU) for the 9/11 attacks.[2] We heard from people who grew up reading children's picture books about Sodom and Gomorrah that said homosexuality caused floods and destruction.[3] Some were taught that "homosexuals" rejected God and were doomed to Hell's eternal torture, and that LGBTQ+ people could stop being that way if they loved God and gave their hearts to Jesus. Kai, a mixed-race Christian in their twenties from a multiracial church, told us about Googling terms like "Christian homosexual" and quickly learning "this is seen as not just taboo, but, I don't know, abhorrent." As Lisa, a twenty-nine-year-old white Methodist lesbian from Texas put it, she grew up knowing that being gay:

> was the one thing that you never, *ever* wanted to be as a Christian. To me, I felt like the church thought it was the worst sin ever. Higher than murder or something. I thought that murder was probably forgivable but being gay wasn't.

While white evangelicals tend to differ from those from Black Church traditions when it comes to questions of politics and inclusion, a strong vein of anti-gay and anti-trans sentiment runs through both. Many Black LGBTQ+ Christians we heard from specifically mentioned a "Don't Ask, Don't Tell," approach in their churches, coupled with an abstract sense that being LGBTQ+ would be unacceptable to the point that they were terrified of their feelings or internalizing self-hatred. In some churches, it wasn't subtle at all. A heterosexual bishop of around seventy years of age, Harold Robinson, spoke of the predominantly Black churches he grew up in, where unlike other sinners, gay and trans people could be ridiculed from the pulpit. He recalled:

> It was always treated with disrespect and mocking. It wasn't that it was just a sin. It was the one sin where you could . . . laughingly talk about it and disparage the people in a mocking way. Now, that's what I grew up in. So you could always get a laugh about sissies or, you know, men sleeping with men or whatever, you'd get a laugh and you could call 'em nasty, you could call 'em filthy. . . . See, I just have to acknowledge it because you did not mock other people the same way. Whether you preached against it or not, they wasn't mocked, they wasn't shamed, and they certainly wasn't made to feel that they weren't welcome. So the fornicator is there and the adulterer is there and the one with the drinking problem is there, and all of that—all of them are there on Sunday morning. None of them feel like that they couldn't come to church except for, like I said, the way that particular community was treated.

People from both predominantly white evangelical and Black Church traditions told us they had always been told that there was no hierarchy of sin—but people's actions spoke differently. Churches treated homosexuality and being trans as worse than *anything*.

Different churches disagree about what counts as "homosexuality." Is it having sex with someone of the same sex as you, dressing or behaving contrary to your church's gender norms, or does just calling yourself gay count as sinful? Rosaria Butterfield, a former lesbian, has argued against even celibate Christians calling themselves "gay" because that adjective would "modify" the noun of their Christianity. Denny Burk of the Committee on Biblical Manhood and Womanhood insists that even feeling attracted to someone of your same sex is sinful.[4]

Some "welcoming but not affirming" churches allow lesbians and gay men to say they're gay but require them to lead a celibate life, but in churches that see marriage as the culmination of a person's relationship with God, celibacy doesn't guarantee that a person won't draw suspicion.

An openly gay, celibate, white woman in her twenties was hired to minister to students at a predominantly white conservative Christian college. A blog post indicating she might be softening her position on same-sex marriage got her summoned to the office of the college president—a much older man—so he could grill her about her sex life. Darren Calhoun was celibate when he was a worship leader in a predominantly white, "welcoming but not affirming," church. He was once called into his pastor's office and questioned by a committee because someone had reported seeing him "on a date"; that is, eating at a restaurant with another man—and a "slip" could cost him his ministry. He told us he had to ask what it meant to be "on a date": "Am I allowed to go out of my house, and have a nice time, with another person? Does it have to be in a group?" Unmarried heterosexuals weren't supposed to be having sex either, but the pastor didn't seem to be calling any of them in for questioning or expressing fear of their potential "slips." A white, heterosexual man we call Jeff, who attended the same congregation, told us he used to pick up women at church and cheat on his wife with them! He didn't have a leadership role, but it seems the pastor never summoned him to his office. He was free to figure out on his own how to live a Christian life.

Gay Christian Network (GNC) founder Justin Lee—a white, cisgender, gay Southern Baptist—writes of having come out to his pastor when he was a teenager in the 1990s. He had never so much as held hands with another boy, but his pastor sent him to a support group for middle-aged sex addicts.[5] A lot of conservative churches won't let LGBTQ+ people collect the offering, teach Sunday School, or read the Scripture lesson for fear that their sin will somehow transfer to others, yet it made sense to send a kid to a group for middle-aged people who had trouble controlling their sexual compulsions?

We heard from LGBTQ+ people whose churches thought they were possessed by demons—a number of trans women in particular spoke of seeking, or being dragged into, exorcism rituals to purge the "demon of femininity." Aurora spoke of knowing, in every church she attended and every ministry she served, that she wouldn't be accepted for who she was. Even a pastor she knew to be in a relationship with another man preached about hellfire and damnation raining down on "homosexuals." A white trans woman we spoke to—so highly respected that she had been a pastoral counselor to many pastors for years before she transitioned—was asked by her clients if she was going to publicize their secrets when she came out as trans, as if she could no longer be trusted. Many churches regularly taught people to discern God's will or calling for them, to become the person God intended for them to be—whom to marry, what career to go into, where to live, how to minister. But it was unthinkable that clearly devout Christians could be answering God's call to become who God intended them to be when they came out as gay, bi, or trans.[6]

Sometimes even intersex people—those in the roughly 1.7 percent of people born with chromosomes, hormones, and or physical sex traits that make it difficult or impossible for doctors to categorize them as either male or female—were subject to gender and sexual policing by their religious communities.[7] We interviewed a white person named Les, who was raised as a girl but who now identifies as a man. In his early fifties, he had been shocked to discover that he had been born with ambiguous sex characteristics. He found that his parents had at first given him a boy's name, only to later cross it off on his birth certificate and write in the girl's name he had always known. This discovery explained the repeated, confusing, and painful genital surgeries he was subjected to without explanation or support throughout his childhood, and the shame that accompanied them. Reeling from all this information, he turned to his pastor for comfort and guidance. His pastor's response? "Change your ways or leave the church." What "ways" was Les supposed to change? The way his body was shaped when he was born? The ways he was trying to make sense of what had been done to him?

How would same-sex marriage threaten the institution of marriage more than heterosexual divorce? How, exactly, is being gay worse than *murdering someone?* By what logic would a pastor think it appropriate to send a teenage virgin to a group for middle-aged men with out-of-control sexual compulsions? Why would conservative church leaders express concern about seeing a Black, gay man in a restaurant with a male friend, even as a white, heterosexual man cheated on his wife with women he picked up in their sanctuary? Why would being trans seem like a threat against the almighty creator of the vast diversity of the universe? Why shouldn't intersex people be able to follow the path of Jesus, just as they are?

The answer to all these questions appears when we realize that a lot of conservative Christians today treat our society's dominant understanding of sex and gender as a commandment from God, more fundamental and important than the Ten Commandments. A number of participants pointed out that in the book of Genesis, God creates the heavens and earth, day and night, creatures of sea and dry land as well as "birds of the air," but no one takes these distinctions to mean that anything in between is abominable or a threat to the order of the universe. At one Reformation Project conference, Eduardo, a Puerto Rican, bisexual Seventh-Day Adventist, led a workshop on bisexuality where he characterized creation as a spectrum. He quoted queer theologian Alan Hooker, saying that God's claim that "I am the Alpha and the Omega" (Revelations 1:8) invokes endpoints to mark a whole alphabet between them—no one thinks God was saying beta, gamma, and the rest were bad letters. Invoking the pairings in Genesis, Eduardo asked:

> Can you stand with your feet in the muddy sand on the beach, waves crashing around your feet, tide slowly rising or falling, and honestly draw a clear line between sea and dry land?

Shorelines, sunrises, and sunsets are beautiful *because* of their in-betweenness. Anti-LGBTQ+ Christian activists often claim that LGBTQ+ people are abominations because they do not fit neatly into the binaries that these activists derive from a seemingly literal reading of the Bible. But, as many have pointed out, there are no amphibians in the Bible either, and no one goes around calling frogs "abominations."[8]

But many non-affirming Christians interpret the Bible to mean that God's most fundamental commandment is that human beings are created in two distinct, opposite sexes that complete each other in heterosexual marriage, and to defy that blueprint for creation is to repudiate the Creator. Theologians call it the doctrine of *complementarity*. Seen through that lens, masculinity and femininity are the eternal essences that define humanity. Anything that challenges or differs from that norm is an inhuman attack on God's order, and those who violate those gendered expectations seem less than human. Theologian James Hamilton describes complementarity as akin to gravity in a story about a plane crash, the obvious but usually unspoken factor necessary for anything else to happen. Albert Mohler, president of the Southern Baptist Theological Seminary, argues that without complementarity, Christians are left "without any authoritative revelation of what sin is" or "what it means to be human."[9]

None of this is to say that conventionally conservative Protestants are against sex or sexual pleasure. White evangelicals in particular don't think sex is bad, and they have published hundreds of books teaching heterosexual married couples how to have satisfying sex lives. Some even state that Christian, marital sex is the hottest because God is part of it. In the complementarian view espoused by many US evangelical Protestants since the 1960s, sexual pleasure is God's gift to married heterosexuals, particularly husbands.[10]

In this view, sex is like fire—necessary and beneficial when contained (by marriage), but dangerous when allowed to run rampant. Accepting "homosexuality" seems to mean "anything goes," and the harms that follow from sexual sin—rape and abuse, for instance—seem to prove that sex is dangerous, even as Christian men's abuses of women, girls, and boys are downplayed. A lot of Christians tend to think of sex outside of marriage as carnal, whereas sex within marriage is "spiritual." Of course, this formulation obscures the rape and abuse that happen *within* marriage, and it posits all sexual abuse and assault as simply the natural result of God-given masculine sexual aggression, which women are expected to rein in and blamed when they don't.[11] Meanwhile, LGBTQ+ Christians are often scapegoated for abuses they would never dream of committing.

To many conventionally conservative Christians, God's condemnation of homosexuality is obvious. In Genesis 19, God rained hellfire down on the city of Sodom. Leviticus 20:13 declares that a man who "lies with a male as with a woman" has done "an abhorrent thing" and "they are doomed to die."[12] In the New Testament, the apostle Paul decried "the wicked" in his letter to the Roman church, speaking of "unnatural" intercourse between women and "shameless acts" between men (Romans 1:26–27). In Paul's letters to the church in Corinth and to Timothy, he listed Greek words often translated nowadays to mean "homosexuals" in his lists of commandment breakers—even though those words were not interpreted as "homosexuals" in English translations of the Bible until 1946.[13]

In most conservative Protestant churches, this link between God and heterosexual marriage goes without saying, and any challenge to that link seems not to be Christian at all. A 2017 analysis of the one hundred largest Protestant megachurches found that *none* allowed LGBTQ+ members to participate fully in leadership and liturgy (including same-sex marriage and ordination). When conservative churches have changed their teachings to affirm LGBTQ+ people, they have often lost up to 90 percent of their members. A church with over two thousand members saw elders resign and attendance plummet to 240 attendees when the pastor announced support for LGBT people and same-sex marriage.[14]

For many who see homosexuality and trans expression as sinful, there is no such thing as *being* a gay person or a trans person. There are only discrete bad behaviors, made tempting by the devil and perhaps some kind of dysfunction in a person's childhood. Pastor John MacArthur has compared the notion that some people *simply are* gay to the notion that some people *simply are* born to be bank robbers, so we should let them rob banks. Pastor J. D. Greear has likened it to the idea that wanting to have sex with someone other than his wife would mean he was born to be polygamous, so she should simply live with it (even if that wasn't the deal they made when they got married).[15]

From the perspective of complementarians, homosexuality (as well as gender transition, which complementarians these days often seem to see as a gender-bending "sexual kink" rather than a genuine identity) is sin, and "identifying with your sin" is a grave mistake. When people argue there is an innate disposition to being LGBTQ+—the idea that people are "born gay"—conservative Christians counter that *everyone* is born disposed to sin; the point of Christian life is to help each other to resist the temptations of sinful thoughts and deeds.[16]

Many conservative Protestants have elevated the "common sense" that two distinct and opposite sexes occur in nature to the level of a sacred commandment—one that predates the Ten Commandments in time and is far more important. Hence the idea that murderers can be forgiven but not gay people. They have elevated that common sense, based on what theologian Robert Gagnon has called "the glove-like physical fit of the penis and vagina," to the level of *God*.[17] But complementarity, and its limited definitions of male and female, are human creations. They protect men's authority over women, and make people of color, LGBTQ+ people, and some cisgender heterosexual white women into sexualized outgroups to scapegoat for everything from poverty to illness to crime, social disorder, and even natural disasters.

Conservative Christians claim that they hold Jesus and the Bible in higher regard than do LGBTQ+ people and those who support and affirm them. No one in our research ever said this, but it seems to us that when they treat the humanly created hierarchy of gender as more important than what *Jesus* said were the most important commandments, they replace Jesus's teachings about love and relationship with the worship of a particular social order.[18] In some Christian circles, equating a human construction with God is called *idolatry*.

* * *

There is nothing timeless about the way we tend to understand gender in the United States today, and this idea does not actually come from nature. Many cultures have treated gender as a spectrum, much like all the other spectrums found in nature. Our society gets a binary conception of gender from interpretations of ancient Greek philosophers' understanding of differences as hierarchies. These interpretations continue to affect how people tend to see white/Black (and nonwhite), male/female (and not-male), hetero-/homo- (or anything "queer"), and countless other seemingly opposed pairs where the first is seen as more spiritual and closer to God and the other is treated as somehow more carnal and closer to animals.[19]

Until the eighteenth century, European experts used to see women's bodies as underdeveloped versions of men's bodies, rather than their opposite. Even then they knew that nature itself sometimes creates intersexed people, those whose physical bodies don't conform to the notion that male and female are discrete opposites. In the Bible, Jesus mentions "natural-born eunuchs," implying that he knew of intersex people then, and in fact, Christian religion scholar Megan DeFranza has found that early rabbis—whose job of circumcising infants acquainted them with all varieties of bodies—had names for four additional categories of people between male and female.[20] Biologist and historian Anne Fausto-Sterling has found records of intersex people in the United States and Europe in the nineteenth and early twentieth centuries, who were part of their communities and sometimes married.[21]

General knowledge about the existence of intersex people has been obscured since the 1950s. Since then, doctors have tended to surgically alter intersex children without their understanding or consent (and sometimes without their parents' understanding or consent) to make their bodies conform to our cultural norms, leaving many with physical, and often psychological, scars. Today, some US evangelicals argue that being intersex is a result of humanity's fall from grace, a problem for which medical intervention and surgery are the solutions to make intersex bodies conform to supposedly "Biblical" teachings about gender.[22] But surgery and medical interventions can cause lifelong pain, scarring, complications, and trauma—some interventions feel like repeated sexual assault, and often those interventions are performed on young children who didn't ask for them and clearly find them physically excruciating. Intersex people have been stigmatized, shamed, and made invisible because of often harmless differences between their own bodies and what our culture thinks of as "Biblical" and "natural." DeFranza and intersex colleagues, such as Lianne Simon, argue that such physical harm, pain, and shame cannot be God's intention for anyone, and argue that it is unethical to inflict those things just to bolster our cultural ideas about gender. DeFranza argues that people born intersex, no less than anyone else, are made in the image of God and don't need fixing; they are lovable, whole human beings just as they are.[23]

After almost three decades of organizing and writing by intersex people about the harms they have endured, some doctors are starting to change the way they treat intersex people. Led by intersex activists and their allies in the church, some Christians are starting to catch on, too.

Most societies around the world and throughout history have had special roles and rituals to provide ways of understanding this fact of nature. Many societies have traditionally recognized that—for biological or other reasons—some people don't fit the roles commonly given to men or women, and they have institutionalized special roles of their own.[24] Almost every Indigenous group in the Americas and Pacific Islands has recognized third (and sometimes fourth) gender roles, such as the Navajo *nadleehí*, the Crow *badé*, and the Hawai'ian *māhū*. These roles have often been forgotten due to the eradication efforts of the federal government and the missionaries, and Indigenous historians and others are working to revive them.[25] These are and were special roles of honor. Throughout Africa and Asia as well, people have long recognized that gender is more of a spectrum than a dichotomy, recognizing third, and sometimes fourth, gender roles. And while many languages assign gender to third-person pronouns (like *he* and *she* in English), other languages (like German) also have gender neutral pronouns. Still others (like Swahili) do not specify gender in pronouns or forms of address; the relative age of the person being spoken about is more important than whether others are male or female.[26]

Our understandings of gender are particular to our culture. As the quote from Aurora at the beginning of this chapter makes clear, even today among US conservative Protestants, churches can differ regarding what counts as a challenge to the complementarian narrative, and what counts as sinful. Clearly, there is not one clear message coming from the Creator.

* * *

Aurora's comments also point to the connections between sex/gender and race. Our culture arranges these things into hierarchies and those hierarchies overlap so they seem to confirm each other's truth, making inequalities created by society seem natural and God-given rather than unjust, human institutions. In policies, science and medicine, employment, mass media, and many other domains, men are treated as the "neutral," "basic" human form from which everyone else deviates. Heterosexuality is treated as natural, healthy, good, and normal, with anything else being seen as deviant. Whiteness is treated as the "neutral," basic human form as well, from band-aids and crayons to textbooks, cosmetics, and beauty standards, not to mention white supremacy in policing, medicine, popular culture, business, real estate, and laws. Countless scholars and others have observed that the American culture leads many people, particularly white people, to assume white people are "normal," better than everyone else, and entitled to the comfort of being the standard by which others are measured and found lacking. But the supremacy of white people is, as James Baldwin once said, a delusion.[27] That delusion has been held in place by powerful institutions—including the Catholic Church and European monarchies.

In the late 1400s, as Europeans were just beginning to travel the world in search of extractable resources, land, and trade routes, they understood their own ways of defining sexual and gender roles as natural and godly. Under the Church's 1493 Doctrine of Discovery, categorizing some people as other-than-human allowed their land to count as undiscovered "no man's land," up for grabs to the monarch who sponsored the voyage. This incentivized European colonizers to perceive other peoples' manner of dress, division of labor, and sexual mores as signs that they were dealing with beings who were less moral and less human than themselves. In the New World, Indigenous people were seen and categorized as sexually animalistic, justifying conquest of their lands and culture to this day—even as white male settlers were brutalizing and raping Indigenous people.[28] When Christopher Columbus's men landed in what is today Puerto Rico and encountered people they saw as men in women's clothing, they threw those people into pits to be eaten alive by dogs, determined to eliminate the Taino people's different ideas about gender.[29]

US slavery was justified with stereotypes of Africans and African Americans as more sexually voracious than white people—stereotypes rooted deeply in our culture that continue to shape how people are treated in many aspects of life. We see this today, in a culture that stigmatizes women of color in ways that are simultaneously gendered and racial and seen as deviating from white women's supposedly God-given "purity." And we see it in a culture that treats white men's sexual urges as understandably aggressive "by nature," while sometimes celebrating but often stigmatizing Black and Brown men as hypermasculine and prone to sexual aggression.

Some LGBTQ+ and allied evangelicals we heard from had studied European culture's role in promoting a binary conception of gender and shaming those who did not conform to it. Using "queer" to refer to anyone whose life did not match the European, complementarian ideal, a gay, Korean American Christian Reform pastor we call David put it this way:

> In Africa . . . there was no problem with queer people until the white people got there. And even in, you know, Japan, they had six genders, like, way, way back before the damn white man came in. . . . In particular, you know, my focus is on Minjung theology which is Korean liberation theology that comes straight out of Korea and was a holistic liberation theology that addressed gender and sexual orientation and everything. And, nobody talks about, nobody engages with it. And there's other theologies from China and from Japan, and knowing the histories of gender and sexual identity from those countries is really, really important.

Because the culture that treats white people's traditions as standard and superior to other people's—that is, white supremacist culture—contains deeply rooted sexual stereotypes about Black people, Indigenous people, and people of color (BIPOC), not even the most "proper" members of BIPOC communities can take for granted that they won't be treated as sexually deviant.[30] Because sexual sin figures so heavily into the stigmas used to disparage Black people, Indigenous people, and other people of color as "beneath" white people, the slightest hint of "impropriety" often threatens to bring shame down not just on oneself and one's family, but the whole group. We see this dynamic in Aurora's comment at the opening of this chapter. In her estimation, public gender expression was more important in Black church spaces, and private behavior more of a concern in the white ones. Aurora spoke of having grown up in predominantly Black or multicultural churches and schools until her mother died when Aurora was sixteen, at which point she moved and began attending her stepmother's predominantly white, Assemblies of God church. As conservative as the white church was, her experience captured the focus on an outward presentation of respectability in predominantly Black churches and multi-race Christian schools she attended. We will discuss this dynamic more in later chapters.

Racism rests on assumptions about white, complementarian sexual and gender ideals as normal and Godly, and nonwhite people as deviant, both sexually and in terms of gender. Black, Indigenous, and other people of color's experiences, and the differences some saw between predominantly white churches and predominantly Black, Asian, or Latinx ones, bear the legacy of the racist culture of sexual stigma and shame. As a response to the sexual stigmas that have fueled white supremacy, some Black Christian communities have, since the early twentieth century, enjoined Black people to display respectability in order to deny fuel to racist, sexually shaming stereotypes. At the same time, Black and other churches where people of color predominate have become primary sites for the community to come together to resist and lament racism, something many find crucial to survival. Analyzing the experiences of African Americans, sociologist Patricia Hill Collins has argued that even though "respectability politics" was intended to procure dignity for working-class African American women in particular, "the politics of respectability basically aimed for White approval."[31] In effect, they held Black people accountable to disprove racist stereotypes rather than critiquing the white supremacist assumptions that (1) Black people are inherently sexually different from whites; and (2) that such differences, if they existed, would justify racist abuse. Scholar C. Riley Snorton has observed that as much as the Black Church has been a place of "refuge, political change, and spiritual fulfillment," it has also been a "place for gender and sexual regulation."[32] Anyone who seems to defy their church's "respectable" standards may feel, and even be treated, as though they're betraying the whole community.

Communities and churches that are made up primarily of people of color are no more homophobic as a whole than white ones, but because there are so many more white Americans and because sexual assumptions anchor racist stereotypes, being a LGBTQ+ or same-gender-loving Christian who is also a member of a racial or ethnic minority group can be complicated to navigate. Like Aurora and Sandra, whose story we shared in the introduction, African Americans and people of color who had spent time in predominantly white churches and ministries spoke of needing to blend in, to suppress the parts of themselves that did not conform to what was considered "normal." Those seen as girls and women were explicitly encouraged to dress modestly to refute others' sexualized stereotypes of them.

Some BIPOC respondents who had grown up in predominantly white churches were conscious of having to disprove white society's stereotypes of them to prove they weren't shameless. Maddie, a twenty-one-year-old Mexican/Salvadoran college student, reflected on what her mother taught her about how and why to always be "ladylike," saying:

> For us growing up it was always just like being very ladylike, and a lot of that goes into respectability, too. Like, she wanted us—because she . . . wanted us to be respectable ladies and respectability is always defined by Christianity here and in El Salvador. So it's just like being a good mother, being a good girl, like not tempting men . . . [M]y mom also was like, okay, you're like a brown girl in the United States, like . . . we grew up in a white community, like, "We don't want them to think that we're any different than them."

Being Christian, properly gendered, and worthy of respect were tied up in constant knowledge of white people's judging eyes. Maddie's mom was trying to help her navigate a world where young white women were assumed to be respectable, while her daughters had to *prove* they were.

For LGBTQ+ or same-gender-loving people in Black congregations, the stigmatization was especially frustrating because it looked so similar to the stigmatization by white society that they helped each other to navigate. Over lunch one afternoon, Darren shared the irony of feeling like LGBTQ+ people in Black church spaces were often treated the same way white culture had treated Black Christians. In the mid-twentieth century, he pointed out, white people considered the music of Mahalia Jackson and other famous gospel singers to be of the devil because it sounded to them like "bar music" or jazz; in their eyes, just to be Black was to be sinful. He continued, "So they should know something about their culture being equated with evil, being inherently sinful, but they turn around and say the same thing about LGBT people."

* * *

A lot of African American LGBTQ+ and same-gender-loving people told us they longed for spaces where they could bring "their whole self," rather than having to downplay their race in some spaces, hide being LGBTQ+ in different spaces, and so on. People often call this *compartmentalizing*. Sociologist Richard Pitt found this pattern in his study of gay Black Christian men, noting that compartmentalizing is neither ideal nor always feasible—to many Christians, their faith is an important part of their romantic lives and vice versa.[33] Darren spoke of a pattern of compartmentalizing among his gay Black Christian friends:

> There's about four churches that are pretty much known as where all the gays go [around here] and they've all been very publicly, actively, politically anti-gay. On any given Sunday somebody might be praying against the spirit of homosexuality or encouraging some hyper-masculine behavior and response to a more effeminate or a less manly expression. . . . [I]n those churches I have lots of friends and when I talk to them about . . . the culture of their church the response I get over and over again is that, "Well, I know they're going to be that way. I know they're going to act that way, but I like the music, or I like the sermons, and so when they do that I just tune out." What I'm hearing them say is that they're effectively leaving entire parts of themselves and their experience at the door, bottling that up, compartmentalizing it.

Respectability politics generates a culture of perfectionism around Black sexuality, which a respondent we call Simone described as "anti-everything," and another respondent, who we call Imani, learned about as "beating back the flesh," and which many respondents described as demanding unreasonable moral perfection. Darren described it as:

> a perspective that's built on these very high, unreasonable, ideals. And it comes from leaders that project themselves as perfect. They only preach about what's wrong with *you guys*. They only preach about how *you* need to get your family together, even though their kids can't stand them. They preach about all these external things to keep the focus on *you* and what's wrong with *you*.

White churches are concerned with appearances, too. But because their whole race is not sexually stigmatized, they often have more leeway to talk publicly about sex and sexual transgressions. Because they don't have the added burden of countering stereotypes of their race, seeking professionalized help from support group leaders and inpatient "treatment" programs has been more common.

The same binary culture that has stigmatized people who don't conform to a male–female dichotomy also leads people to stigmatize women and girls. It stigmatizes women who are not submissive and attractive to men, but also stigmatizes women who have sex, even if they are forced to. This view is often taken as "common sense," but it is made almost explicit in evangelical "purity culture," in which teenage boys are encouraged to pledge abstinence until marriage but are met with understanding when they "slip up," assuming God made men "naturally" sexually aggressive.[34] At the same time, teenage girls are more likely to be held accountable for sex they have with boys—even for being raped—and treated as "damaged goods."[35] Some teenage girls are given purity rings to remind them not to be sexually active until they are married, while they are also expected to cultivate appropriate levels of attractiveness and submission to men. Monica, a white, bisexual volunteer for The Marin Foundation, wrote a blog post about the shame she lived with as a homeschooled fundamentalist adolescent, which manifested as an eating disorder. She wrote:

> As a normal preteen, I started to gain weight and develop sexually. I hated the way my chest, hips and thighs were becoming curvier. I was scared that developing into a woman somehow meant that I would become impure, that somehow my womanhood would make me a bad girl. . . .
>
> I wanted to stay a little girl, the sweet and innocent Christian girl that my parents, my youth group leaders and Christian community wanted me to be. If I could avoid growing breasts, I could avoid the all the negative attention. Not from the boys, but from fearful adults.
>
> So I stopped eating. I thought if I could keep the perfect little girl body, I would finally be able to conquer my sexuality. To demolish it for good. I forced myself to become unaware of my body. I refused to take any joy in it, assuming that any pleasure was sinful.
>
> I became anorexic not to pursue some ideal sexual image, but to avoid one altogether.

* * *

Black people, Indigenous people, and other people of color see every day the effects of white culture's assumptions that white people are not just the quintessential humans, but virtuous. To most white people, these assumptions are so ubiquitous as to be invisible, like the air we breathe. While most white people in America would never want to be thought to be racist, we have benefited from generations of racist policies, laws, and institutions treating us and our ancestors as human beings who matter more than others, including slavery and segregation (and not just in the South), and Depression-era policies designed to create a home-owning white middle class where none existed before. BIPOC individuals have been denied these benefits not just culturally, but by law and policy.

The assumption that to be American is to be white, heterosexual, and Christian could go largely unspoken for over two centuries because it was affirmed everywhere—property laws, banking policies, segregated institutions, mass media, and most white churches. A lot of scholars have shown how white supremacy—and not just the culture of people who don't mind being called white supremacists—has been so taken for granted that it shapes what many white Christians think it means to be *Christian*.[36] Using robust national surveys, sociologists Andrew Whitehead and Samuel Perry found that just under 80 percent of Christians who identify as "evangelical" at least somewhat support the principles of White Christian Nationalism, a worldview that correlates a greater likelihood of believing that God created the social hierarchies of white over Brown and Black, native born over immigrant, and men over women. Many White Christian Nationalist church leaders use their pulpits and religious authority to advance that cause—even if these beliefs are the exact opposite of what the Bible teaches about helping the poor, welcoming the stranger, turning the other cheek, and loving your neighbor.[37]

In Whitehead and Perry's analysis, men's control of women's bodies is part and parcel of White Christian Nationalism much as it is part and parcel of any kind of religious fundamentalism. These authoritarian cultures rest on a vision of men's unique authority and strength for protection from outsiders and the maintenance of social order. A hierarchy of men over women requires heterosexuality and it requires two clear categories of people so that everyone knows their place, and no one notices all the gray areas—all the things that men, women, and everyone else can have in common. From this perspective, blurring that solid-seeming boundary between male and female threatens the sacred social order.

Other scholars see gender and sexual hierarchy as more central to conservative Christianity. Church historian Kirsten Kobes du Mez observes that among white conservative evangelicals, masculine authority seems to take precedence over the teachings of Jesus. Anthropologist Sophie Bjork-James shows how white evangelicals come to see the hierarchies of husbands over wives and white people over those of other races as inextricable from God's love and sacred order, so that working for social equality seems contrary to God's plan. To be sure, Southern Baptist leaders Burk and Mohler have argued that *intersectionality*, the scholarly concept that focuses on how social inequalities of gender, race, class, and sexuality work together, is "unchristian" because it recognizes the power of social dynamics, as if that recognition somehow diminishes God.[38] Does recognizing that human inventions like cars and guns can kill people diminish the power of the Almighty?

* * *

Whitehead and Perry point out that the roughly 80 percent of white evangelicals who support White Christian Nationalist beliefs and the 20 percent who don't all tend to agree that the Bible explicitly forbids homosexuality. These authors argue that gender and sexuality are more "elemental" to religion than race and ethnicity, which they see as more a product of culture.[39] But regardless of what they think about race and racism, LGBTQ+ and allied conservative Protestants argue that the conventional view of gender and sexuality is *also* a product of culture, projected onto the Bible.

Christian theologians and Bible scholars have long debated how to interpret the Biblical passages that seem to address homosexuality. Some Christian scholars point out that anti-LGBTQ+ scriptural arguments rely on inconsistent methods of interpretation and can amount to projecting social prejudices into the Bible. They argue that when evangelical Christians are consistent in how they apply their principles of interpretation, the analytical process reveals that the Bible does not actually say that binary gender, heterosexuality, and or heterosexual marriage are commandments at all. There are a number of books of sophisticated scriptural scholarship explaining these arguments, which we have space only to sum up here.[40] In a nutshell, they point to the fact that few Christians adhere to the hundreds of laws laid down in Leviticus—about not planting different seeds in the same row, not wearing clothing of mixed fibers, not eating pork or shellfish, for instance—even as some cite Leviticus 20:13 to rail against "homosexuals." They argue that the ancient Greek words appearing in some of Paul's New Testament letters (*malakoi* and *arsenokoitai*) refer to the idolatrous (and often abusive) pederastic practices of ancient Greece and Rome, not to the egalitarian, same-sex love relationships of today.

They point out that Paul's use of the word "unnatural" in Romans 1 could mean many things, and in fact, that he uses the same word to refer to long hair on men, to which many Christians today have no religious objection.

But the most fundamental argument has to do with the creation stories in Genesis, where the story of God creating Adam and Eve is interpreted to mean that male and female are incomplete halves that complete each other in heterosexual marriage, the seed crystal that lends its structure to the rest of the universe. Evangelical Protestant ethicist David Gushee has pointed out that the Bible does not say that human beings are incomplete without marriage, and that any notion of human beings as incomplete would weaken Christian teachings about human dignity.[41] Bible scholar James Brownson argues that Scripture actually doesn't say that male and female are only complete in heterosexual marriage. In his view, complementarity has no Biblical basis, and that people ignore differing definitions of the term so that they can proceed as if it's unquestionable.[42] He and Bible scholar Karen Keen have argued that the creation stories in Genesis posit that the problem with the original human being was that none of the other creatures God had made were *similar* enough to stave off the human's loneliness; God created Eve so that human beings could have covenantal kin relationships, not to insist that people try to match binary gender ideals.

When Richard Hays, a prominent Biblical scholar and long-standing non-affirming voice in the church, revised his position in a book co-authored with his son Christopher Hays, he made a Biblical case for affirming LGBTQ+ people and shared personal reflections on what led him to change his mind. Even before the book was released, other vocal conservative Christian thinkers including Burk and Gagnon publicly dismissed Hays's position; Gagnon charged Hays with heresy.[43] It seems that, for these thinkers, complementarity really is the crystal around which God's created order is built, a commandment more sacred than the Ten Commandments or any other Biblical teaching.

* * *

Since the 1990s, LGBTQ+ conservative Christians and their allies have been divided as to what *they* think is the best way for LGBTQ+ Christians to live, even as they have all been susceptible to poor treatment in their faith communities. While proponents of celibacy—often called "Side B" to avoid judgment—tended to maintain the evangelical belief that sex is intended to take place only between a husband and a wife, "Side A," tended for a long time to agree that sex should only take place within the lifelong commitment of marriage—which was why they believed that same-sex marriage should be recognized by the church.

But as many people raised in 1990s "purity culture" have come to realize, evangelical sexual ethics pose problems beyond those of not allowing same-sex couples to marry and thus have sex. It is impossible to separate this cultural narrative of sexual purity from the white racial frame that defined the "true" woman as white and "pure," whose purity must be violently defended to the death by white men against hordes of hypersexual men of color who supposedly covet it. This equation of white womanhood with purity was what justified simultaneously racist/sexist stereotypes of women of color as less-than pure, providing ideological cover for white men, as well as men of color, to treat them as less than fully human. As people who grew up in it, like Linda Kay Klein and Dianna Anderson, have noted, this cultural understanding of sex treats it as something that diminishes a person, particularly if that person is female. Even Joshua Harris, the author of *I Kissed Dating Goodbye*, came to realize that purity culture was not something he wanted to impose on his own children.[44]

Many LGBTQ+ evangelicals have been unfairly stigmatized by a culture that assumes that gay and bisexual people are all sexually promiscuous, that being trans is a "kink." This stereotype echoes the racist stereotypes that people of color are sexually wanton or lascivious, and some LGBTQ+ Christians of all races have sought to prove that stereotype wrong by being ultra-respectable, fastidiously adhering to the tenets of purity culture. Since its inception, The Reformation Project (TRP) has insisted that churches should bless same-sex unions precisely because of their commitment to this teaching, and their belief that in the Bible, the apostle Paul describes celibacy as a rare "gift of the spirit," not something that should or could be forced on a whole category of people.

TRP's founder, Matthew Vines, and Bible scholar James Brownson often repeated their assessment that Genesis 2 means that sex creates a kinship relation, that "You shouldn't say with your body what you aren't willing to say with your life," so sex should be reserved for marriage. Between conference sessions one day, Theresa pushed Brownson on this: thinking of people for whom conservative sexual ethics had become a toxic prison and for whom a period of sexual freedom was healing, she asked him, "It seems like you're assuming that everyone has the same right to determine what their body 'says' that white men have traditionally had. What if what someone is saying with their body is, 'This body is me, this life is mine?'" He took her question seriously, but he wasn't convinced. For him, it was important to be able to say that gay people could be accepted and expected to adhere to the same ethic of reserving sex for marriage—if only conservative churches would recognize their marriages. Brownson, Matthew, and others who spoke about sexual morality at TRP events emphasized the common ground they shared with other conservatives—the belief that sex outside of marriage was sinful.

That didn't mean Matthew espoused harsh judgment about it. While making announcements from the stage before the lunch break one day at the Kansas City conference, he went off book, talking about how conservative leaders had asked him if he "condemned the promiscuity of the gay community." He responded that he didn't think *condemning* anyone was helpful, that gay people had been *condemned* quite enough. Referring to the gay dating app Grindr he continued:

> While I don't *condone* the Grindr culture of "sex first, maybe date later," I think we should meet people where we are and show them that we have a better way, like we do with everyone else. That's what evangelizing is.

For Matthew and some other leaders in this movement, the "evangelical sexual ethic" of reserving sex for marriage is sound—the problem is excluding same-sex couples from it and then shaming LGBTQ+ people for failing to uphold it.

* * *

If we don't understand complementarity as the core assumption underlying much conservative Protestantism, a lot of the arguments against LGBTQ+ people seem contradictory. Is same-sex sex wrong because it can't lead to pregnancy? Many conservative Protestants accept birth control for married couples, and even the Catholic Church allows that married couples can have sex after menopause, or when one of the spouses is infertile. Is the problem that homosexuality is hedonistic, seeking pleasure without making the sacrifices heterosexual marriage demands, navigating the conflicts that emerge in the collision of existential opposites? This argument implies that homosexuality is inherently more appealing than heterosexuality and involves fewer sacrifices. Does God reserve sexual pleasure as a reward to married couples for holding out? Realistically, a satisfying sex life is hardly limited to those who were virgins on their wedding day, or even to those who are married to each other, and marriage is hardly a guarantee of sexual satisfaction.[45] Is same-sex marriage an attack on marriage itself? It kind of looks like same-sex couples want to *join* the institution, not destroy it. And why, again, do so many conservative churches see heterosexual divorce as a call for grace, while refusing to bless same-sex relationships?

From the perspective of complementarity, all those contradictions become invisible; homosexuality, bisexuality, transgender experiences, and even intersex people's existence can seem contrary to the blueprint of creation, and therefore like radical attacks on God's whole plan.

* * *

Guided by complementarity doctrine, conventional approaches to "homosexuality" (generally defined to include bisexuality and even people who are transgender, which is not a sexual orientation) included ignoring it as distasteful and unspeakable, working to "fix" LGBTQ+ people to make them "normal," or demanding celibacy as the price of inclusion in a community. Some churches teach that if someone is *really* Christian, they literally can't be LGBTQ+. Some teach that sexual orientation and gender identity do not exist because God created everyone to be just "normal," meaning heterosexual and cisgender. Those churches have often endorsed or attempted "reparative therapy"—trying to "fix" people's sexual orientation or gender identity to make them conform to the ideal of cisgender heterosexuality. Some have no room for LGBTQ+ people at all; some have practiced exorcism to try to rid people of it.

Some allow that people can claim a gay identity if that is what they are, but they must hope either for a "mixed orientation marriage" to someone of the other sex or remain celibate. These churches might allow LGBTQ+ people to attend, but not to be members; to be members, but not to serve the church; to serve the church, but not to serve in ministries involving children. Paradoxically, they treat marriage as the single most crucial part of life—the part where a married couple could most fully know God by consummating marriage—such that they stigmatize and pray for cisgender heterosexual single people to find someone to marry soon so they can fully know the joy God intended for humanity. And yet, when someone comes out as gay or lesbian, the same churches that see sexuality as so central to one's relationship with God treat it as an craving that should be abstained from, like drinking alcohol, or eating sweets.

When the conservative Christians we spoke with revealed that they were (or someone else revealed them to be) LGBTQ+, other conservative Christians might "pelt" them with Bible verses, as if losing an argument would change their identity. Some pastors and others assumed that they were sexually depraved and open to bestiality, orgies, or whatever other spectacular transgressions of conservative Christian sexual codes they could think up. Some would just cut off the relationship completely, sometimes violently. "Homosexuality" just wasn't considered normal, in a world where being "normal" was often equated to being "good" and "natural" and "acceptable to the all-loving God."[46]

LGBTQ+ people really exist, even among conservative Christians, and clearly Christians disagree about what the Bible teaches them about this fact. So how are people supposed to make sense of these debates over the

Bible? For many people we have heard from, the key is in Jesus's warning about false teachers and teachings in the gospel of Matthew (7:17). To discern false teachings from truth, Jesus said to look at the "fruits" of the teaching; "Good tree bears good fruit, and bad trees bear bad fruit." The conservative church's intense antipathy toward LGBTQ+ people engenders spiritual violence. It is a blueprint for failures of Christian love. It distorts love, making it seem incapable of transcending social constructions of gender and sexuality. It urges people to do violence to those they love in efforts to love them better and make them love according to its script. To many LGBTQ+ Christians and those who love, respect, and listen to them, the overwhelming destructiveness of conventional church teachings seems to be bearing some pretty horrible fruit.

3

A Sacrament of Shame

"I Love You, but Hate Your Sin"

I found myself unconsciously shutting down connection. And that was something that I think a lot of my friends had a hard time understanding. Because I am an extrovert. I do love people. And I can listen to stories and laugh and have a good time. And so it was bizarre to them that, inside, I was crumbling in every moment because I was so fervently policing myself and making sure that I did not let myself go too far emotionally with someone, lest I start to have this idea that I would want to share life with them, and experience intimacy at any level, with them.

And I think that's where the shame piece really began to come clear to me: I was experiencing Christian life in a very different way than all of my other Christian friends were. And it took me a long time to be able to look back on that and say, "Those were days when I hated myself." And I hated myself for the sake of demonstrating how much I loved God.

—Kai

Kai was a teenager in the Southeastern United States when they discovered the evangelical church. A person of white and Hawai'ian descent in their twenties, Kai now goes by gender neutral pronouns and identifies as *māhū*, the Hawai'ian third gender. But when they first became Christian in high school, they embraced their church's "welcoming but not affirming" teachings and identified as a lesbian committed to celibacy. Seeing same-sex intimacy as incompatible with Christianity, Kai spent most of every day trying to be of service to their friends in the church:

> A big part of my Jesus following was this idea of self-sacrifice, self-denial, serve others before self. And to follow Jesus is to pick up your cross and carry it. And, to me, the most significant way in which I'd always been doing that was by what I called "surrendering my orientation," surrendering all emotional impulses that would ever lead me to believe that there could be something God-honoring and life-giving about the love I would have with another woman.... Because, to me, to hate this part of myself so much that I spent eighty percent of my energy every single day attempting to eradicate it—it felt holy. It felt like that was what was making me righteous.

As Kai shared their story, they told us they willingly sacrificed intimacy with others, even friends, despite the suffering they experienced:

> And I can specifically remember instances of crying out to God, whether—in like a corporate worship setting or just in my own private prayer time, and thinking, "Even if you don't take this away from me, this suffering is more than okay. Because I believe you love me that much. I would do anything for this cause. And if the difficulty of my life testifies to the extent of which your love has covered the brokenness of all of humanity, then I will do this for the rest of my life." And, unfortunately, that's sort of masochistic.

Kai reflected that even though they "really believed all of the Christian messages that had been imparted to me about faith coming to us in the form of a gift, believing that God's favor is unmerited, unwarranted," they still felt like they alone had to do something to earn God's favor—"surrendering" not only their orientation, but their need for emotional connection even with friends. Kai spoke of a striking contrast; having a lot of friends and feeling accepted in that church but cutting themself off from anyone they felt too close to, lest their feelings become too much like love. Realizing that their straight, cisgender friends experienced Christianity in a completely different way—with close friendships and intimacies, without hating themselves to prove they loved Jesus—Kai began to rethink what Christianity meant for them. Eventually they embraced the compatibility of same-sex relationships with Christian teachings and non-European ways of understanding gender. And when they did, their church "friends" rejected them.

Kai's story captures the push and pull many LGBTQ+ conservative Christians experience. Their churches preach that God's unconditional love, grace, and forgiveness are available to all, or at least all believers. LGBTQ+ conservative Christians are as excited as any Christian to share that love with others. But, at the same time, they are conscious that something about *them* puts them alone at risk of losing God's all-encompassing love. They certainly lose the love of a lot of other Christians.

Such failures of love—the failure of friends and family to be open to learning from someone and growing by virtue of that connection—can instill profound shame in the person from whom love is withheld. Shame feels deeply personal, but it is actually a social emotion. Sociologists, psychologists, philosophers, and others agree that, at its root, shame reflects a fear of a break in a social bond, a fear of not being accepted by our community.[1] In Kai's case, it wasn't even *fear* but *certainty* that they had to sacrifice their fundamental capacity to love others if they wanted to be worthy of God. To Kai, that suffering felt like a sign of faithful commitment. It felt like a tangible sign of God's presence in their life, almost what some Christians call a sacrament.

But if you demand constant suffering from someone, you're not really loving them.

* * *

Far-right conservatives travel the country to protest funerals, plays, and pride parades with signs that say things like, "**D**on't th**I**nk Ch**R**ist accep**T**s **Y**ou HOMO" and "Fags Die God Laughs." A lot of the LGBTQ+ people who see them may get angry, outraged, or just crumble at the sight of them, and to a lot of straight and cisgender conservative Christians, these spectacular rituals of public shaming are embarrassing and hateful. Many conventionally conservative Protestant churches advocate a position in line with the old saying, "Love the sinner, hate the sin," reminding members that "loveless judgmentalism" isn't any more desirable than saying "anything goes."[2] But however toxic the stranger with the "DIRTY HOMO" sign may be, far greater damage is done when loved ones' commitment to their gendered narrative leads them to break relationships with LGBTQ+ people.

Even in churches like the one in Kai's story, where people have worked to eliminate the harshest human judgment to be "welcoming but not affirming" to LGBTQ+ people, how they actually treat LGBTQ+ people can distort love and harm people. By making a belief—their understanding of gender—a higher priority than listening to and understanding the actual LGBTQ+ people in their lives, non-affirming Christians can impart a particularly toxic form of shame that we call *sacramental shame*. A sacrament is commonly defined as a tangible sign of God's presence, and in some churches, they are considered necessary for salvation. Sacramental shame is when a community demands the performance of shame as a sign of God's presence in an LGBTQ+ person's life.

Because they believe that God created people to conform to binary gendered ideals, including heterosexuality, non-affirming Christians tend to treat variation as a lifestyle choice; that is, something a person has control over. They hope to discourage people from choosing the behaviors and identities they see as contrary to God's plan, so they make it clear that same-sex sex, gender transitions, and sometimes even LGBTQ+ identities are sinful and shameful. But the feelings that most people identify with being LGBTQ+ don't go away just because someone wants them to. People turn to that narrative hoping to combat sin and find "new life" in Jesus. But regardless of intention, that narrative's toxic consequences don't promote life, they destroy it, as Kevin Garcia puts it in the title of their 2020 book, *Bad Theology Kills*.³ But it's not enough to glibly point fingers at conservative bad guys. We can learn from the experiences of LGBTQ+ conservative Christians about the ways lots of people, perhaps even ourselves, might rely on shame and control rather than love.

If shame is the fear of being exposed as unworthy of relationships, *shaming* someone else is a way of telling them they are unworthy of a relationship with you. In a non-affirming church, LGBTQ+ members might end up having to display—and feel—ongoing shame about their gender or sexuality as a sign that they have not rebelled against God. Shame becomes the tangible sign of God's presence in their lives. Life in this dynamic becomes an unlivable paradox: shame—the fear that your capacity to love is dangerous to the people you love—becomes a requirement for even the faintest semblance of love. And this dynamic can be particularly fraught and complicated for LGBTQ+ Christians who are Black people, Indigenous people, or other people of color (BIPOC), where survival in a racist world can depend on faith and family, and faith and family can depend on the complementarian narrative of gender and sexuality. Isaac Archuleta, former director of Q Christian Fellowship, wrote an open letter to conservative Christians, saying "I did the right Christian thing: I hated my sin. But when your 'sin' is loving, you're left with no option but to hate your entire self."[4]

As Justin Lee told us about founding the Gay Christian Network (GCN):

> I wanted people to not have to live with the constant shame. And the option that was available for me when I was growing up was steeped in shame. It was all about, you know, feeling horrible about yourself until you became straight, which, of course, never happened, so you just felt horrible about yourself forever.

As a fundamentally relational creature, a human being, if my capacity to love is my source of shame, if that is what makes me unfit for *any* relationship—then my very existence is the problem.

* * *

Assuming that God can help a person overcome any temptation if they try hard enough, non-affirming Christians might be tempted to think that LGBTQ+ people who can't change their sexual orientation or gender identity aren't really *trying* to change, have not *really* set their sights on God, haven't *really* prayed, haven't *really* wanted it. LGBTQ+ conservative Protestants themselves often started out believing the same things, trying all the Christian approaches they could find, begging God to change them or make their errant feelings go away. They didn't rebel against God or the church—they wanted more than anything to belong in it. LGBTQ+ conservative Christians speak of beseeching God to fix them, of "crying ugly tears on my bedroom floor" while begging God to take away their sinful feelings. And for most of them, the omnipotent and all-loving creator of the universe didn't change a thing.

Kevin Garcia (they/them) tried for ten years to "pray the gay away" by going to therapists and group confessions, having "demons" cast out, fasting, relentlessly praying, and constantly performing acts of penance. None of it worked, which led Kevin to believe that *Kevin* was the problem, that their heart was "incontrovertibly damaged" and their soul "marred beyond any hope of healing." They wrote:

> For ten years I was convinced it was something wrong with me. It had to be me. I wasn't ever going to be good enough for God because I wasn't strong enough to overcome this trial.
>
> This warped view of myself distorted my logic. It caused me to view my life as [worthless]. It pushed me to take my life because a life full of this, what I saw as a horrible pattern of sin, a terrible addiction that I couldn't hope to overcome, was not worth living . . . .
>
> As I worked to suppress and change my sexual orientation, continually being met by failure, I internalized those failures as being my fault. I believed God was displeased with me, that I wasn't doing enough, that I couldn't change.
>
> What was the fruit of that labor? Literal death. I wanted to kill myself and nearly did.[5]

White, transgender Baptist pastor Allyson Robinson reflected on the thirty years she spent "begging" and "cajoling" God to make her *not-be* a woman, seeking others' prayers and an exorcism to free her "of the demon of femininity." But nothing changed. She wrote:

> And when I finally realized that no amount of prayer or fasting, no anointing or exorcism, no method of "relying on God" or "crucifying my flesh" would end my suffering, I gave serious thought to ending it all. Driving my car into a concrete bridge abutment at speed seemed, for a fateful moment, the only way to end my pain without bringing shame upon my church and my family.[6]

Darren Calhoun had been raised Catholic but was saved in a Pentecostal church when he was seventeen, and he devoted his life to the church. When he spoke about his experience of being redeemed as a Black, gay, Christian, his pastor told him he should be ashamed of himself, he should never speak of it again, and that no one would receive him if they knew he was gay. His pastor told him he had to lie "[i]f you really want to be Christian." It was the first time Darren felt shame about who he was. So, he willingly took his pastor's advice to live in an out-of-state building owned by the church. As we've mentioned, Darren slept on the altar, fasted two days per week, cleaned the building for $50/week, and constantly prayed to become straight. He did this for nearly four years. None of that effort ever made him heterosexual.

In an interview, Darren reflected on the years he spent sequestered in his pastor's out-of-state church, and the shame that consumed him there:

> I wanted intimacy, just to be known. I wanted somebody to really *get* me and to really understand me. But the only thing I could think about was the shame of wanting to be known, the shame of wanting to be close, the shame of wanting to be touched even, because we're embodied creatures. If the only thing I could deal with was *that* being shameful, then I could never find out, "Oh, there is some authentic need in here. There are some healthy ways that I could have

my needs met. There are some things that are natural and normal, and that are part of most of human history until now, when we got so homophobic, and so anti-touch, and so isolated. We live alone in ways that are unprecedented in history, you know?" ... Like, that has nothing to do with holiness. That's not the life that Jesus lived. Jesus had John laying on his chest. I promise you that would be problematic in many churches where we're trying to avoid homosexuality, and we're trying to avoid "the appearance of evil."

Shame comes from a fear of being unworthy of love, but when it's your human need for love that seems to make you unworthy of love, the impossible paradox becomes toxic.

* * *

Sacramental shame can urge the people who really internalize it to cut themselves off from relationships. It can make LGBTQ+ people see their very capacity to form relationships and love others as damaged and potentially harmful to those they love, so they cut themselves off from relationships of any kind. This chapter opened with Kai's story in a "welcoming" congregation, feeling like they couldn't get too close to *anyone*. Darren had a similar experience in a more unwelcoming one. When his pastor shamed him for being gay, he came to fear his own capacity to love.[7] In an interview he explained:

> As far as friends, there were a lot of people that I cut off. And I thought I was endangering them. I thought that I was going to poison them, I thought that my struggles were going to disillusion them, because I was ministering, and some people have ministers on some kind of pedestal. So I felt that all the stuff that was going on, would be so harmful, and so from my perspective I felt that I was doing good ... by pushing them [away].

Others shared similar experiences of rigidly policing their emotional attachments, of remaining aloof, and of not letting themselves get too close to anyone—even in friendships—for fear that they might harm others and that they were unfit for relationships. Ron Belgau, a celibate white gay convert to Catholicism, wrote that Paul's New Testament letters make it clear that homosexuality is one among many sins that bring condemnation, saying:

> Paul argues that homosexual acts can 1) keep us from the kingdom of Heaven; 2) defile the temple of the Holy Spirit within us; and 3) place us back under the judgment of the law.
>
> Given the stakes involved, it is not a risk I am willing to take. Even more so, I would never risk inflicting consequences that serious on another man whom I loved.[8]

Some, like Ron, choose celibacy while openly attesting to being gay, which allows them to be honest about who they are. But some Christians stigmatize and shun celibate gay people, too. Another option is to "live a lie"; that is, to keep secret their feelings of love and attraction, and their knowledge of who they are. But if people cannot bring their whole selves to others, to be open and vulnerable, then these relationships are hollow. A white gay man in his twenties we call Greg had poured himself into his faith and tried to build friendships in church and his Bible study, but it didn't work: "I couldn't get close with them because I wasn't being myself. . . . I felt like it was all a lie."

Christian singer-songwriter Vicky Beeching became a workaholic so she would not have to get close to people. As she told a reporter for the *Independent* in 2014, "It was too painful to be around people that didn't understand." She went on to Oxford University and then to become a Nashville Christian superstar at the age of twenty-three. A reporter she spoke to after coming out publicly sums it up: "To avoid the desolation of her personal life, Beeching would perform endlessly, ensuring every birthday and public holiday was booked up."[9] Eventually, the chronic stress of constantly policing her feelings manifested in a life-threatening autoimmune disorder that required chemotherapy to treat.

Beeching isn't alone in reporting physical results of toxic stress from this dynamic. Others report emotional isolation, despair, self-hatred, substance abuse, eating disorders, reckless behavior, and suicide attempts—those who succeeded are no longer around to tell us about it—as a result of attempting to suppress their attractions and cutting themselves off from relationships. An hour into our lunch conversation, Kai recalled that the stress of mandated celibacy had caused them heart failure. As a healthy college student, they had collapsed with a heart rate of 19 and ended up in the hospital for a week. Finding no potential cause except the high levels of stress hormones in Kai's blood, doctors asked if Kai had been under any particular stress lately. At the time, Kai couldn't think of anything. As we spoke, it occurred to them that they had fallen in love that year and cut off that relationship in deference to their theology. "I literally had a broken heart," they marveled, "but to me that wasn't stress. That wasn't anxiety. That was just life." They paused in thought for a second, then said it again, shaking their head slightly: "That was just life to me."

* * *

Human beings are born for the kind of deep, egalitarian connection with other people that can seem to transcend words. The twentieth-century Protestant theologian Karl Barth argued that Christianity is fundamentally about God's desire for relationships with people, a desire that made God want to come to earth in the human form of Jesus.[10] The Ten Commandments prohibit various ways of violating relationships with God and/or other people: worshipping other gods, lying, stealing, and coveting neighbors' wives and possessions. Two of the four gospels report that when Jesus was asked which commandment was the greatest, he said loving God with all your heart, soul, and strength, "And the second is like it: 'Love your neighbor as yourself.'"

Jesus's claim that loving your neighbor "is like" loving God suggests that Christianity recognizes and celebrates human beings' fundamentally relational nature. If I hoard resources and keep them from people who need them, if I steal from or cheat people, my greed has led me to violate others' trust and made me unworthy of my relationships with them. Murdering, stealing, and breaking promises all violate relationships. Other things not listed as commandments can also violate relationships or prevent relational connection: upholding white-centered ways of thinking and acting can do harm or threaten harm to people of color and make a person or institution unworthy of their trust. Failing to show up for people can suggest to them that they don't matter to us and that our relationships with them are expendable.

Dealing with shame a lot, many people we spoke to referred to Brené Brown's distinction between guilt as a feeling of having done a bad thing, and shame, the feeling that "I *am* bad."[11] Often, when we break relationships, we feel not just guilt but shame. Shame is tied to relationships because authentic relationships require vulnerability, being willing to expose who we really are and risk that others might not like what they see.

Feeling shame isn't necessarily always toxic. Because shame is rooted in concern for social bonds, it can serve as an emotional "red flag" holding us accountable to others for who to be and how to behave. The possibility of feeling shame means that we want the people who matter to us to think we're good people. Feeling shame can indicate that we recognize our moral flaws and want to be more worthy of relationships with others. Robbing banks, as in John MacArthur's analogy, or breaking promises you made to your spouse, as in J. D. Greear's, breaks relationships by violating others' trust and treating them as obstacles or objects rather than people whose feelings and trust matter to you. When we see ourselves as the kinds of people who fail our relationships—because of dishonesty, greed, or racism, for instance—feeling ashamed of these shortcomings may lead us to confess, atone, and work to be better people, worthy of others' trust.[12] In that case, shame can build or restore relationships. But that kind of work doesn't change people's sexual orientation or gender identity—things that don't change at will and don't violate our relationships.

There is a huge difference between experiencing shame occasionally and routinely having your worth as a person called into question.[13] In some cases, and not only in conservative churches, shame can become a disposition; that is, a habitual way of approaching the world. Women, people of color, people with disabilities, poor people, people of minority religions, immigrants, fat people, the old, the young, and people in one or more of these groups sometimes come to feel as if there is something fundamentally wrong with who we are.[14] In these situations, we can feel like we are only welcome *anywhere* if we compartmentalize, leaving the unwelcome parts of who we are at the door of every gathering we attend. Progressives and liberals can try to counter that shame by shaming the rich, the white, the male, and so forth—treating social power as a disqualification for trust and connection, regardless of whether that person has proven unworthy of trust. The difference is that institutional power creates more vulnerability for those already at the bottoms of hierarchies.

In the Introduction, we referred to a speech Sandra gave at a The Reformation Project (TRP) leadership training, in which she described growing up in predominantly white conservative churches where she internalized the beliefs that women couldn't lead, that Black people were deviant, and that gayness was a symptom of unhealthy emotional codependency. As a Black lesbian, she strove to downplay those parts of who she was that diverged from her church's social ideal. She described her efforts to "be a good little white boy" as a "living suicide." As she spoke of the traumatically shaming nature of constantly having to hide parts of herself, audience members agreed, yelling "Mm hm!" and "Yes!" It's worth revisiting how she spelled it out:

> To be told in a space that's for healing and wholeness, to be told that I was created in God's image but simultaneously being asked to fit to the image of the white Western evangelical world, that minimizes my gender, that ignores my blackness, and rejects my sexuality. That is an act of violence.

By "hiding" parts of herself, she was trying to be someone else, to fit an image of God that was actually an image of other people—white, cisgender, heterosexual men. She was trying to fit in to meet the conditions others placed on her belonging. She was trying to fit into a space that taught her over and over, probably without coming right out and saying it, that who she was was wrong. How much energy did she spend trying to be someone else? What else might she have done with that energy?

Some might say that it's clearly wrong to shame people over their race or gender, but sexuality is different. Sexual sin is something Jesus actually spoke of when he equated remarriage after divorce and looking lustfully at women with adultery. And yet, while these admonishments might today seem most relevant to heterosexual men, that is the group *least* likely to be shamed for their sexual transgressions.

Sociologist Kelsy Burke has found that in conservative Christianity, white, heterosexual men, in particular, are more likely to be shown "grace"; their sexual transgressions confirm the complementarian narrative of men's "naturally aggressive" libidos, and white men are considered the standard from which other categories of people deviate and fall short. In the 1970s, evangelical authors of Christian marriage guides wrote about sex as the *culmination* of one's relationship with God. Husbands and wives were encouraged to explore their sexual desires, particularly the husbands', and to understand sexual pleasure as God's gift to married people, made all the sweeter by knowing that satisfying sex was God's special blessing and reward. To this day evangelical women are often told it is their duty to "be a blessing to your husband."[15]

In many cases, family and church are entirely overlapping groups, and for people of color, both can provide crucial help in surviving and navigating a racist society's shaming and stigma. Embracing a Christianity that is often defined by white people in white terms, LGBTQ+ people of color navigate families and churches that have dealt for centuries with racist claims that all people of color were inherently sexually deviant. In those communities, being LGBTQ+ might seem to prove the stereotypes right, bringing shame on all of them. Conservative Christian LGBTQ+ people of all races expressed shame and fear of alienating their loved ones, but white people didn't express any fear of bringing shame upon their whole racial or ethnic group.[16] Conservative Christian people of color have accused LGBTQ+ people in their communities of rejecting their people and their heritage to embrace a "white sickness."

In a keynote address at a Q Christian Fellowship conference, a Chinese American, celibate gay pastor spoke of being constantly treated as "not Chinese enough, not American enough, not man enough, not gay enough, not straight enough, not Christian enough." Feeling that you're never enough, or too much, are both experiences of shame.

Relationships are about being vulnerable to others and feeling that they see us, that they hear us, and that they are open to learning from us and growing with us. Rather than helping a person to restore relationships, sacramental shame attacks their ability to form them. What we mean is that in a sacramental shame dynamic, a loved one breaks a relationship with a LGBTQ+ person, closes themself off from listening and relating to them—and the blame falls to the LGBTQ+ person for being LGBTQ+ because the loved one stigmatizes how the LGBTQ+ person experiences love, connection, and their sense of self. Sacramental shame treats LGBTQ+ people as not just broken, but more broken than everyone else. Sacramental shame makes people feel unworthy of the infinite love that God supposedly freely gives everyone. It makes God's purportedly unconditional love conditional for LGBTQ+ people. Christians are taught to "be like Jesus," loving and serving others, but in some Christian communities, LGBTQ+ people are not *allowed* to minister to others, lest their "sin" spread through contact.

* * *

In the book of Matthew (7:15–18), Jesus warns his followers of "false prophets, who come to you in sheep's clothing but inwardly are ravenous wolves," and says, "You will know them by their fruits. . . . A good tree cannot bear bad fruit, nor can a bad tree bear good fruit." For LGBTQ+ conservative Christians who are subjected to sacramental shame, "bad fruits" are everywhere: broken relationships; physical violence; feelings of God's distance; being banished, cut off, or held at arm's length; mental and physical illnesses; addictions; wanting to die; trying to die; and killing oneself.

As we discussed in Chapter 2, complementarity doctrine elevates social conceptions of gender and marriage to the level of Godly mandates. Rigid adherence to complementarity keeps parents, pastors, and friends from loving the LGBTQ+ people in their lives in a relational way. Love requires vulnerability—openness to learning from another, being open to uncertainty. It requires people to prioritize—not control—relationships. Saying, "I love you but hate your shady business dealings" may make sense when talking about someone whose actions violate others' trust. Loving people can mean holding each other accountable to be better at honoring relationships. Saying "I love you, but I hate your sin" when the supposed sin is your capacity to love, and/or who you are—that's not really loving at all. As soon as complementarity doctrine takes priority over relating to another person, then any "love" becomes conditional and the relationship breaks. Rather than learning and growing from their connection to that person, the will to control takes over. Sacramental shame treats people as objects, as problems to be fixed or managed, or as tests of one's devotion to doctrine.

* * *

Christians generally think they're supposed to help people feel closer to God (i.e., to feel God's love), but non-affirming Christians often make LGBTQ+ people feel further from God. A Black, pansexual, genderfluid pastor we call Jamelah lamented that people are afraid to seek the resources they need to live because of what they had been taught about God. She recalled:

> [In Baptist or Pentecostal spaces], I feel like my people are dying. I spoke at a youth conference four or five years ago and we had queer youth present. And people went on tirades about human sexuality and—you can see, when you look in certain people's eyes, you can see, when parts of their soul begin to die or rot.

If you haven't been there, imagine being a young person, sitting through such a "tirade," knowing that the speaker is talking about you. Maybe the friends you came to the event with are sitting all around you, saying "Amen!" and "Yes, Lord" as the speaker goes on. In effect, the speaker is saying that nothing anyone can say will convince them that you're okay, nothing will convince them that you are worthy to love and serve God and other people, just as you are. If nothing will convince them, they're not open to you, to your story. In short, they are not open to *relating* to you, to learning and growing by virtue of connecting with you. Relationally speaking, you're not a person anymore. And it's not just the speaker because the speaker claims to be speaking for *God*. In churches that teach that God craves a personal relationship with everyone, LGBTQ+ people are told that they alone are somehow not good enough for that relationship, which makes God's nonresponse to their sincere prayers for change feel like the profoundest rejection.

A thirty-two-year-old Black gay man we call Lucas told us he needed church to sustain him in a racist world, but he also feared that God's love might not be unconditional *for him*. Lucas remarked:

> I have all the information that I would need to know that, like, same-sex unions would not be a problem. I can tell you right now I'd probably accept a proposal. I'd have the party, I'd have—I'd invite all the people and I'd get to that church—and I'd probably faint. It's still this very irrational fear that's just kind of given in childhood that just hasn't been—it just hasn't disappeared yet. . . . Like, I have all the social references, I have all the relationship models, I have all the ministry models, I have all the organizational models, and I even, like, can sit down and exegete Scripture . . . So, I mean, I know these things but, like, it's not satiated. The fear just still hasn't gone away. . . . I guess that's the fear is that—not that we get there and there's no God, but that we get there, there is a God and this God is this hateful person with this trident and this long beard and this dress and is, you know, crazy homophobic and, you know, that's—that's what's not satiated.

Lucas wasn't alone; a twenty-six-year-old Black bisexual woman we call Iris had largely resolved her religious anxieties by determining that God was not "petty," meaning God didn't punish people for failing to be perfect. Still, she worried sometimes that God would cast her out. She recalled:

> I was so good at being kind of the Christian good girl, I got a lot of validation in that, like, "You're good, you don't have to worry about these things, you're not fornicating, you're not drinking, you're not

smoking, you're not doing any of the things. . . . You're fine, God loves you, you're great." But that's a hard thing to think, "I have to do these things or the bottom drops out." . . . I think I was afraid, but I think in my mind back then, it was just like "I'm not afraid, I'm just trying to do the right thing" as I understood it. I think now I can look back and see, like, I was really scared that, like, petty God was gonna be like "Get out of here!"

Similarly, Greg desperately wanted a relationship with God, but was "ashamed to turn to God," unable to trust God or feel God's love, and lamented, "I want to be one of your followers, but I'm afraid to even talk to you because you're going to hate me."

The concept of *spiritual violence*, named by Christians to capture various experiences in which religious objects, rituals, or authority were used to degrade them in their relationship with God—like sexual abuse by clergy—points to the distinctive kinds of harm done when Christians make other Christians feel separated from God or feel that God hates them.[17] In the course of our research, we heard about a lot of forms of spiritual violence: LGBTQ+ Christians who had been forbidden from worship or told they couldn't pray, who were told that they were sick and irreparable, whose parents couldn't bear to be around them or who said having a gay kid was worse than death. We heard from people who had come millimeters away from suicide, and of course, some people succeeded at it. Some churches publicly shamed LGBTQ+ people by listing their "sins" in the guise of a call to prayer.

Spiritual violence can also lead to physical violence, and those stories are not hard to come by among LGBTQ+ conservative Christians. At its conference every year, GCN/QCF had an evening open mic time, during which dozens of people lined up to share testimonies of how the group saved their lives from countless kinds of suffering, including homelessness, physical attacks, reparative "therapies," and heartbreaking words of condemnation. Church members may have intended to be loving, to rid the person of something destructive that has taken hold within them. If the church believes in demons, they may think a demon needs to be physically exorcised from a person; the failure of the demon to flee could lead church members to repeat and intensify their efforts, at times "laying on hands" in ways that felt like a group beatdown.

At other times, the violence is not even intended to heal, but to express rage. Cal, an Asian American in his early twenties, had published a blog trying to work out why Christians were so hostile to LGBTQ+ people. If LGBTQ+ people were sinning at all, Cal posited, their "sin" was one of love. His college ministry leader ordered him to take it down and told him, "I just feel like punching you right now." We heard testimony from a man whose father punched him in the face and threw him out of the house when he found out he was gay. Sociologist Bernadette Barton tells the story of a gay girl living in the Bible Belt whose mother attacked her with a butcher knife after her sister outed her. Acts of physical violence convey that a person is simultaneously negligible—something, like a mosquito or cockroach, that it is not wrong to hurt—and profoundly threatening—someone so dangerous that hurting or even killing them is justified. In his 1952 book, *Black Skin, White Masks*, Franz Fanon observed that his presence among white people, his insistence on being seen as fully human, provoked violence and outrage because his humanity threatened white people's definition of what it meant for *them* to be human—to be superior to Black people. These violent urges and outbursts seem similar, threatening cisgender heterosexual conservative Christians' very notion that what it means to be human is to be better than (and other than) "homosexuals."[18]

Physical violence is a dramatic way of severing a relationship with a person—an effort to control or eliminate them, an assertion of invulnerability. To the one being hit or threatened or attacked with a butcher knife, it generally doesn't feel like love. But physical violence is not remotely *necessary* to breaking a relationship. Shame is a fear that something about who you are will make you unfit for relationships, and some churches make that fear a reality. Being banished doesn't feel like love either. We heard from people who were thrown out of their church, from others who were allowed to attend their church but not be members, from people who were allowed to be members but not to serve in any leadership capacity, and people who were allowed to lead but were constantly under scrutiny and at risk of losing their ministry. All of this is distancing, or holding others at arm's length.

Church extends through members' lives. At its most active time, The Marin Foundation received calls nearly weekly from parents struggling with their pastor's advice to throw their thirteen- or fourteen-year-old out of the house for being LGBTQ+. In 2014, Pastor John MacArthur recommended waiting to sever all ties until a child reaches adulthood. While exact statistics are hard to come by, the Family Acceptance Project argues that Christian homes are largely responsible for the vastly disproportionate number of LGBTQ+ youth living on the streets.[19]

But banishment does not have to be literal. For some, the fear was of quietly "disappearing" or turning "invisible." We heard about fairly public exorcism attempts in churches of all kinds, and some Black respondents, in particular, reported hearing mocking and scorn for LGBTQ+ people from the pulpit. But among our BIPOC respondents, under the constant threat of being sexually stigmatized by a white-centered culture, we have observed that what dominated their LGBTQ+ experiences were silencing and invisibility. Confiding in loved ones most often provoked well-intentioned, quiet reassurances of "we'll get through this," prayers for deliverance, and warnings not to sin. Imani, a twenty-nine-year-old Black bisexual pastor, described growing up in a Black Church culture that helped her to build a deep well of pride in her Blackness but enforced silence about LGBTQ+ people, compounding the widespread claim that bisexuals didn't exist at all. She recalled:

> I got all that information filtered through [older relatives] it was still very hushed and words people wouldn't use. And people's partners were their "friend" and, . . . no matter how clear the people were about who they were and who they loved, everybody else talked about it as if they could create a secret out of something that wasn't a secret. And then [my cousin] who was in the same congregation, came out. Her mama had a fit, and their relationship was so strained *I* didn't even see her for a while.

Imani experienced that silence as a child and teenager, trying to make sense of her difference, which resulted in her trying to figure out whether she could even *exist*. She recalled:

> You end up thinking for a long time that it's not real or it's not there, and . . . these ways of being these people literally, like, whole people don't exist. . . . I was scared to ask questions . . . because I didn't want to offend anyone, and I didn't want to hurt anybody . . . —I didn't want to disappear, too. You know what I'm saying? Like, "You all are literally telling me whole groups of people don't exist. Like, am *I* going to stop existing, if I ask you these questions?"

When loved ones adhere so strictly to complementarian gender ideology, they connect full personhood to cisgender heterosexuality, and—because racism is anchored by myths about deviant sexuality—ultimately as white.[20] Persistent racist stereotypes can pressure communities of color to demonstrate that their members live up to complementarian ideals to show a racist society that, as a group, they are morally worthy of respect.[21] In Imani's story, that drive for respectability sounds like a confusing stew of fear and silence and love—conditional love.

Similarly, Simone told us that, even once she felt comfortable naming the truth of her sexual difference, the invisibility of Black LGBTQ+ people in broader culture led her to believe that Black people "were not gay" in the sense that they did not outwardly claim this identity or truth about themselves regardless of how they related to others in their personal lives. This invisibility reinforces narratives within the Black Church that gayness is a "white thing," again complicating the dynamic for Black respondents because of the threat that in naming their sexuality they might be perceived not just as sexual deviants, but as race traitors.[22] When Derek, a mixed-race twenty-two-year-old, was growing up in a predominantly white Nazarene church, he entertained the possibility that he was gay because he was partly white.

For others, the "disappearing" took the form of friends all ghosting them at once. Kai told us of their journey from being sure that affirming same-sex relationships was wrong, to thinking the church might have gotten it wrong, which meant they were "ostracized" from most of their faith communities. They told us they lost "80%" of their friends, recalling:

> I had known rich community. I had felt so supported and so cared for [as a celibate lesbian], and looked up to in a lot of ways. And to have all of that come crashing down, without so much as a single conversation with some friends, it devastated me in a way that I thought I was ready for in my mind, but emotionally kinda tore me to shreds.

It turned out Kai's friends' love was conditional after all.

For Kai's community, the problem was that Kai questioned their stance on mandatory celibacy, but in other communities even identifying as anything other than heterosexual and cisgender can cause an entire church to turn their backs on a person, cutting them off from relationships. We spoke with a young, white man from Ohio whose Christian friends all stopped speaking to him when he told them he was gay. Similarly, a white, queer, cisgender man, Brandan Robertson, wrote of his experience with the fundamentalist church that had given his life meaning when he first found it at age twelve—a church that had celebrated what they had seen as his spiritual gifts. In an open letter he asked:

> Dear Church, why is it that the moment when I feel most truly authentic and most truly connected to God, that you have pushed me away and said I am invalid? Why must who I am as a person cause you to fear me so much? . . . When I kept my sexuality hidden, you lauded me. You told me I was anointed of God. That I was going to be used by God to change the world. . . . Now, when I walk into that same church, I only get side glares and people telling me that they're "praying for me." What's changed? That I'm more honest? More authentic? More devoted to Christ than ever before? Yet nothing is the same between us. Instead of a beloved member of your community, I'm a stranger and exile in the house of God.

After he came out, he says he received numerous condemning messages from former friends, mentors, and pastors, including one that said:

> It is safe to say that in [the] current trajectory of your life you will usher many into a hellish existence. And when you need the blood of Christ to wash away your sins, where will you turn, now that you have renounced His redeeming work so thoroughly. But I already know, you have a victim mentality and you use your sense of victimhood to victimize others. Your behavior is repugnant to me.[23]

In situations like these, what had seemed like intimate connection, the solid base they stood on as they engaged the world, was removed in the blink of an eye once they tried to be better known, more honest. Kai's and Mike's friends disappeared; Imani's cousin disappeared. What Brandan had thought was love quickly turned into fear and disgust, until he went away.

*   *   *

Of course, people whose parents throw them out of the house are traumatized. But more "loving" forms of sacramental shame can work a different sort of trauma. Many parents would never dream of throwing their child out of the house (and experienced dismaying conflict when their pastors told them they should). Many wouldn't dream of hitting their kids or attacking them with a butcher knife. At the same time, many conservative Christian parents or pastors, steeped in complementarian messages, are likely to see a child's or church member's being LGBTQ+ as a problem they need to *fix*. Suddenly, the child or friend must be kept at arm's length—someone to pray *for* and not *with*. As lovingly as it's intended, trying to "cure" loved ones of being LGBTQ+, in more subtle ways than physical violence or banishment, cultivates shame, quietly severs their relationship while seeming to preserve it, and has toxic effects.

In response to the sexual stigmatization of racism, BIPOC Christians tended toward private efforts at changing people, such as in Darren's sequestering. After nearly four years in seclusion—certainly an extreme case—Darren eventually heard Jesus telling him to stop hiding from life, and to go out and be among other people. Feeling totally cut off from those who had been at the center of his life, he moved on and found a multiracial but predominantly white "welcoming but not affirming" church, where he could be in ministry and contact with others on the condition that he remained celibate.

Darren had the advantages of being able to feel relatively comfortable in predominantly white spaces and being able to find a church where people tried to respect diverse ways of being Christian. And, having experienced his shamed sexuality as a dangerous compulsion, he agreed with their insistence on celibacy. Even so, he felt that he had to watch himself to be sure he compartmentalized adequately, so that his style of worship didn't draw comments from white people. Not every LGBTQ+ person of color can find a combination with which they can live.

Predominantly white, LGBTQ+-affirming congregations can be found in many places, including some dotted throughout the rural South. They are not everywhere, and the nearby one might not meet a person's particular needs, but they are out there. Predominantly Black or multiracial LGBTQ+-affirming churches exist, like Lighthouse Church of Chicago and City of Refuge in the Bay Area, but they are fewer and farther between. Lucas gave the hypothetical example of a white gay man having to leave his conservative church, saying:

> Let's assume that he leaves that and tries to find a more open and affirming church. He can find another space culturally and music-wise that would totally minister to him. It's really hard as a person of color to find that. . . . Black culture is so tied up in church and it's something that, like, you are born and raised to, like, need, recognize, respect, and even crave. And then to deny them that is just cruel.

Those who find LGBTQ+-affirming churches often only find predominantly white ones, and they endure subtle (or not-so-subtle) racism and ethnocentrism from white pastors and laypeople who treat white traditions and music as "Christian," and nonwhite traditions as interesting variations, distractions, or worse. A Black, same-gender-loving pastor spoke at a conference about her experience in a predominantly white seminary, where white classmates sought to remove all the songs with blood imagery from the hymnal because it clashed with their nonviolent understanding of Christianity. Most of the songs they tore out had roots in the Black American experience.

* * *

There are ways of being visibly unloving, such as refusing to engage in relationships with people and negating them. But LGBTQ+ conservative Christians have also experienced other failures of love, failures that were cast as attempts to love and help them. Complementarian theology can turn efforts to love and help LGBTQ+ people into something harmful.

Some white LGBTQ+ people also came to be afraid that God hated them, and some "disappeared" from their churches as well. It is mostly white people who were sent to, or voluntarily enrolled in, ministries that tried to "cure" people of being LGBTQ+, or at least to help people to resist gender- and sexuality-related temptations. Reparative "therapies"—to try to either cure people of being LGBTQ+ or help them manage it like an addiction—have been thoroughly discredited by all major mental health organizations. Exodus, the umbrella organization for reparative therapy for over thirty years, closed in 2013 when board members and the executive director came to terms with how deeply they had been misleading people. The executive director apologized on national television for the harms people suffered in their ministries. Some ex-gay treatment programs have closed their doors or changed their mission. Garrard Conley's memoir, *Boy Erased*, and the documentary, *Pray Away*, detail the intensely stigmatizing experience of being in programs that treat being LGBTQ+ as sinful, harmful addictions.[24] And, as Alan Chambers, Exodus's last executive director attested at GCN's 2012 conference, a year before he and the board shut Exodus down, these programs don't really change anyone's sexual orientation or gender identity. Some of these ministries persist, mostly in the Restored Hope Network. These therapies showcase the lengths people have gone to live out their belief in the complementarian vision of gender and sexuality.

A white gay man we call Jimmy observed in his time at a prominent residential program that participants were re-enrolling for second and third ten-week sessions, but they were getting no closer to their goal of change. In the meantime, he saw them "hiding from life" rather than doing Christ's work in the world, serving other people. Jimmy, still as gay as when he entered the program, declined the opportunity to re-enroll, and moved to a new city to work with a ministry serving people experiencing homelessness.

Whether they were sent away or simply seeing reparative therapists while living at home, many participants found that the message was the same: until their orientation changed, they would continue to displease God and be unfit to love. They prayed to God to change them, and God never changed them. And in the meantime, those they trusted to guide them and to love them repeatedly told them they were unworthy and that they needed to be fixed. As white Christian trans activist Stephanie Mott put it at a conference, "What Christians fail to understand is that when you tell them that because of who they are they cannot participate in faith, you push them away from God. Why don't people get this—that in the name of Christ they are pushing people away from God?"

Not all white Christian families took the "Exodus" approach of sending people to a particular ministry, and some homegrown efforts to "fix" LGBTQ+ people are quite public. Rob and Linda Robertson are white, conservative Christian parents who have traveled the country telling their story. They published their testimony online to help other Christian parents of LGBTQ+ kids avoid the mistakes they now realize they made. The Robertson family's story helps us to see how efforts to love LGBTQ+ can go terribly wrong.

When their son Ryan, then twelve, told Linda he was gay in an instant message in 2001, she felt shock and fear. She and Rob responded to Ryan with expressions of their deep unconditional love for him—coupled with equally explicit conditions. They told him:

> We *love* you. We will *always* love you. And this is hard, really hard . . . [but t]he feelings you have had for other guys don't make

you gay. You don't know who you are yet. Your identity is not that you're gay anyway. You are a child of God. . . .

We love you. Nothing will change that. . . . But if you're gonna follow Jesus, holiness is your only option. Since you know what the Bible says, and since you want to follow God, embracing your sexuality is not an option.[25]

They write of their years of frenzied efforts to help their son, arranging time for him to spend with manly Christian role models, having the church organize prayer teams, keeping a binder of relevant Scripture in the bathroom so that the whole family could spend their idle moments praying for Ryan to be attracted to girls. Ryan participated willingly, testifying in front of over a hundred area teenagers about his struggle not to be gay, memorizing hundreds of Scripture passages, praying constantly. But nothing changed. His parents recall:

God didn't answer Ryan's prayers—or ours—though we were all believing with faith that the God of the Universe—the God for whom NOTHING is impossible—could easily make Ryan straight. But He did not.

The narrative goes on to detail how, five years later:

just before his 18th birthday, Ryan, depressed, suicidal, disillusioned, and convinced that he would never be able to be loved by God, made a new choice. He decided to throw out his Bible and his faith at the same time, and to try searching for what he desperately wanted—peace—another way. And the way he chose to try first was drugs.

Using heavily, Ryan disappeared for a year-and-a-half. His parents stopped praying for him to be straight and just prayed for him to be okay, and to know that God loved him. Eventually, he came back, asking if they could ever forgive him for things he had done in service to his addiction, and the family did a lot of hard work to apologize to each other and forgive each other. But ten months after his return, Ryan went out with his old friends, overdosed, and died in the hospital seventeen days later.

Treating being LGBTQ+ as a sin or a problem to be fixed does harm, and perhaps the best evidence of that comes from parents who tried that approach and experienced where it led. The Robertson family's story also shows how "love the sinner, hate the sin" breaks relationships. They say:

> Though our hearts may have been good (we truly thought what we were doing was loving), we did not even give Ryan a chance to wrestle with God, to figure out what HE believed God was telling him through Scripture about his sexuality. We had believed firmly in giving each of our four children the space to question Christianity, to decide for themselves if they wanted to follow Jesus, to truly OWN their own faith. But we were too afraid to give Ryan that room when it came to his sexuality, for fear that he'd make the wrong choice.

Once Ryan told them he was gay, his parents stopped trusting him as someone who could find his own way. Linda testifies, "I grieve for what could have been, had we been walking by FAITH instead of by FEAR."

The Robertson family felt love for Ryan. We have no doubt that they wanted what was best for him. They wanted to spend eternity with him in heaven rather for him to stray from God's path. They wanted him to have a good life, full of love like their own. We don't want to add to the regret these loving people clearly feel. They have apologized on the Internet, for all the world to see, because they know they did wrong, and years later, people still post hateful criticisms of their parenting as if they themselves aren't aware of the depth of their error. They know.

But to amplify their own message to others helps to explain how treating being LGBTQ+ as sin violates relationships. Philosopher Martin Buber can help us to see the difference in ways of loving others. In what he called an *I–you* intimate relationship, he wrote, we learn and grow as we connect to others; in what he called an *I–it* objectifying experience, the other does not penetrate our defenses or touch our souls; we might get information from them, but we don't grow and learn from them.[26] We might love ice cream, but we don't have a relationship with ice cream. We love it as an object. We don't learn from it, except for what new pleasures it can bring us or how much we can eat before it makes us feel sick. We take care of it, only so that it doesn't melt and thus stop giving us pleasure. We don't expect our care for it to help it grow and change and be its best ice-cream self—it is not a person. It is an object, ours to eat or save for later.

Ryan's coming out shifted his parents' love from relational to objectifying, the one-sided love for an object. They felt compelled to fix him, to control him. bell hooks defines genuine love as "a combination of care, commitment, trust, knowledge, responsibility, and respect," but when Ryan revealed he was gay, his parents' efforts to fix him amounted to a withdrawal of trust.[27] They didn't trust him or his capacity to relate to others. Rather than learning to experience intimacy with other people while relating to God, they gave him a choice between being loved by God and being a relational person. They write:

> Basically, we told our son that he had to choose between Jesus and his sexuality. We forced him to make a choice between God and being a sexual person. Choosing God, practically, meant living a lifetime condemned to being alone. As a teenager, he had to accept that he would never have the chance to fall in love, hold hands, have his first kiss, or share the intimacy and companionship that we, as his parents, enjoy. We had always told our kids that marriage was God's greatest earthly gift . . . but Ryan had to accept that he alone would not be offered that present.

Linda wrote that when he finally called home after eighteen months of them not knowing whether he was alive or dead, he asked, "Do you think you could ever love me again?" In Linda's telling, "I told him that we had never stopped loving him, not for one second. We loved him then more than we had ever loved him." They felt love for him, but to *him* it hadn't felt like being loved. That's part of what makes sacramental shame so toxic—it looks like love but doesn't feel like being loved. And if you don't feel loved by people who so obviously love you, isn't that proof of how messed up your capacity to love is?

Conservative Christian parents, friends, and pastors usually don't mean to treat their loved ones as objects; they want what's best for them. They want them to live rich, love-filled lives according to what they see as God's will, and they want them to spend eternity in heaven. It's not that his family treated Ryan callously. They felt love for Ryan. Because of their complementarian understanding of gender and sexuality, his being gay filled them with fear, and they acted on that fear to try to fix him—to fix the problem he had become—so he would conform to their church's narrative. At its core, the "love the sinner, hate the sin" approach distorts love, almost imperceptibly shifting from relational love to the one-sided "love" people feel for objects, like ice cream. And that has consequences.

* * *

It's easy enough for a lot of liberals and progressives like us to see how sacramental shame is destructive and wrong, but it's not enough to point our fingers at the people who are trying to be loving and do the right thing but fail in the most important ways. The question we need to ask ourselves is how *we* fail to love. How *we* dispense shame—to people who seem to have it easier, to people who aren't up on the lingo, to people who want to create a more just world but don't know how. And do any of us *really* have all the answers? Those of us on the left often fail to love, too. We often rely on shame to police the boundaries of our own groups. In some ways, this might protect us. Everyone needs safe spaces, especially those who are systematically oppressed. But when we fail to relate to people (even when it's safe for us to do that)—by withholding recognition, by refusing to listen to others and hear their perspectives, we close people off from movements to make the world more just.

In The Marin Foundation's biweekly discussion groups, we saw the value in listening, even to people who disagreed with us. In those open discussions, that cultivated an ethic of listening, no one decided being LGBTQ+ was *more* sinful than they had thought before. It takes time and energy, and not everyone has that all the time. We know. But when someone has started asking questions and wants to work out their thinking and hear your perspective, giving them that care can help them to understand how toxic some of their past behaviors and beliefs have been. It can help them to be more loving. The movement for love and justice can expand and grow. And, as we describe next, people can heal.

4

How Relationships Can Heal Toxic Shame

In Chapter 2, we met Eduardo, who argued that creation isn't actually just pairs of opposites, but beautiful in-betweenness as well. Similarly, Austen Hartke—a white, bisexual, trans, Lutheran, Hebrew Bible scholar—published a video in his YouTube series, *Trans and Christian*, pointing out:

> In Hebrew, in the original language of Genesis, the first human is referred to as *adam* [pronounced *a-DAHM*]. This word *adam* is very close to the Hebrew word *adamah* which means earth or ground. So basically, this first person is named "Thing Made Out of Ground," or "Earth Creature," or "Human." The thing that jumps out at me immediately about this is that the original human is androgynous, it's genderless, it's sexless, it's just *adam*, it's a human, made out of ground and breathed into with the spirit of God. In fact, lots of people have seen *adam* or, "Adam," as a great example of a gender-neutral or intersex person in the Bible. And the cool thing about it is that God is totally fine with it. God loves this first human so much that God surrounds them with animals and tries to find some partner for them, simply because "It is not good for the human to be alone." God isn't concerned about Adam's gender or sex; God is concerned with Adam's need for love and community.[1]

In 2016, Christian campuses debated trans people's use of public bathrooms in light of North Carolina's House Bill 2, which required people to use restrooms that matched the sex listed on their birth certificates. Echoing Eduardo and Hartke, Matthew Vines, the founder of The Reformation Project (TRP), who is white and gay, remarked on Facebook:

> [Y]es, God made male and female. But God also made night and day—and that doesn't mean God didn't make dawn and dusk, too. And ironically, it's typically dawn and dusk that people think are the most beautiful times of day!
>
> Literally no one looks at a sunset and says, "How tragic that the lines between night and day have been blurred in our broken world." Even though night and day are creational categories listed in Genesis 1, just like male and female, with no exceptions mentioned! No, we intuitively understand that God's creation is bursting forth with diversity, with blurred boundaries, and with all the beauty that brings....
>
> So my view: If you think trans and non-binary gender identities are broken, then you should think sunsets are broken, too. And if you aren't willing to say the latter, then perhaps you should rethink the former.[2]

Many conservative Christians would immediately dismiss such commentaries as the arrogant logic of self-interested queer and trans people trying to twist the Bible to serve their own purposes. When LGBTQ+ Christians come to a place of naming and affirming their gender or sexuality, many conservative Christians see it as an instance of sinful people sinfully elevating themselves and their selfish, sinful desires over other people and God's word. The "pride" they see is the deadly sin that "cometh before a fall"; that is, arrogance or hubris.

Other Christians have argued that LGBTQ+ pride is not the same as arrogance or hubris, but the opposite of shame. In a Gay Christian Network (GCN) online devotional published during Pride Week, a contributor wrote:

I've been reflecting on this word: Pride. I grew up being taught that pride was a sin, perhaps the root of sin. Pride was the opposite of humility. But when we speak of Pride Month, pride is not the opposite of humility—it is the opposite of shame.

Some "pride" certainly is arrogance or hubris, which violates relationships by putting oneself over others. But what we'll describe in this chapter is the kind of pride LGBTQ+ people usually talk about, relational pride, which fosters relationships because it is actually connected to humility. Both relational pride and humility allow us to be open to vulnerable connection to other people; that is, to relationships.

Humility isn't the same thing as being down on yourself. In everyday life, people often think of "humility" as something closer to shame than pride—downplaying or not thinking too much of yourself. Others define humility as being willing to say, "I could be wrong," and that is part of it. We define it as a realistic sense of your limitations *and gifts*, which depends on openness to information from other people about yourself.[3] This includes the gift of being a human being (*Adamah*, as the book of Genesis describes it), and thus worthy of relational connection. Humility fosters the capacity to give and receive love that sacramental shame destroys. It is impossible to separate humility from relational pride, which is the ability to *affirm* and even rejoice in your own value and worthiness of love. With humility/pride, I can bring the fullness of who I am, flaws and all, to relationships because I know my worthiness isn't conditional and doesn't depend on fitting someone else's ideals.

Humility is crucial to being an ally. But humility also allows people who have been systemically degraded and devalued to be open to the possibility that they could be wrong about the toxic messages they have internalized—including theologies that diminish them.[4] Openness to being wrong can mean realizing that what you have always known about homosexuality and trans identities—that they are results of demons, the Fall, or a corrupted soul—is incorrect, that sexual orientation and gender variations are real differences in how people are constituted, and that they don't diminish a person's ability to be good and do good.

LGBTQ+ Christians' stories show that the pride they come to experience is actually something that many people, including many cisgender heterosexual Christians, enjoy and take for granted—the knowledge that they are not monsters, but human beings who are worthy of relationships and the joy of being loved unconditionally. When you've internalized harmful messages about yourself, humility paves the way for this kind of pride.[5]

* * *

In the last chapter, we told part of Kai's story, of realizing they had been equating their constant feeling of shame to holiness—to the point of literal heart failure. They also shared with us the story of their transformation:

> So, by being this mixed-race person who has this exclusive same-sex attraction but is still trying to live into the traditional ethic in primarily white spaces, I thought: "This is who I was made to be." You know? And I kind of came alive for a season in that. However, what I began to realize, as I started to meet other LGBT people, was that this was not their experience. And when they started telling me their stories about depression and anxiety and religious-based self-harm, it raised questions for me.
>
> And even though I was finding a lot of support in the faith communities I was a part of, in a lot of ways being put on a pedestal for [chuckles] "How a Gay *Should* Be," . . . I knew that that wouldn't work for so many of the friends I was making. That there was nothing viable about the path I was choosing for them. And that really began to kind of break my heart. Because, to me, the whole reason I felt so captivated by this Jesus story in the beginning, again, was that social justice piece: was the way in which historical Christ interacted with people in the margins, and sort of turned the whole fabric of society upside-down in saying, "Well, actually you thought this was for some and not for others, but really it is for everyone."

Kai moved toward accepting their sexual orientation and gender identity because of their humility—their openness to new information, their recognition that they might not already know everything there is to know. That humility was driven by their love and care for others, and it ultimately helped them affirm their own value and worthiness as a gay, nonbinary person. As Kai tried to share Christ's love with other LGBTQ+ people, Kai was heartbroken to see the destruction that Christianity had caused in their lives. Humility—the consciousness that they could be wrong—drove Kai to learn more about the fruits of the sexual ethic they were teaching and living. They said:

> And the more disturbed I kind of got about this idea, the more I started to look into some different perspectives. And so I began to reach out to pastors, researchers, people who were studying these things in an academic context, but it had very practical implications for how people live their lives and understand this topic. And when I did that, I also began to learn about this epidemic of—suicide, really, is what began to tear away at me. And sort of looking at the numbers around that situation and the way in which it, in all of these research projects, was being directly connected to rejection—more often than not, religious rejection; more often than that even, Christian religious rejection—the more and more troubled I became by it all. And, yeah, I just struggled so hard to open myself up to the possibility that I might be wrong.

Openness to new, potentially transformative information through relationships with LGBTQ+ people—humility—opened Kai to a deeper relationship with God, a "spiritual experience." As they put it:

> It just took building a lot of relationships, and reading materials and resources outside of that world, in order for me to begin opening up a more honest conversation with myself [laughs] about it all. And really, too, with God. It was spiritual for me to actually begin to start wrestling, and to let myself doubt, to let myself wonder. And it was such a vulnerable experience, I think, for me to do that for the first

time; more vulnerable than I've really ever felt. And the more I began to take steps in an honest journey, a true journey, the less convincing the narrative I had been living became. And not only did it become less convincing, but it became more clear to me that it hurt other people. . . . And I thought, "As holy as this feels, it's not the spirit of the Jesus I fell in love with when I became a Christian."

As Kai sought more information from "outside" the evangelical world, they also sought guidance in the Bible:

So, as I continued to study not just the passages in the Bible that seemed relevant to this topic, but just the broader context of the Scriptures, and really looked into who was being rebuked in the New Testament, who were the people that both Jesus and the rest of the apostles had a problem with, it was not the culturally stigmatized groups. It was actually the opposite. It was the people who did have good intentions—they have these hearts, were attempting to follow God but, in the process, it caused them to exclude others. And so, for the first time, I began to identify with *those* people. And I thought, "Something I'm believing about myself is forbidding other people to really experience a whole relationship with God. And if I really believe that relating to Christ is the best thing that ever happened to me and I want that for other people, then I need to start actively working toward breaking down those barriers. I need to start actively working toward removing the obstacles and making this message as accessible as possible to people."

For Kai, healing began with love for other people. But it also required humility, an openness to the possibility that what they had believed about gender and sexuality for their years as a Christian had been wrong. Seeing the harmful effects of those teachings, Kai sought to learn more. Walking in Jesus's footsteps was supposed to be about helping others to experience God's love and justice through relational connection. When Kai realized that it had become about something else, something harmful, they began to dig deeper. They were trying to resolve a contradiction—a conflict between message and reality—out of love for other people.

Kai's pursuit of more information was not driven by arrogance, which cuts others off by saying, "I know everything I need to know, I don't need to learn anything from God or anyone else." Kai's humility, grounded in love, allowed them to recognize and ultimately affirm their own humanity and worth as a person, by recognizing other LGBTQ+ people's worthiness of love. Seeing the harms others had endured unjustly at the hands of people who shared Kai's theology inspired Kai to seek a deeper relationship with Jesus, who criticized people who would separate anyone from God's love. Wasn't that what Kai was doing? They continued:

> It's funny because one of my life verses that I really gravitated toward in my whole experience was a verse in Romans that talks about not being conformed to the patterns of the world, but being transformed by the renewing of your mind. And, for me, all of the years up until these moments of new questions began to happen, I'd thought that related directly to me rejecting society's acceptance of LGBT people. But for the first time I started to focus more on the renewing of *my* mind: being transformed by the renewing of *my* mind. And it occurred to me that if I as a Christian still believed exactly what I believed ten years ago, that maybe I wasn't participating in that transformation process; that maybe I was holding to something that was not, again, reflective of the spirit of Jesus.

The work and vulnerability it took to come to a place that was truly loving to other people led Kai to understand the Bible in a new light and opened Kai to the possibility of being transformed as they had always believed Christians should be. Humility opened Kai to the idea that God could be happy with Kai just as they were, without demanding the "masochistic" experience of perpetual shame and severed friendships they had previously experienced.

* * *

How Relationships Can Heal Toxic Shame

Humility is a great equalizer—it flows from and sustains our ability to see others as our equals, neither diminishing nor elevating ourselves. Humility allows us to suspend judgment and learn from others, including about ourselves. We're not alone in seeing humility this way. Conservative Christian philosopher Bob Roberts argues that humility is a deep knowledge that your worth as a person does not depend on how well you stack up to other people or ideals, which frees you to be honest about your gifts and limitations, open to the possibility that you might be wrong—and open to the possibility of change.[6]

By allowing that, we can always learn more from others. Humility fosters wholeness. When we exhibit humility, others don't have to hide or downplay parts of themselves—their sexual orientation, gender identity, their race or disability, or any part of who they are—for us to learn from them and relate to them. Relational pride/humility also fosters our own wholeness. Addressing the 2018 TRP leadership cohort, Sandra, whom we heard from earlier, spoke of growing up in churches where she stood out for her deep commitment but felt accepted only to the extent that she downplayed what made her different. She described parroting the perspectives of white boys and men—even refusing the leadership positions she was offered on the grounds that she was a woman and therefore unfit to lead. For her, it eventually came to feel like "hiding," silencing her own perspective. And people generally "hide" in response to fear, including the fear of being unworthy of relationships, which is what we call shame.

Eventually, Sandra reached a breaking point. She was struck by a passage written by Reverend Barbara Brown Taylor:

> I thought that being faithful was about becoming someone other than who I was. And it was not until this project failed, that I began to wonder if my human wholeness might be more useful to God than my exhausting goodness.[7]

As Sandra described the experience of finding herself in community, she made an analogy to playing games with her two-year-old, mentioning that his favorites were those like hide-and-seek and peek-a-boo, which gave him the delightful experience of being found, as in, "Where's Robbie? *There* you are!" She said:

> Because he just wants to be seen. I feel like with condemnation or celebration, I feel like a lot of our stories can break into those two categories. You come out, and lucky for me I was in a community here in Chicago where I came out and they said, "There you are!" And there are other communities where they say, "Go into hiding. Not here, not now, go to this place. Go get fixed." And I think that's the difference. What happens when people come out of hiding? We can celebrate them, or we can condemn them.

She continued the analogy, asking:

> Why did it take so long for me to look in the mirror and say, "*There* you are?" Because I had had so many years of investment, and so much investment in my life, with seeds that were bearing fruit, that were going to kill me. . . . And tonight's really special, because the people that were a part of me being able to look in the mirror and see, the ones that said, "*There* you are," are here, tonight. They're here. And it's such a gift, because I couldn't have done it on my own. I couldn't have done it without The Reformation Project, people that were committed. I couldn't have done it without that. So I found people who chose not to be segregated, in order to embrace the fullness of God's creation. . . . I found those people and as a result of this merciful loving community I found myself. I got to choose *me*.

Sandra didn't choose herself *over* God or other people; she was finally able to choose to allow herself to exist, as she was, as God created her to be, in her wholeness. She reflected on how relationships allowed her to accept herself and thrive. Mentioning Darren Calhoun by name, she recalled:

What I did instead is I came to a church community, I developed relationships. They didn't think like I thought because I was homophobic, but I respected them, and then I met Darren, and I was like "What? This is blowing my mind right now" but I was open to it because I had seen the fruit of their lives resembling a lot of the Jesus that we were learning about, so I thought "Well, there might be something there." . . . All I know is that I'm alive now. [Applause] All I know is that I'm here, and I'm alive, and I would do it again. I would do it again. I never knew I could be this grounded in myself. I didn't know this was a part of living. I really didn't. So my journey here was only made possible by . . . people like you. . . . I'm only here because of the people I know here, that were committed to loving me on the journey.

She had disagreed with Darren on whether it was sinful to be gay, but seeing the "good fruits" of his ministry, she was able to listen to him and see that what he was doing actually looked a lot like what she had been learning from and teaching others about being Christian all along. By seeing Darren's goodness, she was able to accept her own "human wholeness."

Christian survivors of sacramental shame have a lot to teach all of us—of any or no religion—about what it means to be relational creatures and how relationships can help us to thrive. They have a lot to teach all of us about how humility (openness to learning and growing in relationships) and pride (joy felt in affirming your worthiness of relationships) undergird love (the emotions and actions that ground and fuel relationships) and make life livable and good.

* * *

Even people who see same-sex intimacy as sinful can promote healing from sacramental shame—to an extent. It's not an either–or situation. While their relationships will be limited if they can't see the double standard of cutting LGBTQ+ people off from the intimacies they allow cisgender heterosexuals to experience, there is a difference between that and cutting someone off from all relational connection. Look at the difference Darren experienced between being required to isolate and hide from life in a church basement and finding a "welcoming-but-not-affirming" independent megachurch where he was invited to lead worship. He was allowed to acknowledge that he was gay *and* serve the church—as long as he was celibate. It was trying at times; the megachurch was predominantly white, and he constantly found himself having to explain racism to white people. He was called to account for himself more than a straight person would have been. But people would listen to him and learn from him. They hugged him. They took care of him. He made friends. He began to heal from the previous four years of trauma.

Jimmy's story was slightly different, although he, too, eventually concluded that God didn't want him to "hide from life." A white, cisgender man, he grew up Primitive Baptist and Southern Baptist, and he was about thirty years old at the time we spoke. When he started college in the mid-2000s, he described himself as having "struggled with same-sex attractions," indicating that he thought even a gay identity was sinful. In contrast to Christian leaders, like Darren's pastor, who cut LGBTQ+ people off from relationships, the InterVarsity Christian Fellowship leaders at Jimmy's university encouraged him to cultivate relationships with other Christian students, with other LGBTQ+ students, and to foster connections between the groups. By building a relationship with him, his InterVarsity leaders allowed him to figure out who he was and to talk about his experience so that he could live his life. They expected Jimmy to be celibate, but they didn't require him to fixate on changing his orientation.

Allowing Jimmy to prioritize relationships—rather than isolate himself until his orientation changed—allowed him to help other LGBTQ+ Christians navigate the same questions he was trying to answer about what kind of person it was possible to be and what kind of life it was possible to live. Once he left the residential ministry that had tried to "cure" his orientation, Jimmy decided he needed to stop focusing on himself and work on serving other people. He remarked that he had been:

feeling like if there is anything to this whole Christianity thing, it shouldn't be churning out individuals that hate themselves, [whose] communities . . . are exporting them to this program because they didn't know what in the world to do with them.

While those churches cut ties to their "same-sex attracted" members, sending them away until they were fixed (which didn't generally happen, so they just stayed away), Jimmy's InterVarsity advisors had encouraged him to cultivate relationships as a way to walk in Jesus's footsteps. Rather than fixate on his orientation and re-enroll in the ex-gay ministry (whose leader later apologized personally to each attendee he could reach for the harm he did by trying to fix them), he remained committed to celibacy and got a job serving others.

Even with his religious commitment to celibacy, being able to *say* he was gay made his life livable. In Chapter 3, we saw how Kai eventually experienced celibacy as shaming; experiences like Kai's were what led many in this movement to see *mandatory* celibacy as destructive. At the same time, ministries that allow celibate LGBTQ+ people to simply *say* who they are allow for vastly better lives than those that regard even *saying* that you're LGBTQ+ as "identifying with your sin" and therefore demand total transformation as the condition for any kind of relationship.[8] Dishonesty would be another option, but real relationships require honesty. In contrast to the view that claiming a LGBTQ+ identity is an act of rebellion, LGBTQ+ conservative Christians and their allies insist that it is simply an honest description—that identifying as gay, bi, or trans doesn't challenge a person's Christian identity any more than identifying as a mother, a heterosexual, or a White Sox fan. Identifying as LGBTQ+ allows people to stop focusing inward and feeling like there's something fundamentally wrong with them all the time so they can focus outward on loving and serving *others*.

* * *

It's not just humility in human relationships that opens pathways to healing from toxic shame. When human relationships fail them, many LGBTQ+

Christians respond to relentless sacramental shaming by humbly turning to God.[9] Conservative Protestant ethicists see Biblically based humility as the trait that fosters submission to God's will instead of one's own, that disposes a person to place total trust in God. They characterize humility as the opposite of arrogance, the kind of pride that puts a person's own desires and will over that of God or other people.[10] In this framework, a humble person trusts and submits to God.

Using the tools their churches gave them helped some people to hear directly from God that they were made to be LGBTQ+. Philip, a Black gay man with cerebral palsy, shared his story at a conference. He and his twin were the youngest of seven children raised by a single mother after their father abandoned them. He was declared stillborn and deprived of oxygen for fifteen minutes at birth. As a child in the 1970s and 1980s, his teachers dismissed him as uneducable, so he taught himself to read by sneaking his sister's books out of her school bag at night. His mother fought for his life, supported him, and instilled in him a deep faith in God. As an adult, he began to hear God calling him to pursue ministry far from his family—a call he found ludicrous because of his disability. He struggled with it but came to trust the voice of God over his own fears, moved out of state, took the job, and eventually earned a master's degree.

But he continued to ignore the reality of his feelings of attraction to men. Again, it was in a moment of prayer when he heard God challenge him to be himself. As he prayed, "God, I worship you with all that I am," he heard God speak to him, saying "No, you don't!" As he told the story:

> I said, "Yes God, I praise you with all that I am." And God said, "No you don't! Why do you hide that you're gay? I made you that way. Until you can give me *that*, your sexuality, you are not praising me with all of who you are." I said, "What, God!? Are you crazy?! You can't ask that of me, it's too much!" and he said, "Yes, that is who I made you to be." [reconstructed in notes]

Guided by his faith and trust in God, Philip answered God's call to minister to others as a Black, gay, disabled Christian man—as his whole self. Setting aside the difficulties he knew would follow, he trusted God. Conservative churches around the country used to host him so he could share witness of God's power in his life, but sure enough, those invitations dried up once he came out as gay. It seems they wanted him to confirm to their own narrative, not to teach them to understand God in new ways.

Shae Washington, a Black queer woman and a former staff member of TRP, shared a similar story. She had spent lonely years struggling to reconcile her sexuality and spirituality, knowing that if she came out, she would lose important relationships. People would question her faith in and relationship with God. After years of praying about this struggle, one day Shae heard God say, "I have already set you free on the cross. Why are you still in the closet? Come out, be who I created you to be." That day, when Shae chose to trust the authority of this message, she said she felt a tremendous peace from God that kept her grounded as she confronted the consequences of her submission to God's voice: former friends who now demanded she show them where in the Bible it said this was okay, or church members who charged her with arrogance for elevating her own experience over thousands of years of tradition. What looks like arrogance to fellow church members can actually be an act of submission to God, a willingness to take the harder path of listening to God and being who God was telling her she was made to be. Shae and Philip displayed not the arrogance of rejecting everyone's guidance, but humble faith in God's guidance—as their churches and families had taught them.

Many, like Kai, spoke of other tools they had cultivated in home churches and campus ministries—methods of biblical interpretation, of discerning God's will through prayer—that equipped them to cultivate an openness to considering that they might be wrong. Sometimes those tools led them to conclusions that challenged social hierarchies, leading other conservative Christians—generally those at the tops of those hierarchies—to accuse them of arrogance. For instance, Bryan identifies as a white, Native American, third-gender, bisexual person who was in their mid-twenties at the time of our interview. In an interview, Bryan shared that their Southern Baptist pastor's emphasis on individual discernment gave them tools to pursue their questions, even as that same tradition called certain conclusions sinful.

Bryan's self-discovery of their identity as a third gender, bisexual person was rooted in their Native American (Cherokee) identity, which led them to question the teachings of their church and their college InterVarsity group:

> I just had all these questions about faith and like a lot of them were rooted in my Native American heritage and like, how is it fair that this religion gets to go to other people in other continents for centuries at a time? How is it fair that . . . the gospels are written about animals and plants that aren't native to us and languages that aren't native to us and cultures? Like, why does everything have to be foreign for some and not for others, and how is that considered fair if that's the only source of truth?

Feeling uncertain about how to reconcile their faith with these questions, Bryan attended a Bible camp where they read the Bible six hours a day for six days. When they returned to their InterVarsity group with more questions and no answers, the group's response was to deny that Bryan was truly a Christian, saying that Bryan's god was rationality, not Jesus. Bryan said, "Straight up they were just like 'No, you're not a Christian.' So I came home that summer like crying, thinking 'Oh my gosh, I want to be a Christian, but I can't lie about [the inconsistencies].'" Bryan had already experienced around race and colonization what many LGBTQ+ people come to experience: that their fellow conservative Christians emphasized humility as submission to God but refused to accept new information about the limits of their own—human—understandings of God's social order.

Bryan searched for a church community that would allow them to pursue both Jesus and their questions without fear, and he landed in an LGBTQ-affirming Metropolitan Community Church (MCC) congregation. They identified as cisgender and straight at the time, and when they eventually came to realize they were third gender (a category of roles historically recognized and defined by each Native American tribe) and bisexual, that church community buffered Bryan from a lot of the shame they knew other Christians experienced.

Bryan's ability to trust their own experience of God helped them to cultivate resilience against the shame their previous church had dispensed toward LGBTQ+ people. Bryan never really experienced shame about being bisexual and third gender:

> I mean just the goodness of the relationships, whether they be sexual or romantic or both, the goodness of those experiences are really clear to me and there isn't a shame that overshadows or questions that.... And I feel like that's also a part of my Baptist background of—I can't count the number of times my pastor used to be like, "Don't trust me, read the Bible for yourself. Don't believe my interpretation; read it for yourself and see that that's what it says." And there was this independence of this way of being, like, "You can discern, you have the power of discernment, use it." And I feel like that's been an important part of not having shame in my life of being like, "No, I know and I feel this is okay and this is good." So I'm not going to buy into this whole scenario that I have to be ashamed when I can feel that goodness myself.

Bryan's pastor gave them the tools to understand Scripture, even though he may have tried to tilt the scales a bit; there is a difference between saying, "Read this and see that *this* is what it says" and "Read this and see what *you* understand it to say." Still, Bryan learned to trust their relationship with God and their ability to discern God's will using Baptist methods of reading Scripture. That gave Bryan the courage to choose God over degrading human narratives.

A number of sociologists have posited that "conservatives" place authority in traditions and institutions and "liberals" place authority in themselves, or that "liberals" "reject the Bible."[11] Many people we have spoken to—scholars and others—assume or even insist that anyone who affirms same-sex sex or gender transition *can't* be "conservative." We find those distinctions to be oversimplified.[12] Most conservative Protestants are taught to communicate directly to God themselves without intercession—Baptists, for instance, call this "priesthood of the believer." Pentecostals routinely cultivate an ability to channel the Holy Spirit. LGBTQ+ Christians who struggle to stay in the church rather than leave it altogether are *not* giving themselves ultimate authority. They yield to the authority of God, Jesus, and the Bible, particularly the Gospels—and they crave the community of accountability they get in church, if they're welcome there. They use the tools their churches and traditions have given them to cultivate a relationship with God, to read the Bible, to follow Jesus, and the feel the movement of the Holy Spirit, and when they arrive at a place of self-acceptance, they do so with the same sense of self-worth that many unstigmatized Christians take for granted every day.

* * *

Many participants come to experience a sense of their own worthiness of connection as healing from sacramental shame. This self-acceptance is not arrogance. The kind of pride LGBTQ+ survivors of sacramental shame experience as healing enables them to stop hiding, to be fully themselves, and to recognize their basic goodness as created and loved by God, as they believe everyone is.

Reverend Elizabeth Edman, a queer Episcopal priest, distinguishes arrogant pride or hubris from what she calls "relational pride," the opposite of which is not humility, but toxic shame.[13] Relational pride is confidence in our worthiness for relationships and the joy we feel in knowing this. This confidence in turn enables people to trust their (human) capacity to relate to other people. Relationships with others enable LGBTQ+ people to claim and sustain a sense of self-worth as queer people.[14] Born in recognition of shared humanity, this form of self-love promotes healing from sacramental shame while expanding the possibilities for loving other people.[15] This pride protects people from internalizing the degrading messages of those who deny their personhood. For LGBTQ+ Christians, pride is the recognition that they are made in God's image, loved by God, and worthy to strive to be like Jesus by loving and serving other people.

It is the recognition of being worthy of love. Relational pride sustains humility because it allows people to be vulnerable and open to being affected by others while maintaining a realistic assessment of our own limitations *and* gifts. Relational pride protects people from internalizing others' demeaning narratives and buffers against toxic shame so that humility doesn't slide into self-hatred.

Edman points out that the Christian tendency to conflate all forms of pride with hubris and to define pride as sinful obscures the healthy forms of pride that buttress self-worth. This is the form of pride that heterosexual cisgender Christians can often take for granted as confidence in their own faith; confidence in their own ability to be Christian friends, parents, and spouses; and confidence in their ability to hear the voice of God, feel the Holy Spirit, and try to be like Jesus. Failing to notice and validate relational pride has devastating consequences for LGBTQ+ Christians because it discourages, and even punishes, cultivation of an emotion they need to live—to love themselves, other people, and God in a fruitful, rather than destructive, way.[16]

When people who think gender variation and same- or multi-sex attraction are sinful think about "gay pride," they equate it with a refusal to be ashamed about things they think people should be ashamed of, because they assume God must intend for everyone to be cisgender and heterosexual. But when people celebrate LGBTQ+ pride, they are often talking about a basic confidence in their personhood and worthiness to love and be loved in the fullness of who they are—self-worth that they can't take for granted because it has been routinely denied to them.

* * *

While a sustaining community might be necessary for the long term, the dramatic change brought by that feeling of acceptance—relational pride—can be most vivid when it comes as a sudden jolt. We heard a story from a white woman we call Becca, who had recently come out as a lesbian. She was in graduate school at a conservative Christian university and developed a powerful crush on a friend. One night they were talking on a park bench, and her friend asked her to put to words the palpable attraction between them. She said she immediately became flustered and nervous, but rather than rejecting her, her friend embraced her. That gesture of acceptance transformed how she saw herself, helping her to overcome a sense of failure and shame that had become habitual.

She had agreed to go to a baby shower the next morning, one of those rituals of femininity that alienates even a lot of cisgender heterosexual women. She recalled:

> I've never felt welcome in the company of baby shower women. . . . I just never fit the girly kinda cute type, and I was just dreading it, and I said, "Well, I'll make vegan muffins." And of course, they came out burned, you know? Of course. Like, everything else was just perfect—'cause they were all married and had kids—you know, it was like . . . But that day—I had went to sleep at 5:00 [a.m.] and had to wake up at 7:00 to make these muffins, which I burned, but *I didn't care!* And that was an amazing thing to feel like—going in, I was dreading this chore, but it was like I was riding on fumes—and good fumes—to the shower like "I don't care. I feel cared for and loved, and I don't care that I don't fit these stereotypical feelings," and—so I was buoyed in a lot of ways.

Before that night, she told us, she had been afraid that her crush would rebuff her, say that she wanted too much, that she *was* too much. She felt shame. But after her friend accepted her, feelings and all, she could just be happy for her straight friend with the baby and all the people who had made the perfect cupcakes and meticulous party favors. She wasn't experiencing the whole ritual of feminine heterosexuality while wearing a cloak of shame. The baby shower women were simply different from her, not a reminder of her constant failure. She didn't feel like an unwelcome imperfection. So what if the muffins were a little burnt? It happens! She tried! Feeling accepted helped rid her of the self-consciousness that had made even a celebration feel like a dreadful chore, as if the imperfection of the muffins was an outward sign of her existential failure as a woman. For the first time, she felt the life-changing opposite of shame; another person's acceptance of her allowed her to feel worthy, even if she wasn't going to win any baking prizes. She felt relational pride.

In a 2017 blog post, Kevin Garcia told a story of experiencing relational pride. Kevin and a guy they were dating were walking to get pizza, holding hands, when someone drove past them and yelled, "FAGGOTS!"[17] Kevin reflected:

> I kept replaying the moment in my mind over and over again. I felt angry and a little hurt . . .
>
> But from somewhere in the core of my spirit, something different was shifting. It was warm and exhilarating and joyful.
>
> It was pride.
>
> Weird, right? Like, super weird. A few years before that, even a few months before that, if someone called me a fag, I would have been reduced to tears. But not this time. This time, I was feeling proud of myself. For the first time ever, I was myself completely. . . .
>
> I had this nasty habit of rejecting people who got too close to [me], who I couldn't bear to come out to, to speak the truth to. I was always keeping my relationship at an arm's length.
>
> I'd never given the world an opportunity to truly know me, therefore no one could truly love me. Conversely, no one would ever know me enough to hate me for all of me.
>
> Until that moment.
>
> And I wasn't super waving a pride flag. I wasn't at a protest or parade. I was going to lunch, holding a guy's hand. It wasn't anything brave or revolutionary. I was just being my honest self. And then I was reminded once again that sometimes being yourself is an act of bravery.

The incident could easily have sunk Kevin into shame—as it was no doubt intended to do. The ability to be seen, named, and shamed by a stranger and feel not negated, but joyful, whole, and "myself, completely"—that grounded sense of their own worth is pride. And it's no accident that Kevin was with someone they liked, expressing affection.

The same love and mutuality that made them visible and subject to others' abuse *also* showed Kevin that they, Kevin, were as worthy of love as the person whose hand they held.

Relationships facilitate pride in that way, but healthy pride also facilitates relationships. As the blog continued, Kevin explicitly connected pride to accepting who God made them to be and feeling loved as that whole, gay person. Both relational pride and humility foster a healthy vulnerability, which enables people to form relational connections. Kevin said:

> Pride to me is an expression of my full self. It is a journey into vulnerability, to hold none of myself back from the world. It is being proud of the person God created me to be because for so long I hated who I was.

Humility paves the way for pride by opening us to new information from others, making us vulnerable. It can slip into self-hatred when the information others give us is that we are unworthy or must hide parts of ourselves, but it can also open us to the knowledge that we are worthy just as we are. Pride allows us to *affirm* our worthiness and wholeness, keeping humility from slipping into self-hatred. It enables LGBTQ+ survivors of sacramental shaming to lean confidently into vulnerability, knowing that they are worthy of love, even with whatever flaws and weaknesses they may have, because no one is perfect. This pride both comes from and enables vulnerability and openness to other people—it enabled Kevin to bring their whole self, with their gifts and limitations, strengths and weaknesses—to relationships with others. Virtuous pride sustains relational connection by enabling the healthy humility that prevents arrogance.

Kevin's story also revealed the joyful component of healthy pride:

> It took a long time to become comfortable in my own skin, to accept the person God created me to be. I'm learning that the road to self-acceptance is hard, and the road to being accepted by society as a whole might be even harder. But it's worth it. I'd rather have the

world burn me at the stake for being who I am than drown in the waters of self-hatred.

I'm proud to be called a gay son of God, a gay Christian because that's the person God created me to be. That's who God loves, and to not love myself, to not accept who I am, to not celebrate the person God celebrates, I believe, is an affront to my Creator.

Who am I to call unclean what God has called clean? Who am I to not love, celebrate, protect, uplift that which God loves, celebrates, protects, and uplifts? That is what pride is!

What Kevin experienced when being harassed on the street, paradoxically, was joy in recognizing their own worth. Philosopher Claudia Mills defines virtuous pride as an experience of joy about an accomplishment or achievement, and in the case of LGBTQ+ Christians, pride is a sense of joy in coming to know *and affirm* one's basic sense of worthiness as a person.[18]

Relational pride is not just essential to a healthy life. Bob Roberts sees it as crucial to a Christian life. He sees this sense of one's basic worthiness as a Christian virtue in itself as well as the foundation of other virtues, such as gratitude—because without it you won't feel worthy of being a recipient of other peoples' generosity or God's unconditional love.[19] For LGBTQ+ Christians, pride facilitates the recognition and affirmation of their own humanity, which becomes the basis from which they cultivate self-trust and trust in God.[20] Shae described the pride of claiming and affirming her identity as leading her to experience the peace of God. She was freed from anxieties of compartmentalized life and could trust God's message about her fundamental goodness even in radically uncomfortable spaces where other people did not affirm her.

Seeing the value in traits that other Christians have treated as sinful is an act of healing. In an address at a TRP conference, Elder Carmarion D. Anderson, a Black trans woman, and a pastor in the predominantly Black, Pentecostal, LGBTQ+-affirming movement known as The Fellowship of Affirming Ministries (TFAM),[21] modeled the journey to recover this sense of self-worth by sharing her own. She told the Gospel story about Jesus healing a blind man (John 9), when the people of the village saw his blindness as punishment for sin. Jesus denied that sin had anything to do with it; he spit into the dirt, and put the resulting mud on the man's eyes, and sent him out of his town—"out of his comfort zone of hurt," as Elder Carmarion put it—into unfamiliar space. Once in that uncomfortable, unfamiliar space, a miracle occurred, and the man was healed. What most people would find disgusting—spit-mud in someone's eye—was transformed by Jesus's love into healing that recovered the man's sight and absolved him of guilt. Elder Carmarion likened that "disgusting" transgression of boundaries to the disgusted reaction people have had to her as a trans woman. She called her transition "a medicine to a hurting generation" because of all the people who looked to her for healing when they couldn't look to any other Christians.[22] Relational pride enabled her to testify:

> [T]here was a Higher Being that blew into our nostrils and gave us life, which means that I have the Creator's same DNA, that I am the hands and feet. . . . [Indicating people in the audience] You're the hands and feet. You're the hands and feet. You're the hands and feet. [To those who have judged her:] And how dare you use the Bible to whup me? How dare you crucify me all over again because you have a different definition of love? . . . Love is so simple. I love you not expecting anything in return.

Relational pride is not the arrogance of thinking you can do no wrong or that you're better than anyone else. Both of those break connection. Contrast that with the humility shown by the twenty-seven-year-old white gay man we call Greg. He told us that after he had worked through his struggle with sacramental shame, claiming and affirming his sexuality, he recovered his ability to experience shame in a healthy way:

> I probably make mistakes, do things that I shouldn't have done, that I'm ashamed of, that's normal. And . . . the reasons I'm ashamed or feel like it's wrong are not because of my sexuality but just normal things any straight person would get caught up in or be ashamed of as well. I see it as, "Okay, this has nothing to do with my sexuality."

For Kevin, the pride of fully claiming their identity as a gay child of God led them to feel compassion for the person who harassed them. They wrote:

> I feel sad that [people] are unable to just free themselves to love more, care more, embrace more of God's creation. Because . . . if that guy who drove by sat down with me, shared a drink with me, we'd find out that we're both nothing special. We're both humans with hopes, dreams, emotions, families, ambitions, fears, insecurities, and we're all asking the same question: "If . . . I let you know all of who I am, will you still love me?"

In contrast to what we, following Edman, call relational pride, hubristic pride, and arrogance depend on debasing others to make yourself feel superior. But Greg isn't feeling superior, he's feeling equal to "any straight person." Elder Carmarion sees herself and her audience members as the "hands and feet" of Jesus, which she believes *all* Christians are called to be. Kevin didn't come to feel superior to the person who displayed hatred or disgust toward them, justified though that might have been. Kevin's disposition as a Christian led them instead to feel compassion and sadness. The pride and humility that Kevin experienced caused them to see themself and their assailant as equals; this pride enabled them to perceive shared humanity and to feel pain for the one who denied it.

* * *

This kind of pride only appears arrogant to those who think others really *are* of lesser worth, including in situations of systemic injustice. Like saying that "Black Lives Matter," this pride is not an assertion of superiority. It is an affirmation of the value of those who have been unjustly treated as expendable. The concept of intersectionality is crucial here.[23] It makes no sense in any sphere of life to treat race, gender, sexuality, disability, social class, immigration status, and the like as discrete variables.[24] If you relate to a person, you relate to them as a whole person, to all of who they are. Relationships, according to Martin Buber, are "unbounded" connection.[25] If you affirm someone as a Christian, but not as gay, you are not affirming them. If you affirm someone as a Christian, but not as Black, you are not affirming them. And if you affirm someone as, say, trans *or* as Black, but not as a whole, Black trans woman, you are not affirming her. You are closing yourself off to the possibility of learning from her experience and growing. You are not relating to her.

While cisgender, heterosexual conservative Christians often see "gay pride" as the arrogance of sinners, a lot of white LGBTQ+ people see it as simply being about being "gay," as if sexual orientation and gender identity are separable from race. But that attitude is only available to white people. Speakers at conferences regularly make the point that for LGBTQ+ people of color, affirmation of LGBTQ+ identities didn't mean much if it was not accompanied by liberation from racism. Oppressive cultures, such as those of racism, sexism, ableism, and anti-immigrant sentiment, all stigmatize and deny people's full humanity. In addition to being anchored in systems of structural inequality, all of them prevent relational connection.

People who are not chronically stigmatized and shamed can often take relational pride for granted—sometimes not even recognizing it as pride—so that anything anyone actually has to call "pride" seems like arrogance. Church members often fail to consider the arrogance of their own claim to know with certainty what God thinks about LGBTQ+ lives, gender diversity, and same-sex or multi-sex attraction, and the hubris of taking themselves to be arbiters of God's will. But sometimes, they decide to prioritize love, to be humble, and to learn. And when they do, their relationships grow, they and their loved ones thrive, and everyone is more able to do whatever good it is they have to contribute to the world.

LGBTQ+ survivors of sacramental shame and their allies help us see something vital about humility that most everyday and scholarly accounts of humility miss. Humility is neither just about the self nor just about others; humility guides us to prioritize relationships between ourselves and others. It fosters community. Conservative churches' insistence that LGBTQ+ people not identify as LGBTQ+ keeps LGBTQ+ people isolated from each other, which can keep them from recognizing and valuing their whole selves. In community, people can develop the healthy pride that can heal them of their perpetual feelings of shame. As Edman points out, relational pride both grows out of and fosters a sense of community, a sense that "we're in this together." Community involves a dynamic of recognition, of seeing another's similarities—and differences—and feeling seen in the process, as Becca was the night before she burned those muffins.

Humility enables and sustains love and connection between whole people. Genuine humility leads you to decenter yourself by suspending your certainty, embracing vulnerability, and holding open the possibility that connection to another person might lead you to learn, grow, change—even if you believe you already know the truth or have the full story. Humility fosters honesty about yourself because it leads you to prioritize relationships with people who may share in your gifts or, at worst, be harmed by your limitations. When we don't prioritize relationships, we're not as motivated to take responsibility for our limitations, even if we are acutely and accurately aware of them. The relationships we value make it important for us to be honest with ourselves and others about ourselves.

LGBTQ+ Christians teach us that humility and pride are the beams and girders of the emotional scaffolding that enables and sustains love. For many LGBTQ+ Christians, it is their humility before God—submission to God, following their experience of God's voice—that helps them recover or develop healthy pride, that sense of their fundamental worthiness as beings created and loved by God that sustains their ability to be open and vulnerable to others. That kind of healthy pride reflects a person's wholeness, not only parts of them that others deem worthy, because true *relationships* are between whole people, not fragments. Pride/humility in being LGBTQ+ cannot be separated from any other aspect of who a person is; if you know you are a human being worthy of love, that can't apply to only a part of you.

LGBTQ+ Christians' experiences make vivid what often escapes notice: that humility—openness to new information, awareness of our own possibility of not already knowing everything, *and* awareness of our own human worth—are important aspects of social life—for everyone. Humility helps *everyone* to thrive. How often do we approach a situation with arrogance instead of curiosity and willingness to learn? How often are people so certain—of whatever—that they close themselves off to new information?

How many progressives and liberals think we *get it*, that we're the good ones who are not racist, not sexist, and we are great allies to sexual minorities and trans people—distancing ourselves from *those people*, those bigots? What does that certainty obscure from our vision about our own words and actions? The humility to admit that we are not perfect either, that we, too, are capable of combining power with ignorance in dangerous ways, is the only thing that will help us to make the world safer for those we profess to love.

And how many people are burdened by a sense that there is something about them that makes them fundamentally unworthy of relationships? LGBTQ+ conservative Christians light a path to a society in which everyone is treated as fully human and worthy of love, in which *everyone* is open to learning. For anyone, Christian or otherwise, knowing you are worthy of good things can give you the confidence to be open to other people, to growing in connection with them, to learning from them, and to wishing good things for them—even those who torment you.

5

Becoming an Ally

As Kai showed us earlier, true allies understand that something in themselves—their interpretation of Scripture, their understanding of how the world works—may have to change if they are to truly love others and stand with them. An ally doesn't treat people as issues or abstractions. An ally is open to learning and transforming in order to be worthy of trust, to be a better friend, a better parent, sibling, family member, a better neighbor. Allyship requires humility, learning and growing in sometimes unpredictable ways in connection with others.

But relationships and personal growth are not enough. An ally can't be patient with white supremacy, heterosexism, trans antagonism, and the like. As David Gushee pointed out in a 2015 keynote address, an ally risks something they have—personal security, resources, institutional power or prestige—to protect those who need protection. When people are systematically oppressed by institutions and/or devalued by culture, an ally is open to changing those dynamics, even if it means losing the benefits they get from it.[1]

The anguish so many of our respondents have endured has arisen when loved ones would rather sacrifice their relationship than lose their certainty about their interpretations of Scripture, their understanding of their own privileged place in God's order, and the respect of others who cherish that certainty. Conversely, people's testimonies demonstrate that sharing personal narratives and building relationships are what inspire others to become allies and work for concrete systematic changes.

Humility—the willingness to listen, learn, and grow—promotes love. Love isn't about being "nice." Love requires letting go of the certainty that you have nothing to learn, so that you can learn to see the world through another person's eyes, in new ways you might never have imagined. Humility fosters our ability to learn from others not just about themselves, but about ourselves. Humility enables allies to perceive stigmatized people as *people*, even as their church's narratives would have them question this, and to risk their own standing in the community and their own self-understanding. Beyond this, humility allows allies to see how their very understanding of the world and who they are in it may be built on hidden assumptions that who they are is closer than others to their own ideal—or for Christians, to God's ideal. It allows them to question whether the way they think and see the world is the way God thinks and sees the world.

To be an ally, it's not enough to make relational connection your priority—wanting to be worthy of trust and feeling love for people who are stigmatized or oppressed in ways you yourself are not. Being an ally requires us to sacrifice our own authority and our certainty that the way we have always seen things is the only or best way. It means working to make the world a safer place for people who are systematically harmed and giving up our comfort with and control over the way things are. Allyship starts with relationships, but it can't end with them. That's because relations of power distort the way we see the world and the social hierarchies that shape our lives—social hierarchies that people can change, but we can't just wish away.

* * *

People's efforts to be allies go horribly wrong all the time. Sociologists have repeatedly found that multi-ethnic congregations tend to cater to white members' expectations and preferences at the expense of Black people, Indigenous people, and people of color (BIPOC).[2] Countless observers have noted that, for people of color, belonging to an "integrated"—predominantly white or "mixed"—congregation often means internalizing white people's ways of thinking and doing, and accommodating white people's desires to seem "not racist." Sociologist Korie Edwards studied an interracial church and found that even in a community that white people joined because they wanted to worship with Black people, they would only remain members so long as their whiteness remained "transparent," meaning they could take for granted that their ways of worshipping and thinking about race were just "normal."[3] Similarly, LGBTQ+ Christians often find themselves feeling tricked by churches that claim "All are welcome!" only to reveal the conditions of that welcome once they've grown invested, a problem pervasive enough that there is a website, ChurchClarity.org, to help people access information regarding a church's policies so that they can make an informed decision.[4]

Predominantly white evangelical churches have a long history of seeing *everything* in terms of individuals—not just the individual's relationship with God, but to the extent of denying that social forces even exist and decrying efforts to promote social justice.[5] In the extreme forms of this worldview, *any* problem a person has is a question of their own faith and relationship with God. For many of those invested in changing how evangelical churches treat LGBTQ+ people, the hope is that, if people who see individualism as a sacred worldview learn to listen better to LGBTQ+ people, this will lead them to acknowledge that systemic oppression exists and results from a failure to love. Certainly, some have grown in that direction. That humility is rooted in concern to protect and care for others—setting aside concerns for one's own ego, comfort, and privileges, to become more worthy of others' trust.

People often treat "relationship building," "dialogue," or "reconciliation" as the key to making a more peaceful and just world—but they have failed to change much at all. Scholars have repeatedly observed the limits of "reconciliation" and "dialogue" efforts—largely because they neglect the institutional changes required to stop the injustice and lead to truly equal treatment. In many cases around the world, efforts at reconciliation seem limited to creating warm feelings among some of the people who participate, not restructuring relations of power, as if the only problem is that people haven't been nice enough to each other. In the United States, sociologists Michael Emerson and Christian Smith noted that white evangelicals' refusal to recognize structural racism often leaves Black members of racially mixed churches to feel that "reconciliation was cheap, artificial, and mere words. It was rather like a big brother shoving his little brother to the ground, apologizing, and then shoving him to the ground again."[6] Jennifer Harvey has argued that what is missing in white mainline churches' efforts at reconciliation is repentance and atonement, so efforts to "reconcile" end up asking Black people to trust white people who have yet to recognize what harms they benefit from. These efforts have thus failed to disrupt white supremacist structures and institutions.[7]

It's not that all white Christians intend to be racist or exclude people of color. Many predominantly white churches try to be inclusive and even antiracist, and many people of color choose to worship in these mixed spaces. But racially mixed churches, including those that affirm LGBTQ+ identities, same-sex marriage, and gender transitions, can be plagued by a white-centrism that is invisible to white people who assume their own ways of doing things are "neutral." Predominantly white churches often try to welcome BIPOC members, but that welcome tends to be on white people's terms. BIPOC individuals in mixed church spaces spoke of the constant feeling of needing to "tone it down," to worship in white ways, to not be too loud, to not be too different from what white people took for granted as "normal." They often must apologize for and tone down their differences from whiteness and support or downplay the existing racial hierarchy—like a Black visiting pastor in Sarah Diefendorf's study of a predominantly white megachurch, who received a standing ovation when he said from the pulpit that the Black Lives Matter movement was of the Devil.[8] At nearly every event we attended—all predominantly white—prayers or praise music in languages other than English or from nonwhite traditions were prefaced with an explanation that it may be new to some people, but that this is a way of welcoming diverse people into the fold.[9] The explanations were clearly responses to previous criticisms from white attendees.

Efforts to be an ally or "reconcile" go wrong when people don't rethink the paradigm that gives them social power; true relationships call on you to sacrifice your power, authority, worldview, your insistence on your own virtue, your sense of yourself as central.[10] It can be hard to be patient with people who declare themselves allies and keep messing up.

Institutional change also fails to produce better outcomes if the people doing it lack humility. Even those who embrace systemic change for justice can fail as allies if they lack humility, an openness to learning and growing. If you're trying to be an "ally" to people you won't even listen to, how do you know you're advocating for the right changes? You need to take the time to keep humbly educating yourself.

As scholars of intersectionality point out, most people stand in some kind of relationship of privilege compared to *someone* else. We can learn from others' failures as well as our own, but to do that we need to take a posture of humility ourselves. We need to be able to reimagine the world and our place in it.

* * *

A relationship, in Martin Buber's sense, is more than simply knowing someone or being on friendly terms. It is an intimate connection built on openness to learning from another, to growing, and to changing by virtue of that connection. Like the humility of LGBTQ+ people who have moved beyond sacramental shame, the humility of allies allows them to question what they've always assumed or believed. Many evangelical churches, particularly those that are predominantly white, assume that white power and privilege are just how God made things, that the way they see the world defines the "true" Christianity from which other Christians deviate.[11] Most evangelical and historically Black churches treat complementarity doctrine and compulsory heterosexuality as foundational to Christianity. In relationships with the people they have treated or allowed others to treat as less-than, perhaps unintentionally or without even noticing, true allies come to question the assumptions they have never questioned and see how those assumptions dehumanize and diminish people they should love as equals. They then put something they have—their authority, their power, maybe even their jobs—on the line to work to repair the damage their church's conventional beliefs have caused and to prevent it from happening again.

* * *

Mark is a young, white, gay man from Missouri. As a college student, he had studied the Bible extensively and concluded that it really wasn't talking about loving, egalitarian, same-sex marriages because those didn't exist in the era when the Bible was written. He agreed with The Reformation Project's (TRP's) argument that requiring celibacy for gay people didn't square with the Bible, because the Apostle Paul saw celibacy as a rare gift of the spirit, not a mandate. He shared what he had learned with those who mattered to him, including an older, heterosexual couple from the church he grew up in. The man in that couple had been like a second father to him.

The couple took him out to dinner on the main strip in their town, a busy, six-lane suburban street lined with restaurants, coffee shops, and tasteful strip malls, with parking lots separated from the traffic by well-tended grass and flower beds. The couple could agree that Levitical law didn't apply to Christians; that Paul's letters weren't referring to the egalitarian, loving same-sex marriages of today; that the "sin of Sodom," as Ezekiel 16:49 made explicit, wasn't homosexuality but being "arrogant, overfed, and unconcerned; they did not help the poor and needy." But they still couldn't get behind the idea that God could be okay with him being gay. They couldn't give any reason not to support him as a gay Christian and his hope to one day marry a man; they just didn't feel that they could. He ran out of the restaurant in tears, and to their credit, he said, his friends quickly covered the tab and sat with him for half an hour on the parkway by the parking lot as he cried so hard there were broken blood vessels in his eyes for a week.

As devastated as he was, the conversation gave him hope. Their *belief* that homosexuality was contrary to Christian teaching was more important to them than his wholeness as a person. To him, that was clearly "a failure of Christian love." His problem wasn't that he was gay and God hated it—they *agreed* with his interpretation of Scripture! His problem was that some of the human beings in his life were imperfect vessels of Christian love. *That* was something he could work to change.

* * *

Over and over, conservative Christians who had become allies to LGBTQ+ people shared with us their own stories of change; all of them involved humility, usually rooted in a desire to be as loving as they felt Jesus called them to be. Many respondents who have become allies can recall a moment when they realized they were failing to live up to this ideal.

Earlier we shared Alicia Crosby-Mack's story of learning her college friend was a lesbian and responding by "pelting her" with Bible verses. When her friend called her back to reality, she realized that she needed to let faith overcome her fears and "step back into love." Not everyone who chooses the path of love automatically affirms LGBTQ+ identities, same-sex marriage, and gender transition. But foregrounding relationships buffers against arrogance and leaves people open to learning and changing the things they can change to minimize harm to LGBTQ+ people. Again and again, we met parents who sacrificed their church friendships out of love for their LGBTQ+ kids and who came to conferences to learn more about LGBTQ+ people, the Bible, and how to be better allies. Some had not called into question the inherent sinfulness of same-sex sex, but they still came to see something profoundly wrong in their churches' conventional approach of treating sexual orientation and gender difference as more problematic than their own sin. They started to see the arrogance of assuming that their own sin did not make them unfit to love and serve God but being LGBTQ+ does.

So, they practiced a willingness to learn, grounded in their commitment to loving others as Jesus taught them.[12] A church leader on Chicago's South Side who had taken a stand in defense of LGBTQ+ people connected us with Bishop Harold Robinson. As we discussed in Chapter 2, Bishop Robinson noted the strange double standard that had existed since he was a child, that LGBT people were mocked and made to feel unwelcome in a way no other category of sinners was. He explained, "So fornicator is there and the adulterer's there and the one with the drinking problem is there, and all of that—all of them are there on Sunday morning. None of them feel like that they couldn't come to church except for, like I said, the way that particular community was treated." He told us about his change of heart, locating it in relationships, saying:

> So, at a certain point, even though my stand as far as whether this is righteous behavior did not change, my attitude toward how it should be dealt with did change because I had to deal with a sister that was close to me who I had to sit with, dealing with the lesbian issue, and so I got a chance to look in her eyes and look at the pain, look at the shame that you just described, look at the fact that that's still a full human being with all of the feelings that everybody else has and all of the struggles—in other words, making her life of non-effect is just cruel. . . .
>
> It's made me to pray. It has made me to be compassionate. It has made me to study and to acknowledge God and to consult God and consult the Scriptures to see if I'm on a firm foundation and if what I'm standing on is actually true and will hold up. It has also made me say that, "Absolutely do not participate in mocking, do not build up barriers that won't allow someone who's struggling with sexual sins or sexual issues—" 'cause I know they don't, some don't consider it to be sin, but whatever your struggle is sexually, to not build up walls where they can't come in and pray and work out they soul's salvation just like the one that with the crack habit or the brother who is addicted to pornography, which is something I know personally about. So I know what sexuality can do and I know the depths that it can go.

Bishop Robinson recognized that his own sinfulness was no better than that of those he had seen mocked his whole life; it was his relationship with a parishioner that showed him the peculiar arrogance of singling out sexual sins as worse than all other sins. He recognized that he had struggled with a habit he knew to be wrong, and it didn't disqualify him from praying or leading a church. His sin was no different from or better than anyone else's.

Relationships could inspire some to humbly reevaluate the hierarchy of sin. For others, humility could inspire openness to relationships with LGBTQ+ people, to applying the often-repeated principle of "meeting people where they're at" to LGBTQ+ people, those despised by the "righteous" today. Jeff, for instance, was a white man in his forties who had once served as a missionary, traveling to cities to teach passersby on the sidewalk about alternatives to depravity. He eventually determined that yelling at strangers was less effective, and less Christ-like, than befriending a person who needed something and helping them get what they needed. This same insight would eventually help him to think through what he had always known about homosexuality, once he put his own sinfulness into perspective. He told us about having used church as a place to meet women, his life as a "dating maniac," and eventually, cheating on his first wife, then cheating on his second wife and having a stroke during that affair. While he did not think that God gave him his stroke, it prompted him to read the Bible, where he was "stopped cold" by reading I Corinthians 6:9, "Don't you know that the unrighteous shall not inherit the kingdom of Heaven?" followed by a list of unrighteous people, including adulterers:

> And it just broke me and I just confessed and repented of all that, came back to Christ with my whole heart. And then just started really saying, "You know what, I've got to be way more compassionate for people that are going through the same thing, whether whatever sexual bent they're in." And really take the judgmental face off and say, "You know what; we're all going through struggles whatever it is. And whether it's, people are gluttons or they're liars or they're gossipers, whatever, . . . wherever they're at, that's where they're at.
>
> And I really started seeing, Christ was really down with the people that are struggling. And he did stuff that was just like so anathema to culture. . . . He was with the woman at the well who was a known prostitute, came to him, and he was talking to her. And when the

disciples saw him they just freaked out. . . . And she felt so accepted she wanted the whole town [to know] "Let's go meet this guy, he told me everything I did but he didn't stone me!" or whatever. . . . He just blew away all tradition.

For Jeff, realizing his own sinfulness helped him to see that LGBTQ+ people were no worse than him. In fact, like Kai in Chapter 3, he realized that Jesus was more critical of self-righteous judgmentalism than of any particular rule violation. He said:

And in his strictest stuff or things he had to say was against the religious people. The bigots. The people that thought they were "holier than thou" and were following all the rules, all the laws, and he was really strict on them. He called them "whitewashed sepulchers" and "You prevent people that are coming into the kingdom and you want to make them strain at gnats in soup," and "You're more sons of hell than they," so he really nailed them.

Wendy VanderWal Gritter ran an ex-gay ministry in Ontario, Canada, and led it through a process of coming to affirm LGBTQ+ identities. Her change of heart emerged from her relationships with participants in the ministry. In her 2014 book, *Generous Spaciousness*, she gently echoes Jesus's condemnation of lawyers and pharisees, the "whitewashed sepulchres" who said all the right things, remarking:

I've grown weary of triumphalistic warriors for truth—who know and believe all the "right" things but exude pride, self-centeredness, and a devaluing of anyone who disagrees with them. I would rather engage someone who might have some spotty theology but who oozes humility, kindness, generosity and true and deep love for their enemies. And while this may sound a little too hippy-drippy, this isn't just about warm fuzzy feelings—this is about walking in the way of Jesus.[13]

For her, walking in the path of Jesus requires Christians to be humble and open to learning from other people. Jesus may not have had to be humble, but for human beings who are not divine, learning to be like Jesus does require the virtue of humility. It demands relationships. And it demands action.

* * *

We have encountered many ways that heterosexual/cisgender conservative Christians come to affirm the validity of same-sex marriage and transgender expression—or barring that, to regard LGBTQ+ people as fellow human beings and not monsters. In every case, humility has made the difference. In many cases, that humility inspired them not to throw away the Bible, but to appreciate that they might not have understood it fully. Just as true relationships help LGBTQ+ Christians to understand their own essential worth, relationships help straight/cisgender allies to understand the conventional conservative Christian view as both harmful and misguided, and to love others in a way that feels to them like being loved. That love caused them to approach the Bible with humility, with an understanding that they—and the church—might not already know everything there is to know about it or everything Jesus has to say to them. It opened their eyes to understanding the Bible in different ways.

Monte Vines, the father of TRP's founder, Matthew Vines, described his thought process to an audience at a TRP regional training conference. His desire to preserve his relationship with his son led him to rethink his stance on homosexuality. He looked at the subject with fresh eyes, replacing his "distaste" with an attitude of love and respect. His story gives a clear example of humility—admission that, as certain as he felt, he didn't actually know much about the subject. Humility did not inspire him to reject the Bible, but to understand it more fully. When Matthew came home from college, saying that he was gay and still wanted to follow Jesus, Monte faced a dilemma that was firmly anchored in the conventional view. He was afraid that accepting Matthew's desire to one day marry a man would lead to his own and his son's eternal separation from God. But he didn't wish to harm their relationship. He continued:

> But even though I was confident that God's will, that God held a non-affirming view of this, I also knew that I had never really studied this issue. . . . As a straight man, this whole issue was something that was distasteful to me, to really even think about. And I had never been forced to think about it, and so I had managed to avoid it my entire life. And I realized that. . . . And I knew that if I was going to have any influence over him in this, it needed to be in some basis other than the fact that I was his father and he was my son. . . . I needed to be able to speak from a position of authority, meaning that I knew what I was talking about, and I knew that I really didn't. Not that I had any question that my position was right—of course it was right. [Audience laughs]

So, Monte committed to studying the Bible together so Matthew could see for himself what God had to say about being gay and Christian. Monte reflected:

> I thought if we studied the Bible together, he would see that from the Bible itself in God's own words that this is not what God approves of and he was going to have to deal with that himself.
>
> So we undertook a study that took about six months for us to go through this together. And to my great surprise, it was I that found myself changing my understanding about this and being able to see it in a different way. As we went through the Bible passages, and really tried to dig underneath them, not just scratch the surface but dig the depths, and see what's really there under these passages, and not just these six passages, but all of the doctrines of our faith and how they relate to this. . . . So I was surprised I was the one who ended up changing my view on this, but I'm so glad that I recognized that I really did not know what I was talking about, and committed with him to undertake a real study about that.

Becoming an Ally

Monte's story exemplifies humility—openness, however slight at first, to the possibility that he didn't actually know what he was talking about. That openness to learn was sparked by his commitment to his son. That led him to realize that he didn't have to choose Jesus over his gay son; his son had also chosen Jesus.

At the same conference, Kathy Baldock told the story of a lesbian friend she met while hiking who set her on the path to questioning what she had been taught about the impossibility of being gay and Christian. Her friend was an agnostic, so even though she helped Kathy to see that lesbians weren't terrible people, she didn't challenge Kathy's assumption that gayness and Christianity were incompatible. But late in 2006, Kathy reported, she read an article about the Gay Christian Network (GCN) that made her feel compelled to learn more and attend their conference in January 2007. She continued:

> So who knows why, but three weeks later, I went to Seattle just to see gay Christians. I mean, that's all I went to see. I went to see them. [Laughter] Because I couldn't even imagine, honestly, that they existed.... And it was the first night in worship, standing behind 200 gay Christians, worshipping the same God that I had worshipped, that I knew I had been wrong, and that what I had been told about the incompatibility of being gay or transgender—forget the word transgender, I couldn't even comprehend that one then, but being a gay Christian could actually be something that could coincide. So it was then in 2007 that I began to investigate my own theology. It was really difficult to unravel what I had been told and to try to see this, but I had to find the truth, because what I was seeing in the lives of gay Christians completely confounded what I had been told.

Like some of the LGBTQ+ people described in the last chapter, Kathy and Monte described Studying scripture to see what it really said, a skill they learned in their churches. Another respondent we call Kyle—a white, heterosexual, cisgender man in his late thirties—told us explicitly how his quest for deeper understanding was built on the skills he taught young

Christians in campus ministry. Kyle had been a racial justice educator for an evangelical campus ministry that took a "Side B" position, meaning that "people with same-sex attractions" could identify as gay or lesbian, but they had to either seek out a "mixed-orientation marriage" to someone of the other sex or pursue a life of celibacy, and bisexuals could say they were bisexual but could only marry someone of the other sex. This position started to seem untenable to him because of what he saw in the ministries of LGBTQ+ people:

> So being like the multi-ethnic social justice guy in our region, students and other staff workers started coming out to me, and I think they probably picked up on me being a safer person to talk to. Usually, they were not quite sure how safe I would be, but kind of needed a place to talk and took the risk. And so, as that was happening and I was starting to apply a lot of cross-cultural learning skills that I'd be teaching students—spending more time listening, naming my own assumptions so that I could put them on hold while hearing other perspectives and then reevaluating, like, "Where is truth in this? What is good? How do I learn from people who are not like myself?"

Kyle began by using the tools of humility that he taught his students. He then used the tools of conservative Bible interpretation to understand God's word:

> But it was just finding that [the Side B position of his employer] was really hard to uphold in terms of a lot of the conversations I was having, where people who were seeking same-sex relationships were still bearing fruit in their ministry, and that [the ministry's position] kind of flies in the face of Scripture. It's been apparent in Scripture that you'll know the movement of the Spirit by the fruit that is borne, and that when people continue to see—like lead people to Christ and do stuff like that, that like that's evident that they're bearing good fruit in their lives, you know. And it's been my experience that people

who are engaging in sinful activities have a hard time doing that; that times in my life where I've been, you know, let's say engaging in sexual sin, that my ministry fruits have been non-existent. So that's where—those were the circumstances that were really challenging in traditional understanding of Scripture on same-sex relationships.

For Kyle, not only did his employer's interpretation of Scripture not cohere with his experience of other people, it did not even cohere with other parts of Scripture. Like Jeff and Bishop Robinson, Kyle humbly recognized that he should not cast stones. And using Jesus's own tool for determining true prophets from false ones, he could see people who were open to same-sex sexual relationships bearing fruit in their ministries, just as Jesus indicated "good trees" would. So, he pursued his study of Scripture, again using the tools of conservative Biblical interpretation:

I wanted to be able to do my own study on it. So starting with concordances and lexicons and stuff, doing like root Scripture studies of the words in the six passages that talk about same-sex acts. And then I kind of extended from there to engage commentaries and stuff. And even the commentaries or the biblical scholars would say things that, to me, created space for same-sex relationships, even though they themselves were not affirming. I was like, "How do you get those conclusions? It doesn't make sense." But eventually landed in a spot where I was affirming same-sex relationships.

Kyle knew that studying the Bible on his own might take him to a place where he could no longer work for a ministry that demanded adherence to a policy that conflicted with what he found in the Bible. He did it anyway, lost his job, and eventually got a job at an affirming ministry. Others spoke of the risk of taking a position contrary to the conventional view. We spoke with pastors who knew that to say that same-sex sex wasn't sinful would cost them their jobs and livelihood, who felt God telling them to wait, but who knew that eventually their lives would change. All around the country, pastors and congregations have been decommissioned from evangelical denominations, and independent megachurches have seen their memberships and donations plummet when their pastors publicly avowed that God would bless a same-sex marriage. They suffered severe consequences, but they knew and could feel that God was on their side, and they were walking the path of Jesus.

For an Arab American megachurch pastor we call Edward, it was realizing that not taking a position broke a friendship that made him, and the whole staff of his multi-campus megachurch, take an explicitly affirming stance. He and his colleagues—his spiritual community—had gotten to the point of understanding that Scripture did not really hold today's LGBTQ+ Christians in the contempt often displayed by the church. But it was seeing how deeply a friend feared telling him she was gay—fear that he would fire her on the spot, fear that he would cut her off—that "wrecked" him:

> She leads music at one of our campuses. And when she told me—and I'm the executive pastor so I have pretty much authority to hire and fire at will if I want to, and she told me on my couch at my house as a friend, with my wife and her girlfriend [who is also] my [kids'] nanny, through tears, basically terrified that my next thing was "You're fired, you can't sing tomorrow," and that just wrecked me. It was over from there.
>
> Because [as a church staff] we were already there, theologically, intellectually, whatever. But we weren't there politically, we weren't there—we weren't open and affirming, we were just—we were quietly affirming, which isn't good enough. When one of your best friends who is as close to the "inner circle," whatever that means, as you can be, is still afraid . . . we couldn't go another day with that.

His church did come out as affirming of same-sex marriage and LGBTQ+ identities, and they did lose a lot of members and come under public criticism. But they did not regret the change of policy because they knew it was the right thing to do. They knew it was what Jesus would do.

Some of those who have changed their minds did not only use the tools of conservative Protestant religious teachings; some have even written them. David Gushee, a professor of Christian ethics, changed his mind publicly by publishing a book explaining his reasoning.[14] Having co-written one of the main textbooks conservative seminaries used to teach Christian ethics, Gushee holds a position of some stature in certain evangelical circles. But his change of heart and mind earned him some insulting words. In an op-ed for the *Washington Post*,[15] he discussed his situation, pointing to relationships with actual LGBT people:

> It is hard to describe exactly why my moral vision shifted in this way. But undoubtedly, it had much to do with my move to Atlanta in 2007 and my growing contact with LGBT people, especially fellow Christians. I hardly knew anyone who was gay before that move, but afterward, they seemed to be everywhere, and a few became very dear friends. It became clear to me—in a deeply spiritual place that I will allow no one to challenge—that God was sending LGBT people to me. The fact that one of these LGBT Christians is my dear youngest sister, Katey, has made this issue even more deeply personal for me than it would have been. The fact that one place where she developed a deep struggle with her sexuality was in evangelical churches has contributed to my new moral commitment to make evangelical families and churches safe places for LGBT people.
>
> Evangelical Christians, such as Denny Burk and Robert Gagnon, are criticizing me because I'm now "pro-LGBT." They want to shift the discussion immediately to the debate on same-sex relationships and the proper interpretation of those six or seven most cited Bible passages. I want to move right back to what really matters the most to me—loving this particular 5 percent of the population in exactly the same way that Christians are called to love everyone. That means attending to what most harms them and doing something about it. And that means offering full acceptance of LGBT people, ending religion-based harm and contempt, helping families accept

the sexual orientation of their own children, and helping churches be a safe and welcoming place for every one of God's children....

I am pro-LGBT in just the same way I hope I would have been pro-Jew in 1943 and pro-African American in 1963. I stand in solidarity with those treated with contempt and discrimination. And I do so because I promised in 1978 to follow Jesus wherever he leads. Even here.

While Gushee changed his mind from a relatively safe position, many leaders of conservative churches, ministries, and seminaries, like Kyle and Edward, knew that to change their minds would cause them problems, and possibly cost them their jobs. Certainly, few pastors want to see their posts as mere jobs; they are supposed to be doing the work of Jesus, after all. But that work also pays their bills, puts a roof over their kids' heads, feeds them and their families. We spoke with a pastor in an evangelical denomination who "took it hard" when her teenage child came out to her as gay, for fear that having to support her kid would cost her her job. It did, but she was glad that she had chosen to love her child. Those with whom we spoke to followed their consciences, even if it took them a while to really hear God telling them it was time to make the move. They did so at a price, but then, feeling that they were walking in the path of Jesus—who was often at odds with the religious establishment of his day—gave meaning to those sacrifices.

* * *

As we discussed in Chapter 3, Linda and Rob Robertson have traveled the country sharing the story of how their relationship with their son, Ryan, went wrong when he came out to them at age twelve. Rob and Linda were doing their best to ask for help with what they and their church believed they should be doing. They weren't particularly arrogant. But Rob's reflection helps us to see the dynamics of arrogance often at work. The couple now realize that trying to fix Ryan was never God's intent, that the dogged efforts that felt like love to them at the time were actually a form of control, driven by fear.

In an interview eight years after the Robertsons went public with their story, Linda reiterated that when Ryan came out "fear just took the wheel . . . and I lost the ability to see him with radical love." Hearing Monte's story at the Reformation Project conference, Rob remarked:

> I didn't even consider the fact that I might be wrong. I was certain that I knew what the Bible said. So of course I'm going to do the thing that is most right in my heart and that is pursue the best for my son, and that is stand against what I thought as an encroaching evil, and so I just launched into my ex-gay mode thinking I was absolutely right, and there's no chance that it was going to be found to be different.
>
> So thinking back on that, had I stopped and paused and really sought counsel from somebody who had more understanding in relationships with or a gay individual who's a believer, what it means to be gay and a Christian, then how cool it would have been if I had formed a relationship? . . . Or better yet, in our own church, seek out somebody that's gay, take them to coffee, say "I'm just really struggling here, I've been taught all my life this, and now people are saying, this, what do I even do here?" But I think a degree of humility is really important in all of this, too. Without that, you're just going to stay stuck.

Rob reveals how being closed to relationships that could shake his worldview with new information worked to mitigate his fear of evil. Being closed off in this way is actually what we would call arrogance—something we're all capable of. It can feel like a protective layer, a shield to create a feeling of safety from what we fear. Humility is vulnerable. But arrogance is an unreliable shield, because it carries its own fear with it, the fear of being unmasked as wrong—which, if you've been arrogant, appears "humiliating." Interestingly, Christians often say that *faith* is what helps conquer fear, not arrogance. But in this case, complementarity doctrine makes the stakes so huge that arrogant belief in that doctrine feels like a safe shield. Arrogance feels like faith.

To some who have become allies, it's hard to miss the arrogance of insisting that homosexuality and trans expression are more sinful than heterosexuality and cisgender expression. As a white, cisgender, heterosexual pastor we call Bill remarked:

> I just don't think God condemns people because of where they put their private parts. I think he condemns people because of their attitudes about how they use their sexuality, their attitudes about how they love. That's what leads to condemnation, you know, sort of false humility and arrogance, and things like that. Those are sinful. Loving the wrong person is not sinful.

In his book about the need for Christians to reconcile with the LGBT community, Andrew Marin talks about what happens when Christians stop feeling like they must control or fix LGBT people: they don't just show humility with respect to LGBT people, they show humility with respect to God. He says:

> Christians look at a gay or lesbian person and see a potential behavioral change instead of a person longing to know the same Christ we seek. If we could only release control of what might happen down the road in a GLBT person's life when Jesus enters, I promise that God loves his children enough to always tell each of them what is best for their life.
>
> So then why not start peacefully pointing gays and lesbians in the direction of learning how to have an intimate, real, conversational relationship with the Father and Judge instead of trying to put all of them into 12-step programs?[16]

By promising that God can speak to LGBT people without other people's help, Marin points out the arrogance of Christians to think that it is in their own power to "fix" anyone.

Gushee drew a striking parallel between the way Christians used to think of and treat Jews—based on a handful of Scriptures—and what we are calling "the conventional approach" to LGBT people. He explained the difficulty of this shift for Christians, saying:

> There is the issue itself, with all its complexity, but then there's also the authority problem in the Church, and the difficulty of admitting we were wrong. So it's never just about a few Bible passages and how they should be interpreted. It's about capital A Authority—of scripture, tradition, and contemporary church leaders, and who gets to say who has got it right. It's also about the general unwillingness of Christians to admit that they might have gotten something wrong, either individually or collectively. That idea is very unsettling, and it's hard to face, and those responsible for institutions especially struggle with admitting prior error. But admitting prior error is called repentance, a concept we should be familiar with. And the Church has repented before. It's really important to remind people that the Church has gotten some key things wrong before, has repented, and has recovered to enter a more faithful path of discipleship. We did it on slavery, race, and antisemitism. We can do it now.[17]

For these Christians, the call to love is a call to reject arrogance (I Corinthians 13:5)—the security of knowing that one understands it all perfectly—and foster relationships. Those who have changed their minds on this issue feel more at peace than they did before, even though many lose their jobs or are rejected by former friends or churches. Exercising humility—which is rooted in and sustains love—they no longer feel tension between being Christian and heeding Jesus's and Paul's emphases on love. They no longer let fear control their responses to their loved ones, but feel free to relate to them, to learn from them, to humbly admit they were wrong. Saying "I could be wrong" expresses openness to other people's perspectives. They don't just feel closer to their loved ones; they feel closer to Christ, that they are being like Jesus. They feel as though they understand God better, understand Scripture better, understand the beauty and complexity of creation better than they could before. The change that comes makes allies feel closer to God too, because they're not envisioning

God as someone who's just looking for reasons to cast people off. Love doesn't feel like a struggle against anything. It just feels like love.

For Gushee, the Christian principle of repentance is an act of the kind of humility the church claims to cultivate. He also reflected on what it feels like to change:

> We must listen for and be ready for the Spirit of God—which looks like our hard hearts melting, our calcified minds changing, our spirits repenting; it looks like our churches growing more inclusive, our courage deepening, and our love for unwanted strangers growing fierce. It looks like joyful cross-bearing for Jesus' sake. It looks like solidarity with the oppressed. It looks like strangely abundant joy.[18]

* * *

For many of those who have experienced "failures of Christian love," it starts to become apparent that Christian love means listening to others who are being harmed, learning from them about the nature of their suffering and how to end it. In January 2016, GCN director Justin Lee, a white, cisgender, gay man, gave an impassioned Sunday morning talk, drawing from the parable of the Good Samaritan, a story Jesus tells in Luke's gospel in response to the question, "Who is my neighbor?"[19] Justin said:

> It's easy for us who have been hurt or marginalized to read the parable of the Good Samaritan and think about ourselves in the position of the man on the side of the road. We've been hurt. We've been beaten. We've been marginalized and people are passing us by and they don't seem to care. But . . . [a]ccording to Jesus, the question isn't, "Who is my neighbor?" but, "To whom will I be a neighbor? To whom will I be a friend? To whom will I be family?" See, we are called to be allies to the marginalized and the hurting in our world. Not just allies, but neighbors. Not just neighbors, but friends, as Jesus was a friend of even the sinners—and aren't we all the sinners? Not just friends, but family. Brothers and sisters. Not just family, but to love them as we love ourselves. It doesn't get any more intimate than

that. And that's empathy, isn't it? To love someone as you love yourself. To see the world through their eyes and have that much love for them. That takes a lot of intimacy. . . .

[W]e must not be so focused on our own marginalization that we fail to care for others . . . I believe social justice in whatever—whatever terminology we want to use to talk about it—is something we've got to talk about, because this is a Christian concept. It's Biblical.

Justin explained that as a white man with a comfortable upbringing, being gay helped him to realize that some of the assumptions he had taken for granted could contribute to harming others without his intention. Seeing how the heterosexuals in his life had gotten it all so wrong with him—even while trying to be loving—helped him to realize that he too might have some things to learn about how to be loving to people who were "marginalized in ways I'm not." He told a story about a conversation he had had with an African American friend in high school:

> I said something about being color-blind, and he just looks at me, and he's like, "I don't want you to be color-blind." And I was like, "What are you talking about? Of course you do. *[Laughs, then pauses]* What?" [Audience laughter] And he's like, "No. No. My race is an important part of my experience in this world. My lived experience in this world is impacted every single day by my race. I don't want you to not-see this part of me. It is part of me. What I want is not to be judged or treated poorly, but I want to be known." . . .
>
> And then—then, years later when I came out and I had experiences of people saying to me, "Well, I want to know you and I care about you and I love you, but do you really need to talk about being gay?" I was like, "Oh!" and a lightbulb went on. [Audience laughter] I mean, I don't know what it is like to be a person of color in this country. I will never know what that is like. But there are moments when my own experiences of being marginalized in different ways give me little bits of insight and I go, "Oh. This is what he meant. He wants to be known." And it's moments like that over and over that

have consistently made me realize that the more I know, the more I know that I don't know. And the more I need to learn.

For Justin, loving others the way Jesus taught meant empathizing, and empathizing required openness to learning what the world really looked and felt like from someone else's standpoint.

But power gets in the way of even the best intentions to empathize. We can too easily think we understand when we don't, like Justin assuming that his friend would welcome a color-blind response to racism—that the obvious response to racism was to deny race. Following the path of Jesus requires constant humility because the work of understanding and of love is never finished. Humility keeps us open to ongoing understanding, like Justin saying that he will never fully know what people of color go through. Humility keeps us from ever thinking that we're done learning from others, or that having one moment of insight gives us full understanding. Humility buffers against certainty, and certainty is the enemy of love.

Over and over, conservative Christians who had become allies to LGBTQ+ people shared with us their own experiences of having mistreated LGBTQ+ people by treating them the way they had always believed God expected them to, such as demanding they justify their sexuality or seek to be cured. These approaches reflect a certainty that they couldn't possibly be mistaken when it came to gender and sexuality. Letting go of certainty is difficult, because it means questioning an entire worldview and with it an understanding of yourself built on a particular understanding of God's created order and your own privileged place in it. For white people, including white LGBTQ+ people, recognizing that their understanding of race is rooted in a system with privileges built into the very definition of "white people" similarly means relinquishing an unacknowledged order and their own privileged place in it—including the privilege of not being made to feel uncomfortable by discussions of white supremacist systems and institutions. Prioritizing relational love requires Christians to relinquish certainty over the narrative they have long seen as just how things *are*. It requires admitting that they might not fully understand God's intent, that their understanding might not be the foundation of life they have believed it to be.

Our respondents shared the fears that had motivated them—fear of damnation, of contagion, of being seen as too "liberal" or "condoning sin" and losing membership and respect in their Christian communities. For church leaders, supporting LGBTQ+ people often jeopardized their livelihoods, as church memberships declined or the denominational hierarchy "defellowshipped" them. But they made other sacrifices as well. At a TRP workshop on healing from spiritual abuse, participants were assigned to work in small groups to write a prayer that allowed everyone in the group to feel included. Some people could not hear the word *God* without feeling traumatized, while others didn't know how to find connection without the word *God*. Some couldn't connect with certain images and terms; others couldn't connect without them. The task of being as inclusive as they felt God called them to be required humility, vulnerability, and the willingness to radically transform their own relationships with the divine. It's not easy.

What caused people to risk all that and face those fears? It was love, and a conviction that walking in the path of Jesus is to love people, including people that others despise and condemn. Given the choice between institutional and doctrinal demand, and loving the people in their lives, these allies chose the path of love. That love for the real people who were being hurt by their churches made these allies open to the possibility that what they had always known just might be wrong. They humbly opened themselves to learning new information from others with the goal of being worthy of their trust, and actively committed to reforming or creating institutions that affirm the worthiness of all—where all really are welcome.

Gushee, who has written about Christians who sacrificed to save Jews from the Holocaust, understands solidarity as concrete, institutional change.[20] Justin Lee's speech mentioned the Movement for Black Lives and the physical threats to life experienced disproportionately by Black people at the hands of police. And at the same time, they are white evangelicals, speaking to audiences of evangelicals accustomed—as a matter of faith—to seeing the world in terms of individual souls and sins, not oppressive social systems and institutions. Justin tried to make the case that "social justice" is not just a liberal pet project but is central to Jesus's teachings. As we will explore in the next chapter, tensions like this characterize this movement.

LGBTQ+ people are parts of families and communities before anyone knows of their sexual orientation or gender identity. Homophobic and transphobic oppression can be painful in a particularly intimate way when they take place within relationships with people you love. At the same time, those existing relationships can pave the way for a shift in paradigm—for loved ones to shed their certainty and look back at the Bible to see if it really says that the order of the universe hinges on marriage being between one man and one woman. LGBTQ+ people can push back against their loved ones' erroneous claims and associations, and say, "You know me? Do you *really* think that's true?"

But relationships alone can't create a more just world. For that, we need concrete institutional changes. And those changes depend on acknowledging institutional injustice and taking action to alter the structures that sustain it.

6

Inside and Outside the Evangelical Bubble

Productive and Destructive Tension

As he tells the story, when Andrew Marin—a cisgender, straight, white evangelical—realized three of his friends were gay, he felt God pushing him into uncomfortable territory. He found himself on a mission: to go to the predominantly white gay bars in Chicago's Boystown and hear gay people's stories. To listen, and maybe to tell his own story. When his fellow Christians asked if he wasn't concerned about condoning the "lifestyle," he went back to Billy Graham's famous response to questions about his continued support for President Bill Clinton: "It is the Holy Spirit's job to convict, God's job to judge, and my job to love."[1]

He founded The Marin Foundation (TMF) in 2005, staking out a position of "intentional neutrality" on the question of whether same-sex sex was always sinful. Because its primary identity was as a "Christian" organization, founded by a white, heterosexual, cisgender man—that is, not a "gay" organization—it helped mostly white, heterosexual Christians to find ways to resolve that tension created when people they loved turned out to be LGBTQ+. At the height of TMF's activity, its Director of Pastoral Care received roughly one phone call each week from parents in distress. In many cases, their pastor had told them that Jesus wanted them to throw their thirteen- or fourteen-year-old out of the house. They wanted what was best for their child, but how does a parent know what's best—the "tough love" approach, or a gentler one? If they didn't throw their child out, would God hold *them* accountable for choosing their child over Him? They could call TMF because it was *not* explicitly gay-affirming. It was a *Christian* organization. "Intentional neutrality" made it a safe place to call, where they would hear someone on the other end of the line saying, "I don't think Jesus wants you to throw your child out on the street. I think Jesus *loves* your child, and wants *you* to love your child."

When people felt thrown into conflict because someone in their church or family came out to them, they could go to TMF's "Living in the Tension" discussion group, which also attracted LGBTQ+ Christians, other heterosexual/cisgender conservative Christians, and even a couple of LGBTQ+ atheists. They could hear others' perspectives and share their own, without anyone feeling the need to convince or convert anyone else. In a meeting room in a non-affirming church in a predominantly white neighborhood, predominantly white groups of people with diverse viewpoints showed up regularly to talk about the day's topic, or just to listen.

Acknowledging and accepting tension allowed them to move to a place that prioritized relationships. People could speak their minds and just hear what others had to say. New allies who wanted to help their church to have less-hostile conversations about LGBTQ+ people could come to see how it was done. No one was pressured to adopt any particular view, but we never heard anyone say that hearing about the experiences of LGBTQ+ Christians led them to believe their church needed to be *more* hostile or controlling. The tension allowed some to forge relationships, to listen to others' stories, and to see for themselves that LGBTQ+ Christians had not "turned their backs on God" or "given themselves over to sin." People new to the conversation might leave a gathering with a book recommendation or the email address of someone they could continue to talk to.

Some would apologize publicly. For many years TMF organized a large, highly visible contingent of Christians on the sidelines of the Chicago Pride Parade. Wearing matching "I'M SORRY" t-shirts, participants held up handwritten signs saying what they were sorry for: making people feel like God didn't love them just as they are or seeing LGBTQ+ people as issues rather than persons, for example. When they showed up at the Chicago Pride Parade, they showed courage and humility. They got and gave a lot of hugs on those days.

By setting aside the need for any definitive answer besides "my job is to love," TMF created a space that was, in some ways, more inclusive than explicitly LGBTQ+-affirming groups. The mostly white participants could experience love and forge friendships across the divide. They could feel respected—even the non-Christians. Like many predominantly white groups, TMF wanted to be racially inclusive and diverse. Some noticed that the group was run entirely by white people and did little to challenge assumptions coming out of white-dominated churches about white Christians' "real Christianity" in contrast to other "variations." It seemed to us that Black people, Indigenous people, and other people of color (BIPOC) might show up once or twice or from time to time, but they didn't come back regularly, if at all. The group remained predominantly white.

The "intentional neutrality" that fostered relationships across the divide meant that people who worked for TMF had to publicly claim to be "neutral" on the question of whether same-sex marriage and gender transitions were fundamentally sinful or not. But the same relationships some staff members cultivated there made "neutrality" untenable for them. Jason Bilbrey, the white, heterosexual Director of Pastoral Care, had toed the organization's line. But his job put him in a position to hear story after story of the effects of church people refusing to affirm LGBT identities, same-sex marriage, and gender transitions. Eventually he came to a breaking point. How could he remain neutral in the face of those harms? He remarked, "It just doesn't feel right to say I'm *neutral* on the question of whether God loves my LGBT friends just as they are, or that God approves of their marriages. How can I be neutral on that? I need to be able to say I affirm them." The Acting Executive Director had had a similar struggle.

Eventually, word got out that while Andrew Marin was pursuing a graduate degree in Scotland, the organization had become "LGBT-affirming." On one dramatic evening, people who showed up for TMF's Living in the Tension gathering found themselves locked out of the building, and after some milling around on the sidewalk, the group met in a staff member's nearby garage. With no one else to run the biweekly gatherings, the group met for a time in Jason's living room. Alicia Crosby-Mack had just begun an internship there, so soon she and Jason founded the Center for Inclusivity (CFI).[2] Resolving the tension around intentional neutrality, CFI was explicitly LGBTQIA2S+-affirming. Resolving the tension around TMF's whiteness, CFI was explicitly antiracist.

But it faced different tensions. As CFI explicitly affirmed same-sex sex as compatible with Christianity, celibate LGBTQ+ Christians didn't feel welcome anymore. One time, a discussion facilitator dismissed the view that Christians should abstain from sex before marriage without seeming to have established whether anyone in the room would feel belittled. CFI's office and gatherings moved to an under-resourced and more racially mixed Chicago neighborhood, closer to public transportation. Some who had attended at the previous location didn't feel safe walking around the new neighborhood. With one white and one Black co-director, conversations became more racially integrated, less Christian-centered, and more explicitly focused on the intersections of race, gender, sexuality, and religion. Diverging from conventional evangelical teachings, it was harder to get the kind of funding TMF had been able to secure. Compared to TMF's discussion series, CFI gained more people of color and more non-Christians, and had room for different kinds of questions. In effect, it became a space for a different group of people—people who may have needed that space.

As it created a new kind of space, some others lost the haven that TMF's gatherings had provided for them. We don't know where conservative, white evangelicals went with their questions about how their churches could be less hostile to LGBTQ+ people, but they didn't go to CFI as often as they had gone to TMF. And we're pretty sure those Christian parents whose pastors wanted them to throw their kids out on the street weren't going to call the explicitly LGBTQIA2S+-affirming CFI for advice. Who could they call now?

* * *

A central tension structured all the groups we observed: how to affirm LGBTQ+ people and still be recognizably conservative.

Many, if not all, worldviews are animated by inherent tensions. Contemporary liberal thought holds a tension between tolerance or acceptance for everyone, and not wishing to tolerate or accept those who seem "intolerant."³ Without that tension, liberalism would cease to exist—because it would include either everything or nothing. As Bernice Johnson Reagon put it over forty years ago, there's a persistent tension among progressives between needing safe spaces to be with people like you and needing to work in coalition with others who might not "get" you as well as you would like. Without those tensions, progressive movements can reproduce the same exclusive dynamics they're trying to change in the broader society, or else they will dissolve completely into tiny, homogeneous cliques.⁴

For Martin Luther King Jr., "constructive tension" was "necessary for growth." In his 1963 Letter from Birmingham City Jail, which was quoted at the beginning of every TMF Living in the Tension gathering, King distinguished constructive tension from "covered," festering tension. For King, the constructive tension sparked by nonviolent protest worked to "overcome the bondage of myths and half-truths," by prompting people to explore such questions as "Why?" "Is this true?" and "How do we resolve this tension?" Answering such questions can lead to growth and wholeness, while suppressing them, in King's analysis, leaves the infection of unjust social hierarchies to fester "like a boil," creating increasing pain until something broke and it could be healed with messy exposure to air and light. He wrote:

> Actually, we who engage in nonviolent direct action are not the creators of tension. We merely bring to the surface the hidden tension that is already alive. We bring it out in the open, where it can be seen and dealt with. Like a boil that can never be cured so long as it is covered up but must be opened with all its pus-dripping ugliness to the natural medicines of air and light, injustice must be exposed,

with all the tension its exposure creates, to the light of human conscience and the air of national opinion before it can be cured.[5]

In King's view, nonviolent civil rights actions helped people to see for themselves the violence—the violation of others—inherent in their unexamined worldview, opening the door to negotiation and dialogue. These tensions can be constructive, especially when people with institutional power approach them with humility, being open to new information, and vulnerable to being affected by it, willing to learn and grow. And when we try to cover tensions, in King's imagery, the pus accumulates, and the pain grows.

* * *

All the groups we observed faced the same tension, centering on the question of what it means to be LGBTQ+ or an ally *and* still be a conservative Christian. While there can, of course, be all kinds of debate about what it means to affirm LGBTQ+ people and relationships, the bigger question is what it means to be a conservative Christian. The classic definition of evangelicalism by David Bebbington emphasizes such things as a personal relationship with Jesus, the authority of the Bible, the need to evangelize and convert others, and the belief that Jesus's crucifixion atoned for the sins of humanity—which many LGBTQ+ Christians believe.[6] Conservative Protestants may be rationalist, conducting a detailed study of every word of the Bible, or more charismatic, emphasizing the movement of the Holy Spirit. They may be Republicans or Democrats. For some, evangelicalism is about the movement of the Holy Spirit through contemporary music and a culture that emphasizes Christian identity. Analyzing robust national surveys, sociologists Andrew Whitehead and Samuel Perry found that about 80 percent of white evangelicals adhere to the cultural beliefs of White Christian Nationalism, which they define as a subculture that "includes assumptions of nativism, white supremacy, patriarchy, and heteronormativity, along with divine sanction for authoritarian control and militarism."[7] To those white evangelicals, those tenets *define* Christianity to the point of being invisible (until someone challenges them).

Scholars have found repeatedly that the gender and sexual binary is the one thing that truly defines religious conservatives—so much so that a fellow panelist we spoke with at a conference once scoffed at the idea that the people we're talking about could be or could affirm LGBTQ+ people and still be considered conservative. Don't "conservatives" by definition *not* support LGBTQ+ people?[8] And yet some conservative people—Christian and otherwise—find themselves being LGBTQ+ and having to ask if it's even possible to exist as themselves. The groups we observed formed precisely because there was a need for someone to say that conservative Christians could go on living after they realized they were gay, bi, or trans; that is, to keep loving Jesus and keep trying to walk in his footsteps. And to say that other conservative Christians could keep on loving them, and still love Jesus, and that in fact Jesus would love them too.

When Justin Lee created the Gay Christian Network (GCN) in 2001, it was an online space where mostly white, mostly male, conservative Christians could go in a moment of need to find support in discerning their identity as gay and Christian; in coming out; and in navigating churches, parents, spouses, and Scripture. Gay Christians needed a place where they could go to breathe, to think, to pray, and to figure out that they didn't have to kill themselves, that they could exist, as gay and Christian, without having to try—or to continue to try without success—to change their orientations. That they could be gay and still adhere to an ethic of no sex until marriage—without having to marry a woman and then try to dissociate enough to have undesired sex with her for the rest of their lives. Even celibate gay Christians who agreed with their churches' teaching about marriage and sexuality, "Side B," needed somewhere to turn because a lot of them were in churches and families that saw even just *saying* they were gay as "identifying with their sin." These churches demanded lifelong celibacy but offered little support or guidance for life without marriage. "If you [the Church] want me to live by this ethic," a celibate Christian remarked in a conference speech, "you need to offer me a future that isn't dying alone and being eaten by my cats."

* * *

Even just modeling the compassion you wish the church would show you can spark tension. White evangelical conservative churches, in particular, tend to see "social justice" as out-of-bounds for Christians. By the time of GCN's 2016 conference, the organization seemed to have seen beyond its white origins. The four keynote speakers, including Justin Lee, connected the LGBTQ+ struggle to antiracist struggles. Justin closed with a Sunday morning speech called "Two Dirty Words," in which he echoed King's letter from Birmingham City Jail, speaking of how white evangelicals, in particular, tend to see "social justice"—the two "dirty words"—as taboo and unbiblical. Relating the struggle for Black lives to Jesus's parable of the Good Samaritan, he argued that "social justice" is what results when you do what Jesus taught—truly love your neighbor as yourself and go out of your way to help them when they lie bleeding in the road.

Justin had experienced firsthand how heartbreaking and destructive it was when his loved ones refused to listen, learn, and grow after he shared his experiences as a gay Christian. He *knew* that he would be failing to love as Jesus commanded if he failed to listen and grow in relationship with others when they shared how his worldview hurt them. He reflected on how being gay changed the way he understood this often-cited parable, helping him to understand what Black friends had been saying to him all along:

> This took me some time to figure out. I'm white. I'm male. I'm cisgender. I come from a reasonably well-to-do family. I never had to worry about where my food was coming from. Lived in a house in the suburbs. Got a good education. I'm able-bodied. If I hadn't been gay—right? [Audience laughs] . . . I don't know, if I hadn't been gay, if I would be thinking about any of this. But because I have experienced what it is like to be on the outskirts, I have to care about people who are on the outskirts in ways that I'm not, or people who have been hurt or marginalized in ways that I haven't.[9]

For Justin, "social justice" turned out to be what Jesus was teaching all along. The parable of the Good Samaritan was Jesus's answer to the question of what it meant to adhere to the most important commandments, which are to love God and neighbor. It meant providing for others' real, even physical needs, like the Samaritan did for the beaten man.

The other keynote speakers at that conference connected the struggles of white LGBTQ+ conservative Christians to the struggles of Black people, Indigenous people, and people of color of all orientations and gender identities. One person gave a heartfelt speech connecting the Movement for Black Lives to the struggles of LGBTQ+ people of all races abandoned by their families. Reverend Allyson Robinson heard white conferencegoers saying that racism wasn't GCN's issue to worry about, that the organization was losing focus.[10] She addressed that concern in her own keynote address, pointing out that Jesus transgressed human-made hierarchies and divisions as he brought the message of God's love to the world. Seven years into the Obama administration, shortly after the Supreme Court legalized same-sex marriage, looking toward a solidarity anchored in Christian love—love even for those who dissented from that opinion—may have seemed like the only way forward.

But to some, GCN had gone too far, seeming to support the claim that affirming gay people would make them stop being "Christian." To people for whom conservative faith and conservative politics are intertwined, embracing things like the Movement for Black Lives was not "Christian." The following year's conference felt like a whole different organization's event. Donald Trump was about to be inaugurated after being elected with the help of the 81 percent of white evangelicals who said they voted for him. The conference theme of "Stories Matter"—which seemed to call people's attention back to individual experience—had been decided the previous spring, but speakers and workshop leaders were asked to "avoid politics" in their remarks and focus on personal testimony.

We asked around about the change. As Darren, who served on the board, quickly grabbed some lunch alone at the far end of the conference corridor, probably enjoying a few minutes of solitude, Dawne made a beeline to him and asked whether something had happened to yield the change. He said:

Of course people complained last year. Someone complains every year. Regarding last year in particular, you have to understand, there are people here who voted for Trump. Gay people, yes, and some parents of gay people, who wonder if loving and accepting their children means they have to abandon everything. We need to be a place for them, too. [reconstructed in notes]

To some, no doubt, the 2016 keynote addresses had confirmed their worst fears about affirming LGBTQ+ identities: that accepting "homosexuality" makes a person "liberal," that it's the first step down a slippery slope away from their Christian ideals, and that it isn't really possible to be gay and a conservative Christian. Sharing stories was a way to depoliticize the organization *and* had the advantage of focusing on the personal relationships that do actually change hearts, minds, and maybe even policies.

By the following year, the organization had a new name, Q Christian Fellowship (QCF). The board and Justin parted ways, and QCF established a new executive director, Bukola Landis-Aina, a Nigerian American queer woman. The new mission statement identified the group as "a diverse community with varied backgrounds, cultures, theologies and denominations, drawn together through our love of Christ and our belief that every person is a beloved child of God,"[11] a position embracing more than "conservative" Christians, and possibly alienating those who found its definition too expansive. Its mission statement embraced "Seeking life-giving relationships and partnerships that prioritize considerations of intersectionality; that value reconciliation and liberation of the marginalized; and creating content which inspires the community to seek relational justice," using keywords certain conservative Christian leaders have found particularly objectionable.[12] By 2022, the group was hosting a meet-up for polyamorous families, something many Christians find unchristian and, in fact, have foreseen as being on the "slippery slope" that was begun by accepting the existence of gay people. Some LGBTQ+ Christians would find it objectionable too. And yet, others would ask, is an honest, loving, mutual, sexual relationship of more than two people really at odds with an ethic built on love for God and others? Or is it just at odds with a social order built around a particular view of gender and sexuality? And whose job is it to judge?

* * *

The Reformation Project (TRP) navigated this tension in a different way. It began eleven years into GCN's existence because its founder, Matthew Vines, was dissatisfied with GCN's "hearts and minds" approach and wanted to advocate more directly for institutional change within churches. He has argued that conservative methods of interpreting the Bible aren't supposed to yield the toxic mess found in so many conservative churches; in fact, interpretations reveal support for same-sex marriage and trans people. As a teen, he had felt abandoned when a slightly older boy came out as gay and disappeared from the church. He wanted to help people in churches like his to be *better* Christians—to be better at Christian love—so that future generations wouldn't have to go through what he did.

In TRP, Matthew pointed out that the church once believed—because of the Bible—that the earth was at the center of the universe. Just like Galileo's discovery that the earth moves around the sun, learning new things doesn't threaten God or the Bible, but instead helps people to better understand God's creation and message. People now know what we didn't know before, that there are such things as sexual orientation and gender identity. Gay, straight, and bi+ people exist. The Bible mentions intersex people. Some people really just *are* transgender and/or nonbinary. TRP created a space where LGBTQ+ Christians and their allies could meet and study the Bible, using conservative methods of interpretation to equip themselves to engage their churches until those churches adjusted to this new information and let them have full membership.[13]

For Matthew, being a conservative Christian meant retaining a "high view" of Scripture and studying it carefully for God's guidance in life. It meant being part of evangelical and fundamentalist communities, doing what they do, singing what they sing, and supporting each other through hardships by showing love and spreading the Good News of Christ's sacrifice for the sins of the world. It meant loving God, the Bible, and the

Church, including adhering firmly to the Church's teachings that sex before marriage diminishes a person. Being a white, highly educated, and financially comfortable cisgender man who espoused many distinctively evangelical premises, Matthew could get a place at the table with prominent evangelical leaders and make some progress in diminishing the church's harmful effects. He could explain to them directly why the church needed to get rid of its toxic idea that same-sex sexual activity, gender nonconformity, and even LGBTQ+ identities are sins worse than any other sin. He could show them that the church needs to meet LGBTQ+ people who aren't Christian where they are, just as it meets other non-Christians where they are, to help them to overcome their actual sin (tendencies that separate them from God), not their sexual orientation or gender identity.

TRP was different from GCN. Having the explicit goal of changing institutional policies and practices, Matthew hired experienced social justice organizers to help teach people how to create social change. He acknowledged publicly and frequently that he held his place of authority because of the respect church leaders—and members—afforded to him as a white, cisgender man from a well-off family. In the mid-2010s, TRP leaders taught people that because 33 percent of LGBTQ+ people are also Black, Indigenous, or people of color, neglecting racism fails to liberate a huge part of the LGBTQ+ community.[14] The TRP conferences we attended all began with an Academy for Racial Justice preconference where participants learned about some of the connections between homophobia, transphobia, and racism, and about the need for intersectional justice work.

But hiring people with experience in organizing for social justice created tension with Matthew's commitment to the predominantly white, conservative church. Social justice organizers tend to see racism as a foundational injustice in US society. Some of these activists saw TRP's hierarchical, white, male-headed power structure and commitment to conservative Biblical interpretation as rooted in conservative Christians' racist, sexist, ableist, classist, and anti-LGBTQ+ teachings and practices. Some employees balked at the number of white men invited to speak at conferences and at the fact that a white man set the agenda and boundaries of acceptable discourse. Some found the emphasis on abstinence before marriage to reinforce some churches' harmful teachings on purity and insistence that sex diminishes people. They struggled productively with Matthew for years, but in 2019, the entire staff resigned when they realized TRP would never share their priorities.

The following autumn, Matthew publicly reaffirmed his vision of a church that could remain unchanged except for allowing that LGBTQ+ people exist and belong inside, affirming TRP's "love of God, love of the Bible, and love of the church." He reaffirmed his commitment to the evangelical church's distinction between body and soul. He remained committed to inviting marginalized people to share the stage with white men, without pushing anyone to the side.[15]

To stay in conversation with white conservative evangelicals, Matthew retreated from the antiracist work the staff and board had previously led the organization to do. Instead of using "academic" terms like "intersectionality" to talk about their experiences of systemic racism, TRP would focus on "love for neighbor" and the Bible's witness to Jesus standing with the oppressed and marginalized.[16]

We agree that racism is a failure to love, but as social scientists, historians, and others have repeatedly found, white evangelicals' notions of racial reconciliation have long remained focused on individual sin to the exclusion of acknowledging systemic power and injustice, or structural sin.[17] Matthew himself seems to have seen TRP's potential to help "those who are becoming affirming" of LGBTQ+ people to make the connection to "broader concern for those who have been marginalized." His 2019 statement said:

> Moving forward, we will be intentional about clearly and directly connecting the imperative for Christians to care about those on the margins to the teachings of Scripture. The Bible contains an abundance of passages to that effect; by consistently framing conversations on these topics with biblical parables, verses, and teachings, we can help Christians who are becoming affirming see how a broader concern for those who have been marginalized flows directly out of and

is a requirement of our faith. We have done this in various ways before, but our hope is that increasing the emphasis on our grounding in faith as a motivation for caring about and advocating for other marginalized groups will help more Christians deepen their vision of inclusion.

On the one hand, he hoped that the language of "loving your neighbor" could inspire white conservative Protestants to "care about and advocate for other marginalized groups." And he was committed to retaining a diverse and inclusive board and including diverse speakers in TRP events. At the same time, he acknowledged that TRP couldn't be for everyone:

> The LGBTQ Christian community critically needs an organization that engages non-affirming Christians the way that TRP strives to do, and we are excited and energized by the clarity of our focus and vision moving forward. At the same time, we recognize that the work TRP does is not the work everyone is called to do and that organizations with a focus on communicating with non-affirming Christians cannot serve everyone.

Staff and board members of color saw the profound ignorance of systemic oppression that characterizes white evangelicals' fragility around the discussion of systemic racism rearing its head. Seeing Matthew use the language of "diversity and inclusion" instead of the antiracist concepts people of color had developed to explain racism's intransigence, some people of color who had served and supported the organization felt that he had just jettisoned everything they had built over seven years. To some, it was not TRP's advocacy for change that created tensions, but what it advocated keeping the same. And, as with The Marin Foundation and GCN, the question remained: if the organization started to look like a "social justice organization," how effective would it be at reaching the white evangelicals Matthew and many members wanted to reach? Revealing the connections between racism, homophobia, and transphobia had alienated many of the white conservatives Matthew wanted to engage. Antiracism stopped being a priority.

To the people of color who had worked closely with him over the years, who had invested in him and TRP with the hope that it would be a truly "inclusive" organization that called white evangelicals' attention to systemic racism, he seemed to be saying, "I'm not actually for *you*." When he released this statement, some followers were shocked. On social media, some likened the move to divorce or a death in the family. One former board member, a person of color, said, "I don't want to call it a betrayal, because I've been there all along and maybe I have *not*-noticed things" but wondered what signs they had failed to see, and how they could have failed so spectacularly to see it coming. This person didn't want to call it "betrayal," but that was the word that came to mind because when Matthew felt like he had to choose between the journey he had been on with people of color, who saw racial and sexual justice as inseparable, and cultivating relationships with white evangelicals who didn't see racial justice as a priority, he chose the latter. TRP committed to meeting *them* where *they* were.

At the following year's conference, Darren, who served on the board of this group as well, stood on the stage, looking out at an audience that was significantly whiter than it had ever been. He felt like he was the only person there who saw that as a problem. He decided to step back from his position on the board. He recalled:

> I said my assessment of what TRP will function as, which is, "we reach white evangelicals." And I've said to Matthew personally and to the whole board that my stepping back is not necessarily disagreement with that, but just clarity that it's never going to serve me. To do what it's intending to do, or do what it's doing well, isn't going to serve me directly. I'm going to indirectly benefit from white evangelicals getting better, conservatives getting better, because they have power and can affect my life in ways that I can't affect theirs. But, who this conference will be for, will not be for me. And I'm gonna let y'all do that, because I've got other stuff to do. I've given 20 years of my life

to this same dynamic, of being respectable and acceptable, and it costing me everything, and it just being a data point for them.

Matthew expressed the hope that emphasizing Biblical teachings would make clear to white Christians, eventually, that racism was unloving. But the price of getting white churches to be affirming seemed to be preserving white evangelicals' comfort, not calling attention to the social privileges that have made that comfort possible or who must be "uncomfortable" to secure that comfort. It seemed to mean not calling attention to the ways that white supremacy has become as central to white evangelical Christianity—or even more so—than the teachings of Jesus. Confronting white people with the history of white supremacy—and the ways it conflicts with Jesus's teachings and practice—would make his organization seem too "liberal," as would questioning the dynamics of evangelical purity culture. That would make it seem "antiracist" or "sex positive." By shutting down the conversation about "intersectionality"—which would require people to actually think about the lives of LGBTQ+ people of color—TRP basically sought to "cover over"—in King's words—the foundational tensions in the conservative worldview.

At the 2022 joint conference of CenterPeace and TRP, several middle-aged white men who belonged to the host church wore T-shirts that said, "We are Christian first, everything else second," a common slogan at the time. Where did their whiteness fit into that equation? A man of color at the conference struggled with the slogan during a workshop discussion, saying:

> I'm not any one part of who I am first. I am Black, I am multiracial, I am a husband, a parent, a pastor, a Christian—I am all of those things at once, all the time. I'm not sure what being Christian even means to them if they can separate that from everything else they are.

When he spoke at the conference, Matthew quipped, "We can assure people that the church's foundation is sound. We just need to get the asbestos out of the room where all the gay people are." But if the churches with which Matthew engages consist of people who are only willing to think about affirming LGBTQ+ loved ones as long as it doesn't mean that they have to think about America's foundation of legally granting rights and benefits to white people that were denied to everyone else, what does being Christian mean to them? Can they even begin to separate their Christianity from their white supremacy? Do they really think God favors white people over everyone else? Do they elevate the social system of white privilege and power to the level of the Creator?

* * *

So, what does it mean to be a conservative Christian? Clearly, to many, it has gone without question that to be conservative—or even to be Christian at all—means that you must believe that a binary hierarchy of male over female is God's way of ordering the universe, and without it we would hand Satan the keys to the kingdom. For decades, the one thing that was clear was that conservatives were definitely antigay. But now groups like GCN, TRP, and the theologians and Bible scholars they draw from, have gained supporters who agree that you *can* be a conservative Christian and affirm same-sex marriage, gender transition, and LGBTQ+ identities.

Where does that leave "conservative?" After 81 percent of white evangelicals seemed to spectacularly contradict Jesus's teachings by embracing Donald Trump in the 2016 presidential election, a number of books came out explaining that white evangelicalism has always, in fact, been less about Jesus's teachings than about men's authority over women and white people's supremacy over all others.[18] Ethnographers have found that white evangelicals tend to equate Christianity with white comfort and privilege; a social order in which men have the ultimate authority; low taxes and a rigidly individualistic understanding of where personal wealth and good fortune come from that eschews any look at institutional and governmental policies, systems, and culture; a "law and order" understanding of the criminal justice system as ultimately fair; and an overall cultural preference for individual-level change at the level of hearts and minds, rather than any attention to social systems, institutions, and power.[19] Is that what it means to be a conservative Christian? Many conservative Christians would say it means regarding the Bible as God's word as a guide for their lives, or rigorously adhering to the teachings of Jesus. TRP's negotiation of that tension made it seem that to be a conservative Christian means not to question our society's racial order, to allow white people to be content with "blessings" such as protection by police and the law; generations of federal mortgage protections; and educational, employment, environmental, and healthcare hierarchies, without thinking there might have been some human error involved in creating today's institutional realities.

White evangelicals often think of their good fortune as blessings from God. What does it mean to tell them that their good fortune is the result of the political creation of a racialized underclass? Or to tell them that their authority and their blessings don't come from the all-seeing, all-knowing, benevolent creator of the universe but from changeable and unfair social dynamics?[20] Would they believe it if you told them Jesus wants them to pay higher taxes?

When they're forced to think about it and look to the Bible for guidance, it seems to strike a lot of Christians that Jesus breached social hierarchies and lines between us and them, pure and impure, forbidden and allowed, in favor of loving people, healing, feeding, and restoring them.

Some leaders try to keep the lines of conversation open, the tension alive. They point out that if being Christian means following the teachings and example of Jesus, that path might include violating social convention, transgressing social boundaries, and breaking the rules when love takes another path. They gently nudge people as if to say, "See guys, this isn't left-wing radical stuff. It's just what we've been reading all along. Nothing to be scared of."

* * *

To those who objected to the LGBTQ+ Christian movement's focus on racism, it probably seemed like GCN had proven that affirming LGBTQ+ people puts you on a slippery slope to perdition. We asked the CFI's Jason Bilbrey about this tension once, and he acknowledged that it was a big first step: "Once you start revisiting how you read the Bible, then all these other pieces do come into it." But, he said, it's not actually a slippery slope because you aren't really swept downward. It's more a series of steps, prayerfully and thoughtfully taken, each bringing more clarity to Jesus's message. "The Gospels beautifully dismantle those themes, like clean versus unclean, chosen versus outsiders. And then Jesus dies and the whole curtain is ripped down; the class, race, and gender boundaries are gone." Jason had Galatians 3:28 tattooed on his arm: "There is neither Jew nor Greek, neither slave nor free, nor is there male and female, for you are all one in Christ Jesus."

Others, too, felt like they were "taking baby steps, proceeding *conservatively*," as one person said: taking a step, seeing how that went, prayerfully reflecting before taking the next step.

A number of observers have spoken of the "Evangelical bubble," the cocoon of predominantly white evangelical institutions and rhetoric, that creates the appearance of safety from the threatening world outside—the world of scary immigrants, dangerous non-Christians, racialized criminality, sexual license, and gender deviance.[21] For some LGBTQ+ and allied Christians, coming out came to feel like they were being pushed out of their "bubble"—the safety and security of their church—where they had felt loved and cared for. At that critical moment, many of them needed a place to just figure out how to *be*. For them, these organizations formed a little bubble attached to the big bubble, a little vestibule—a vesti-bubble?—where they could still feel connected to Christianity as they knew it, even as they felt other Christians pushing them out. They could see inside, even if they weren't treated like they belonged there as they had before others knew about their sexual orientation or gender identity. Maybe they couldn't go to their church anymore, or they could go but not pass the offering plate, or pass the offering plate but not teach or lead worship, or lead worship, but only as long as no one reported them under suspicion of "homosexual practice." In countless ways, they were kept hanging on, so long as they constantly established that they knew they weren't really worthy.

Many of the LGBTQ+ Christians we talked to had experienced the comfort and safety of the bubble even as they were hindered or harmed within it. Kevin Garcia described the comfort and familiarity of the bubble, what they called a "comfort zone of hurt" which nearly suffocated them—and almost cost them their life—as they tried to resolve the tension created by the seeming contradiction of being both Christian and gay.[22] Sandra spoke of the comfort of the bubble, and the rewards and uplift she experienced even as it was also slowly killing parts of her. In sharing her healing story, Elder Carmarion D. Anderson recounted the Gospel story of Jesus leading the blind man out of the village, out of the bubble—the protective, familiar space that was comfortable but also harmful to the man, the place that blinds him. Once away from the village, Jesus heals the blind man with his spit and tells him not to go back to believing or internalizing the harm of toxic shame. When healed, transformation happens so that even if people go back to the bubble, they are changed in ways that keep the tension alive and out in the open and creative, rather than hiding it, covering it over, or trying to avoid or deny it.

For some, that experience and the work of having to figure out what it really meant for them to be Christian *and* LGBTQ+ put them into a position to reevaluate what they had always known, to ask questions, to critically examine other examples of what King called "myths and half-truths" they hadn't thought much about before.[23] Some came to question major premises of the Christianity they had always known—whether sex outside of marriage really destroyed people, whether Islam really posed any kind of existential threat to Christianity, whether someone could really claim to follow the teaching of Jesus if they were content to allow people to starve in the richest country in the world and allow police to kill unarmed Black people without any consequence.

In King's analysis, equality is an equilibrium state, and oppression creates tension. It takes work to keep supporting the lie that God likes white people and white people's ways of doing things better than God likes people of color and their ways of doing things. It takes effort to keep producing the idea that men are one way and women are another way—reading James Dobson's books on what men and women are like, and you'll find them unintentionally telling you about all the *work* it takes to produce that fiction: Men are insecure and need women to affirm their superiority and dominance by constantly reminding them of how unlike women they are, what powerful men they are. Women need to constantly remind themselves not to be too "manly," too direct, too certain, too capable.[24] The alternative, allowing that people are all the same in some ways and different in other ways and that all of those differences are beautiful, is a worldview that contains its own tensions—what if my way of being different hurts other people?—but it does not contain the tension created by trying to invisibly maintain false social hierarchies to make them seem like they're just "nature" and "how God made it."

Keeping tension constructive requires love. And love requires openness to new information, including the new information that some people might suffer from unequal treatment built into our culture and the structure of our institutions in ways that benefit you. To try to suppress that information, to keep it "covered," in King's terms, is to cut off your relationship with the people telling you that. When you stop listening and being open to growth and change, that's when you start treating people as objects, as props to prove how not-racist you are, or how "loving" you can be to "homosexuals" by telling them that God hates their capacity to love.

If you love someone, you listen when they tell you that you are part of a system that is crushing them—even if you can't see how you benefit from it. You are open to trying to figure out what your role can be in dismantling that system. If I'm stepping on your foot without realizing it, and you tell me I'm stepping on your foot, how would you like me to respond? The loving way for me to respond would be to move my foot, apologize, and ask if you need anything to help your foot feel better. It wouldn't be to keep my foot on yours and say, "Why are you always complaining? Why do you think all your problems have to be someone else's fault? Have you even *tried* to make your foot less sensitive? Have you prayed to God for deliverance so that your life isn't so full of suffering?"

A bubble exists because of surface tension. King saw some tension as violent and other tension and "productive" and "necessary for growth."[25] For some of those we spoke to, the tension of trying to stay inside and help maintain the bubble gave way, and they experienced a "whoosh" outward into the world they had been taught to fear—the world where LGBTQ+ people are loved just as they are, where racial and ethnic differences are celebrated rather than subdued, and where social hierarchies are seen as unjust rather than God's justice. To be sure, being vulnerable to new information and living your life in a new way is the opposite of feeling "secure." It isn't comfortable to step out into the unknown. For those Christians who have taken that step, that was where faith came in—the faith that they would still have God, even when they *didn't* know what to expect.

Love doesn't stop at the point where it becomes uncomfortable; it just keeps going until the equilibrium King had in mind is reached, until people are equally loved, equally cared for, equally able to grow and change in loving relationships. In the unjust meantime,[26] navigating those tensions can be tricky. But refusing to navigate them is to place faith in your own power and privilege over others. It is to favor control over love.

Power can get in the way of even the best intentions to love and seek solidarity with others oppressed in ways that we are not oppressed. We need to meet people where they are, but in order not to reproduce white supremacy or other unjust power dynamics, white LGBTQ+ Christians who are called to do this work need those most affected to hold them accountable for doing it well. If the message of the Good Samaritan is going to help people see their own unconsciously white-supremacist assumptions, white people need to remain in conversation with antiracist activists who can point out missteps or wrong assumptions we might not notice—a lesson Justin Lee learned when he thought he knew that loving and supporting his African American friend meant being color-blind, which felt to his friend like not being seen at all. All of us who benefit from systems that harm others need to be challenged to see what we can't see and to unlearn what we think we know. It requires actively seeking the perspectives of those affected and embracing their critique even when it feels uncomfortable or is difficult to see for ourselves. And being thankful for their trust and investment in us.

Throughout our observations and conversations, it became increasingly clear that part of what makes LGBTQ+ conservative Christians' stories so compelling is what they reveal about the centrality of relationships in human life. People thrive when they feel worthy to love and take care of others, and to be loved and cared for. They wither and suffer when their capacity to do those things is cut off or shut down, when they are told they are not worthy. And internalizing that shame is toxic. The key to loving others is being vulnerable and being open to learning and growing by virtue of your connection to them. Without that vulnerability, your connection is more likely to be an effort at control or simply going through the motions.

Focusing particularly on Christians of color who are LGBTQ+—people oppressed in more than one way at once—reveals that if you only love part of someone else, to them that doesn't feel much like being loved. Forcing them to segment off parts of themselves and shut them off into separate compartments doesn't allow them to experience wholeness. It is a way of putting conditions on your love, saying "I love you on condition of shielding me from the parts of yourself that I don't actually love," or "I love you, the image of you in my mind, but I'm not willing to grow and change because of our connection. I won't let you affect me except to make me feel good about myself." And if the parts you're not willing to hear about are the parts where they suffer, possibly because of dynamics or institutions that benefit you, that doesn't feel like being loved *at all*. It feels like being used or controlled.

Similarly, to some LGBTQ+ conservative Christians, it becomes clear that if you love someone, then you can't be content to let them suffer. Many of the people we heard from had experienced "failures of Christian love"; that is, friends and family who wanted to be loving, but just couldn't bring themselves to learn, grow, and change by virtue of their connection once they realized the person was LGBTQ+. Those experiences helped many of them to realize that they, too, needed to be better at listening and learning so they, too, could grow better at loving others. A number of people in this movement have come to see the connections, that Jesus's message of love for outsiders and enemies alike meant that refusing to see the injustices inherent in social systems was a failure of Christian love.

For anyone interested in making life more livable for others, the work is never done. David Seitz tells a story about his friend Martine, a Black Christian member of the predominantly white Metropolitan Community Church of Toronto, who was annoyed when someone removed a sign from the front of the sanctuary that quoted Isaiah—"My house shall be a house of prayer for all people"—and replaced it with one that said, "Welcome home." What annoyed Martine was the change of verb tense that signaled a problem with white, "nonracist" culture in general: rather than constant striving to find who else is excluded and expand the house of prayer to include them, too, "Welcome home" suggested that the mission had been accomplished. Everyone was welcome now. By extension, it would follow that anyone who didn't feel welcome was on their own.[27]

The common desire to resolve tension—to come to a place where everything can be declared "all better"—misses the important work of welcoming and the solidarity that happens in the tension, where we must be open to negotiation and therefore new insights.[28] Approaching the world with humility, we acknowledge that we'll never be perfect and will always have things to learn from others.

When conservative Christians do that, they might not look very "conservative" or even "Christian" to important people in their lives. But are their judgments the ones that matter?

7

Love, Shame, Humility, and Justice

Indeed, all the great movements for social justice in our society have strongly emphasized a love ethic.[1]

Oppression functions not simply by forcing people to submit . . . but also works by rendering its victims unlovable . . . In this context, resistance consists of loving the unlovable and affirming their humanity. Loving Black people . . . in a society that is so dependent on hating Blackness constitutes a highly rebellious act.[2]

On the front lines of the so-called culture wars, at the points of contact between faith, gender, sexuality, and race, the people we have heard from have had to figure out a lot—some just to keep on living. They have had to navigate the pulls and pushes of love and its failures, of toxic shame, life-giving humility, and the healthy pride it takes to acknowledge one's own humanity and worthiness of love and relationships. They've had to navigate the pull of loved ones they don't want to leave behind and the call toward a space of abundant love and justice. Listening to and learning from LGBTQ+ and allied conservative (and formerly conservative)

Christians (and former Christians), the two of us have learned a lot about how shame, humility, pride, and love interconnect. And we have been changed.

Some of what we have learned might not have been what some participants themselves believe. Many LGBTQ+ conservative Christians just want to be part of a church that feels like home, where the love they've been promised is available to them. They want to serve it in the ways they feel called to. Many of them aren't radical and aren't trying to change the system. They're conservative. For some, that means appreciating an upbeat service with a minimum of nineteenth-century organ music. But for others, it means finding comfort in the sense of order that conservative Christianity cultivates and the promise of eternity in Heaven rather than in the promise of a better world on earth.

But being who we are—two progressive feminists, one a straight, cisgender Catholic and the other a queer, disappointed humanist—their insights combined with our own to give us a better understanding of what so many social activists have emphasized for decades—that love is necessary for justice, and justice depends on love. Living out an ethic of love calls for you to listen to those who have been denied justice. Creating a just society requires a deep revolution of values anchored in love. This is not an easy lesson, and it is often misunderstood. It has taken us a while to grasp this point ourselves. But LGBTQ+ conservative Christians are offering an example for our time. They show us how love as an ethical practice can foster justice and thriving for everyone.

The movement of LGBTQ+ and allied conservative Christians shows us just what it means to say that human beings are relational creatures and just how deeply we depend on love, how much we need connections that allow us to be vulnerable to new information from others (including about ourselves), and where they can be open to the same from us. They've propelled us to really think about what love is—a practice of connecting with others that transforms us and calls us to help them thrive. Jennifer Nash's definition of love as "actively reorienting the self," and James Baldwin's claim that love involves openness to growing in connection with others, best capture how we have seen people practicing love in ways that allow themselves and others to thrive.³ We have seen people transforming or "reconfiguring" their sense of who they are and what it means for them to be Christian in order to be better Christians, better at loving others. Reorienting ourselves to be more loving requires humility. It does not require you to be a Christian.

* * *

Participants have shown us just how destructive and toxic it is to be told that you are unworthy to love and be loved. We've learned a lot about the complicated dynamics of shame, which we define as the fear of being seen as unworthy of relationships, of love. Many conservative Christian LGBTQ+ people have been shamed for being who they are, for things about themselves that foster relationships rather than breaking them. They are told they are unfit to love and that their ability to love other people is dangerous to the very people they love. And try as many of them might, there is nothing they can do to change who they are. Life can become unlivable when the very people you love and who claim to love you treat you as unworthy of love.

People tend to think shame is the lowest of the low feelings, and that nothing good can come of it. Shame can propel addictions, abuse, and all kinds of harm to ourselves and others. When there's no way to repair the social bonds that you have been accused of breaking—when people break bonds with you simply because of who you are—shame can make life literally unlivable. But sometimes shame is brought on by something you can and want to do differently. You can repair relationships you've broken. People who have been spiraling in addiction can be moved—sometimes by the same shame that caused them to spiral—to enter recovery so they can be there for others. Twelve-step groups are all about facing what you've done, acknowledging and atoning for it, and putting in the constant work to be different, and to repair and maintain relationships.

If shame is a fear of being unworthy of relational connection, sham*ing* someone else is a way of saying, "You are unworthy of a relationship with me, or with anyone. Get fixed or get lost." And it is not just when conservative Christians shame LGBTQ+ people. Liberals and progressives often seem to relish shaming others for their racism, sexism, homophobia, transphobia, ableism, ageism, and ignorance. But shaming others rarely leads to progress. In fact, it can make people feel like there's no point in trying to be an ally at all, and it may sever movement for change.

A lot of us know, either intellectually, in our bones, or both, that who we are—if we're white, and/or male, and/or cisgender, and/or not poor, and/or not disabled, and on and on—grants us privileges that are systematically denied to other people—privileges we didn't ask for. Sometimes we might feel shame because of those privileges. In our individualistic society, these systems of oppression are often treated as individual moral failings, that certain people—racists, sexists—are bad people, deserving of shame. And, of course, some people don't feel any shame at all about social hierarchies from which they benefit; if they see them as God's will or the natural order of things, then they might just think they deserve everything that life gives them, and that other people deserve whatever suffering they get.

But the rest of us might find it harder to know what to do. We know that we exist in an unjust system that benefits us at others' expense. The shame that results from that might propel changes, but it can easily lead us down a spiral. It can be tempting to try to bypass it. When we don't look at that shame head-on, we can end up yelling loudly about others' worse failings while refusing to constructively consider our own. It's a way of deflecting our own shame, but it also deflects from the unjust systems most of us benefit from in one way or another, systems that people can collectively change to make them less harmful.

Or we might try to bypass our shame by focusing on proving that we really are good people by performing allyship to feel better about ourselves and make others like us. Feeling ashamed of the way we benefit from systems of institutional oppression can lead us astray when it drives us to care more about appearing good than about actively working to reimagine and transform institutions, which may mean calling into question deeply held beliefs about ourselves.

For people with some level of privileges granted to us unjustly by institutions and culture, the first step to becoming better allies—to being more loving people—might be allowing ourselves to examine that shame and confront how white supremacy, sexism, homophobia, biphobia, transphobia, capitalism, and/or the marginalization of people with disabilities or immigrants, religious minorities, and others has shaped our own lives and who we are. When we acknowledge these dynamics, that acknowledgement can start to make us more worthy of the trust of those to whom we want to be allies. But the point isn't just listening and understanding; it is going on to do the work to change our institutions and culture so they don't continue to harm people. Men who aren't trans can do that work so that women, trans, and nonbinary people can thrive; people without noticeable disabilities can do that work so that people with noticeable disabilities can thrive; white people can do that work to overcome racism; straight and cisgender people of all races can do similar work so their institutions and culture aren't harming people as well. In fact, those who are given institutional privileges can have special roles to play in dismantling institutional discrimination—it takes humility to listen to those who have been systematically harmed in ways we haven't, and who can see better what those changes need to be and what those who have those privileges can do about it.

While shame is a perpetual sense of unworthiness, humility is a realistic sense of our gifts and limitations, grounded in openness to feedback that fosters growth. We have learned a lot about humility from LGBTQ+ Christians and their allies. We've observed that humility is rooted in a desire to protect, restore, or build relationships. When Kai listened to other LGBTQ+ people and *cared* that the celibate ethic Kai was living out was harming their friends; when Alicia stopped and listened to her friend who had just come out to her; when Edward and Kyle, straight, cisgender men, stopped and listened to the actual LGBTQ+ people in their lives and reflected on the ways they, and their ministries, were blocking others from flourishing—their commitments to listening and learning reflected the choice to enact an ethic of love. By listening humbly, they prioritized others, opening themselves up to the possibility that what they had always known about LGBTQ+ people and how God viewed them could be mistaken.

We have benefited from this example, and we think other liberals and progressives can, too. How often do we assume we know just what another person is thinking and dismiss them before they've said anything? How often do we speak for others when we don't really know their story? Our belief in our own rightness or authority can cause us to act out of arrogance rather than humility. We need the tempering effect of humility to keep us anchored in reality. Recognizing that our perspective is limited and that we can learn more, asking questions before pronouncing answers, can make the left less toxic and therefore more successful. Humility means never forgetting that what we know is always incomplete, limited by our own perspective and experience of the world. Prioritizing relationships with others helps us remember to learn.

* * *

Jeff Chu reflected on all the work conference participants had done before he gave his keynote address at the 2022 CenterPeace conference. Attendees learned about the inaccurate translations of certain words in the Bible and the effects of and treatments for spiritual trauma. But he argued that while this was important, it was not enough:

> You can rehash your trauma all you want, and there is value in that.... You can exegete the heck out of a passage, and there is worth in that as well. But I don't believe any of it matters if you do not believe in your heart of hearts that you are loved. If I do not believe in *my* heart of hearts that I am loved. If *we* do not believe in our heart of hearts that we are loved, above all by the God who created us in love, who redeemed us in love, and who accompanies us, in love. Nothing else we have heard or said will matter apart from a soul-deep understanding of that love. That patient love. That gracious love. That equalizing and healing and boundary-breaking and transgressive love. Do you believe in your heart of hearts that you are loved?

For Jeff, the deep conviction that the creator of the universe knows Christians' hearts and flaws, and abounds with patient, gracious, equalizing, healing, boundary-breaking, transgressive love for them allows them to share *that* love with others. He continued: "You'll never be able to corner this love for yourself. But you are called to testify to it. To bear witness to it. To radiate it out into a world that craves its healing and its transformation." Many Christians want to share that vision of God with the world, and they firmly believe that the creator of the universe knows their hearts and loves them. That love enables them to share their love with others.

And yet "Christian love" often seems remarkably exclusive. Sometimes manipulative. Smug. Cruel, even. Some Christians seem to feel as though God has chosen them alone for that love and have the hashtags to prove it. Some Christians have no desire to share that love with *certain* people, at least not without conditions. Some see a transgressive, extravagant, accepting love for everyone—just as they are—as chaos. To them, God's love is an orderly love that puts heterosexual, cisgender, white, Christian men at the top of God's human hierarchy and demands that others submit to them for everyone's safety—even if they're really only protecting their own authority.[4]

If this book is about anything, it's about how the language of love can be used to mask something that feels completely unlike love to those on the receiving end. People can think they're being loving and still get it horribly wrong. Someone who grows up with abusers might not think twice about a God they've been told loves them so much it will really break His heart to have to send them to the Lake of Fire to be tortured forever. Sometimes people consciously disguise hatred as love, effectively saying, "I love you so much I have to force you to be worthy of love."[5] Efforts to love can end up seeming arrogant and self-righteous. Or they can be attempts to manipulate or control others. The problem with treating it as an article of faith that life is supposed to be horrible for some, less horrible for others, until the Second Coming, is that it makes it seem like God just *wants* some people to suffer, so those who inflict that suffering, or let it continue, are God's agents on earth. If that were the case, then the hero of Jesus's parable about the Good Samaritan wouldn't have been the Good Samaritan at all, but the people who crossed the street and let the beaten man slowly bleed to death on the road—or the robbers who put him there. Jesus's explanation of the most important commandments, to love God and neighbor, said that the loving thing to do—the way to live up to God's most important commandments—is to help the stranger who needs it, regardless of who they are, regardless of who you are, and, as Martin Luther King Jr. pointed out, regardless of what might happen to you.[6]

* * *

Saying we all have things to learn about love from evangelical Christians might make it seem like we're proselytizing, but we're not. Most, if not all, of the world's religions profess some version of the Golden Rule to love your neighbor. This is perhaps the closest thing to a "universal" that exists across human cultures, suggesting that human wisdom continually comes down to people being relational creatures. You don't have to be Christian to cultivate a patient, gracious, equalizing, healing, boundary-breaking, transgressive love, and we have observed that many Christians don't practice love when they're dealing with people who are too different from them. While people who belong to religious communities might argue that it helps to have a group of people to hold you accountable to love better, there is no rule that says you can only love people, and try to love them better, if you have accepted Christ as your personal lord and savior.

Civil rights activists and thinkers, including Martin Luther King Jr., June Jordan, James Baldwin, Audre Lorde, bell hooks, Toni Morrison, Grace Lee Boggs, and Valarie Kaur, among others, repeatedly conclude that love, including loving one's enemies and oppressors, is the key to creating a more just world. And yet love repeatedly falls out of the equation as people strive for justice. It is as if love is a narrow fence to balance on, and it's difficult to imagine balancing on it without falling to one side or the other. On one side, love seems—for those with power and privilege—like it calls for nothing more than being nice. On the other side, love seems—for those at the bottom of a hierarchy—like Stockholm syndrome, accepting the abuse and your abuser's right to keep on perpetrating it.

But as Kaur says, anger is not the opposite of love; anger is the force that protects that which is loved.[7] The opposite of love is indifference, a point King made sixty years ago when he noted that the number-one barrier to racial justice in this country was not the hatred of the Klan but the indifference of white liberals, their failure to be *moved* to act, to work for justice.[8] This is why love is necessary to bring about justice. Love of others motivates us to act, to care about their plight and their suffering enough to do something about it. Without love we can easily remain indifferent, sitting back in our own privilege and comfort and feeling bad for people without changing anything. We need love to act. But if we act without love, we can also go astray. Working for justice without being anchored in love can lead us to reproduce the toxic dynamics we aim to change. Acting without love can lead us to dominate or shame others instead of ushering in a revolution of values. We just replace one toxic dynamic with another.

Still, it feels dangerous to write about love because of how it can turn into a seeming admonishment to love those who do not deem you worthy of love. As many people in this movement constantly remind each other, grace and forgiveness do not mean staying in an abusive relationship. If someone has traumatized you, it takes a lot of work to get yourself to a healthy place, particularly to stay healthy around them.

There are times when someone who has been traumatized, particularly if they have experienced some healing around it, can see their traumatizer's own trauma and forgive them in a way that actually allows that other person to heal and do better. It's not a requirement, but it can happen, and when it does, the world becomes a little more peaceful. We are not saying that love requires forgiveness. Love requires countering the temptation to dehumanize others, including those who dehumanize us.

Beyond those complications, writing about love can instantly seem like an idealistic cliché, and we don't want to fall into that trap. Part of the cliché problem is that "love" can so easily be read as "have good feelings about" or "be really nice." A pastor speaking in a conference discussion reflected the danger of cliché when she said:

> Our church used to end our children's service with this "Love Everyone!" thing. When I started there I said we had to get rid of

that. The point isn't "Love Everyone!" but to *love. Everyone.* It's the difference between a feeling and a verb.

The change in her tone from high-pitched to low conveyed the profound difference between an empty, feel-good slogan and a difficult and powerfully transformative discipline.

Platitudes like "Love Everyone!" demand very little of anyone in terms of change, growth, or action. We've seen that when people claim to feel love but fail to listen, to learn, to change when they're hurting someone, it doesn't feel like love to those they're hurting. Even if they didn't mean to hurt them. Even if they were trying to help them. Even if they wanted the very best for them. That's why love demands humility.

People who complain about "cancel culture" are often those who want to be able to say and do whatever they want without consequences, no matter who it hurts. Creating social consequences for mistreating others can be a step forward. But sometimes, "canceling" takes on a quality of revenge or acts as a shield so we can ignore and hide our own shame about ways we ourselves have been that ignorant or benefited unknowingly from privileges we thought we deserved. Sometimes we "cancel," "call out," or even dehumanize people for ignorance when it wouldn't really hurt us to teach them, and "calling in" would be more productive. It takes strength we might not always have, and also humility to call people in. When we "call people in" we don't decide we're better than them. We prioritize our relationship with them and the hope that they can do better. And when you're the one being "called in" and you feel ashamed of what you didn't know but should have, it also takes strength and humility to be vulnerable enough to listen and learn instead of bypassing your shame and getting defensive or checking out.

Linda Robertson told us a story about a time when she was tempted to relieve her feelings of shame. It's a story that highlights both her humility and the humility of the person who confronted her about her racism. At a post-conference Q Christian Fellowship (QCF) board meeting, Darren confronted Linda about how a session she had led was racist, even though she was trying be antiracist. Speaking to us about it later, Linda described feeling overcome by an awful sense of shame in that moment, joined by the impulses both to defend her good intentions and to get back on the sidelines. But she caught herself and opted to sit with the discomfort of realizing what she could not see at the time, to listen, and to work to incorporate the feedback. She was grateful for Darren's faith in her, his hopefulness that telling her about the racist assumptions she had displayed would help her to grow and keep growing. He wasn't shaming her capacity to form relationships but showing her how she could be better at it. She was worth his time and energy, and he could be friends with her even though she had done him harm. He called her in. Sitting with that discomfort helps people to grow and learn how to do and be better. It is an investment in relationships.

* * *

Perhaps surprisingly, we heard no hate coming from people we encountered over the ten years of our research. Overall, they continued to love those who hurt them— sometimes from a distance. Kaur argues that a sense of wonder helps her to understand her enemies—curiosity about what made a group of white male strangers say hateful things about her fellow Sikhs helped her to listen to them and understand better how to be loving to them without succumbing to their hatred. And, she added, that sense of wonder made her a more strategic activist because it helped her to know what she was up against, and how to recruit or navigate.[9]

LGBTQ+ conservative Christians don't need to *wonder* what made their oppressors that way. Kevin Garcia knew exactly why that passing motorist called him a faggot. Aaron completely understood why members of his church needed his patience—because his own "certainty walls" had taken a while to come down. Darren Calhoun didn't wonder why Trump supporters might need the Gay Christian Network (GCN); he knew they needed to know that if they were gay, they could go on living, and that if their kid was gay, they could go on loving them. These perspectives can help us all to understand and address the barriers to creating a more just and loving world.

Justin Lee was once asked how he learned to forgive those who had hurt him. He cited Lewis Smedes, saying:

> even if someone is doing active wrong and has not repented, we can forgive in so far as we can let go of the hatred inside of ourselves toward that person and free ourselves from that burden of hatred, while still acknowledging that this person is doing harm. And we're not in any way excusing their actions or the harm that they're doing. . . . [F]orgiveness is not the same as excusing someone's bad behavior.

A lot of people—including us at first—question the idea that people should practice love instead of contempt toward those who oppress them. To respond with love seems so hard—even outrageous. People who have suffered oppression or abuse don't owe anything to those who harm them and continue to actively perpetuate those harms or remain indifferent to their suffering. Rather, as Kaur notes, people owe it to themselves to be able to live and act in their world without the burden of hate, without internalizing the values of those who hate them. She quotes a line from Toni Morrison's novel, *Love*, that expresses this idea: "Hate does that. Burns off everything but itself, so whatever your grievance is, your face looks just like your enemy's."[10]

Civil rights leaders have been saying this since long before the civil rights movement. Ruby Sales speaks of growing up in the Black church with spirituals that instilled this love ethic: "I love everybody in my heart, I love everybody in my heart, you can't make me hate you. You can't make me hate you."[11] Kaur quotes Booker T. Washington, saying "I shall permit no man, no matter what his color might be, to narrow and degrade my soul by making me hate him," when she writes about the people who murdered Sikh loved ones in the wake of 9/11 and the police officer who injured her while arresting her as a legal observer. She writes: "The more I listen, the less I hate. The less I hate, the more I am free to choose actions that are controlled not by animosity but by wisdom. Laboring to love my opponents is how I love myself. This is not the stuff of saintliness. This is our birthright."[12] Learning to wonder what made some people hate her and everyone like her was what helped her to see them as fallible people rather than terrifying monsters. It gave her the courage and strategies to make a better future.

To love others is to *do* something, not just feel something. In fact, love as a practice engages many emotions—as Kaur puts it, "Joy is the gift of love. Grief is the price of love. Anger protects that which is loved. And when we think we have reached our limit, wonder is the act that returns us to love."[13] But the labor of loving others takes a community. Those of us who are not directly harmed by abusive or toxic dynamics need to labor for others who are, to act as "accomplices in listening" to those who spew hate so that those who suffer directly don't necessarily have to be on the front lines of revolutionary love toward those who harm them.[14]

Choosing to love others, including our opponents, is a labor that is harder than hatred and violence. We can kill with a single, swift act, whereas it takes a lot of time, energy, and labor to grow and nurture human life.[15] In choosing love, many LGBTQ+ conservative Christians come to see that the people who have hurt them have also been harmed by their churches' teaching that only the perfect are truly worthy of God's love, and that because they are not perfect, God's love for them is constantly in danger.

Non-affirming Christians may be ashamed that they themselves don't match the impossible gendered ideals they see as the seed crystal that structures all of creation—because no one can match those self-contradictory ideals. They may be ashamed that their sexual desires don't match the narratives that would make them "truly righteous," in their church's narrative. Linda Robertson told us about how she grew up, praying thanks to God for loving her despite how disgusting she obviously was. She wasn't gay, bi, or trans; she just knew she was disgusting to God, who somehow held his universal God-sized nose and tolerated her.

Similarly, if they are white, they may be ashamed of the ways their whiteness has led them to cut off avenues of love for other people, or that their lives don't match their fictional ideals of whiteness. If they are poor and believe deprivation is always deserved, they may be ashamed about whatever they have done to deserve deprivation or they may resent those who seem to have cut in front of them in line. If they are rich, they may be ashamed of the ways they have failed to be generous as Jesus modeled—or that they aren't even richer. These shames can be bypassed, unacknowledged, and come out in weird ways—including tormenting those the ashamed see as even less worthy of love than themselves. Maybe they finally see an opportunity to beat back the devil by beating him out of the queer child in their midst. The religion of fear controls them, and scapegoating LGBTQ+ people, people of color, poor people, and people with disabilities becomes a way to reassure themselves that they are less unworthy than someone else.[16]

None of this excuses such behavior—it makes them human. Understanding where they are coming from—for those in a place to do it without falling back into the hole they're pulling themselves out of—can help build relationships and live out the ethic of love so many people claim to value.

* * *

The LGBTQ+ Christians and their allies we have heard from show their churches how to be better at loving others. Whether they meant to or not, they have taught us about the radical potential of love to enact a more just world in which everyone can thrive. That lesson has implications far beyond the world of churches.

LGBTQ+ Christians offer us a model for the transformation of society. Through their stories and experiences, we have gained a deeper understanding of what it means to say that humans are relational beings, and a deeper understanding of just how central love is to human life. In a world where so many of our problems can be traced to dehumanizing others, which is a fundamental failure of love, we are inspired to think that a movement based on love has the radical potential to remake our inhumane, dehumanizing systems. To do this, we need to think of love not just as an individual feeling or even an individual ethical practice, but a collective ethical practice embedded in policies. By centering the voices of LGBTQ+ Black people, Indigenous people, and people of color, we see that working for systemic, institutional change is crucial to showing love;

if we aren't working for that, we are not truly caring for those who are harmed systemically by institutions.

We're not alone in wanting to cultivate this ideal. David Kyuman Kim has called on people to think about how "to revive, reclaim, and replenish the public life of love," saying, "Love is the expression of an aspiration: the aspiration to overcome the alienation and estrangement among people."[17] Love seems idealistic as a sociopolitical ethic only when we assume that reality has to be unloving, or that love can only be isolated into individuals' relationships and not the driving force behind more humane and truly egalitarian institutions. Kaur describes revolutionary love as a both a personal and political practice:

> "Revolutionary love" is the choice to enter into wonder and labor for *others*, for our *opponents*, and for *ourselves* in order to transform the world around us. It is not a formal code or prescription but an orientation to life that is personal and political and rooted in joy. Loving only ourselves is escapism; loving only our opponents is self-loathing, and loving only others is ineffective. All three practices together make love revolutionary, and revolutionary love can only be practiced in community.[18]

What does this labor look like? What kind of labor it is? We can keep our eyes on the task of cultivating and implementing a vision of social justice that replaces systemic oppression with systemic love. To paraphrase Jeff Chu, what might it mean to enact *systemically* a patient, gracious, equalizing, healing, boundary-breaking, transgressive love?

The trickiest element might be patience. Oppression, by definition, does not foster anyone's well-being, not even that of the oppressor, and we are absolutely not interested in reproducing Jim Crow-era calls for people to be "patient" with oppression. King spoke directly to those white clergy who urged "patience" with segregation, brutal violence, and other forms of second-class citizenship, saying their approach was a greater barrier to equality than Southern sheriffs with firehoses. Oppressors have no more footing to demand patience than they may *demand* trust or forgiveness. As

Jennifer Harvey argues, if you're demanding that someone else be patient with you while you're dragging your heels on making reparations, that is not love. It bears repeating that being patient and loving to your enemies does not mean staying in an abusive relationship. And, at the same time, leaders in this movement have argued that there is a benefit not in passively waiting, but in adopting what Olúfẹ́mi Táíwò calls "revolutionary patience," which recognizes that the work of making the world more just is ongoing and imperfect. We may not see the full fruits of our labor for justice in our lifetime, but we work for justice nonetheless, holding out the actively patient hope—from a distance if need be—that people and systems can improve or change.[19]

Graciousness might be easier to think of in systemic terms. It might include systems that give everyone's mistakes not a pass but understanding and the opportunity and support to do better. It calls for implementing restorative approaches to discipline and justice that allow people to repair relationships and give everyone the kind of leniency and support that wealthier white people are already more likely to get in court, the kind of leniency that prescribes and publicly funds drug treatment and safe housing rather than prison.

This systemic, love-driven politics would have to include systemic equalizing—the steadfastly humanizing insistence on equitable treatment and equal respect in institutions and interactions, such as equitable schools structured around the belief in all students' potential, with the funding to match, and systems that ensure that everyone's basic needs are met. It puts the brakes on any calls for patience and graciousness that have the effect of furthering oppression or that ask us to stay in relationships or institutions that harm us. Humility includes recognition of our own humanity and right to safety and thriving, as well as the same for others. Like a white woman that Jennifer Harvey describes going to a concert where all the attendees of color were being frisked, systematic equalizing might involve demanding to be frisked along with everyone else; however, the longer-term vision needs to be on equalizing policies, based on leadership from those who have been most oppressed by them. Dean Spade has written about how people can restructure organizations to allow leadership to come from those who are most intimately familiar with the ways our current hierarchies fail to treat people equitably.[20]

A system that expresses these ideals would also have to foster systemic and personal healing, recognizing that all human beings are equally worthy of wholeness and recovery from injury, illness, and trauma. It would enact policies that recognize that our current systems fail to work the way they're supposed to and need to be radically restructured. This is important because without healing, people will continue to enact hatred, a fear-based reaction to people who they perceive to threaten their sense of self or place in the world. Shawn Ginwright argues that we must create institutional spaces for people and communities to heal.[21]

Clearly, this restructuring would systemically break the boundaries of what's currently possible. A lot of this vision might sound kind of impractical, but the question is, what do we have to do to *make* it practical? It would also include systemic transgression of the social boundaries of who's in and who's out; who is worthy of respect, care, forgiveness, and who is not; and who is human and who is monstrous. If, as Alicia Crosby-Mack put it, everyone needs and deserves to be accepted "in the fullness of who we are," the task for each of us, as we feel our talents guide us in the spheres where we have influence, is to ask what it would take to make that love a systemic reality. What would it look like if we worked for systems in which strangers were entitled to the kinds of education we demand for our own kids? To the kinds of parks and playgrounds, municipal services, health care, and food access that the most fortunate of us take for granted? What other option is there?

* * *

Thinking back to our story from Chapter 1, Darren's statement of love made Dawne feel like maybe she could try to lift people up like that, too, without having to sign her soul over to anyone. What would the world be like, if every one of us loved every single other person as we love ourselves? Even people who hate us. Even people who smell bad, or people who scare us, or people we don't understand? Even people we've been taught to try to avoid? What would it look like if we all took the time to find out what each other needs and did what we could to help them get it? What would the world be like if we could listen to each other with humility, hear, and then truly begin to understand how we have harmed them, or how our own good fortune has come at their expense, to own up to it, apologize, and pay back what we owe? And what if we found ways to practice that love not just on a personal level, but as we set up systems for distributing resources?

If we love other people, we will listen to them and we will fight for them.

ACKNOWLEDGMENTS

We are grateful to many people who have helped to bring this book to fruition. None of this would be possible without the patience, openness, insights, and hard work of the LGBTQ+ conservative Christians who are working to make their churches more loving and accepting of LGBTQ+ people and to make our communities more just for all. It takes so much courage to do this work. We are grateful to those who allowed us to witness and learn from their lives and extended to us the radical love that we talk about in this book.

Our immediate families made room for us to work on this project, listened to our thoughts, and endured time without us as we traveled to do this research and took time to write it up. We are very grateful to our partners, Searah Deysach and Rich Tobin. As we started collaborating on our first grant proposal—the letter of interest for the Self, Motivation, and Virtue project (SMV)—Dawne's child was three and Theresa's twins were three months old and she was still on parental leave. Our kids have literally grown up with this project, and often figured into our conversations with participants. We are grateful to Asa Deysach-Moon, Maeve Tobin, and Merielle Tobin, for getting by without us from time to time, and for inspiring us. We hope that what we have learned has enriched your lives, and that this book helps to make a better future for you.

We also thank our extended families for inspiration and support in this work. This whole project began when a member of Dawne's family, Gabe Ericksen, began a prolonged conversation about evangelical Christian responses to homosexuality late in 2012, and began sharing articles and blogs with her from the evangelical LGBTQ+ movement. Timmy

Turner walked along this path with us for a bit, including sharing his apprehensions about and first impressions of GCN's 2016 conference in Houston. Without Timmy and Gabe, this project would never have gotten started. Theresa grew up in a church environment that does not affirm LGBTQ+ people and never imagined those she was taught to shun would become some of her greatest teachers. Her extended family, including her dad, aunts, and grandmothers, nurtured her faith in a God that prioritizes love over certainty, which has opened her up to learning from LGBTQ+ Christians and inspires her ongoing commitment to this research.

Jodi Melamed introduced us, and Jim Holstein encouraged Dawne to apply for the Templeton Religion Trust's SMV research grant, which required her to work with a humanities scholar. The initial phase of our research collaboration, "The Motivation to Love: Overcoming the Spiritual Violence of Sacramental Shame in Christian Churches," was funded by the SMV initiative and made us a team. We are grateful to Darcia Narvaez and Nancy E. Snow, who ran the SMV initiative, along with the board and staff who administered it, and gave us encouraging and helpful feedback at the conferences. Special thanks to SMV board member Owen Flanagan who was especially encouraging and supportive of us developing this project. The funding from that project and the meetings with other grant recipients were instrumental in shaping our perspective, and it provided the impetus for us to start working together. Other funders, including the Association for the Sociology of Religion's Joseph R. Fichter Research Grant and Marquette University's Committee on Research grants, helped us along, and toward the end, a Sabbatical Grant from the Louisville Institute helped us to pull it all together. We are grateful to Aimee Moiso, Briana Zeitz, Keri Liechty, Jessica Bowman and to other 2023 fellowship recipients for their support.

A number of colleagues and friends provided insight, ideas, support, and feedback throughout this process. We are grateful to Ali Abunimah, Orit Avishai, Ruth Braunstein, Karl Britto, Kelsy Burke, Jonathan Coley, Penny Edgell, Lynne Gerber, Golshan Golriz, Maria Kefalas, Deborah Jian Lee, Brian Lowder, Gerardo Martí, Lain A. B. Mathers, Mignon Moore, Michelle Panchuk, C. J. Pascoe, Jane Peterson, Raka Ray, Michael Rea, J. E. Sumerau, Bil Susinka, and Grace Yukich. We gathered ideas and feedback from a number of conferences and colloquia over the years, including the faculty and students at Fordham University's Carpenter Lecture Series, the University of Arizona Sociology Department, Tulane University's Sociology Department, Marquette University's Department of Social and Cultural Sciences, the Queer and Trans Studies in Religion conference organized by Melissa Wilcox at UC Riverside, a Workshop on Philosophical Theology at the University of Notre Dame Center for Philosophy of Religion, and the University of Memphis Department of Philosophy.

We are also grateful to the editors and anonymous reviewers of *Hypatia, Gender & Society, Journal of Moral Education,* and *Political Power and Social Theory*. Members of Marquette's LGBTQ+ Studies Research Group, particularly Max Gray, Jason Farr, Allison Efford, Ben Pladek, and Desirée Valentine, gave us feedback on our book proposal, and we are thankful to our agents—Amy Bishop, Andrew Dugan, and Kendall Berdinsky—for shepherding us through this process. Marjorie Struck provided research assistance early on. Many thanks are due to our editor at Oxford, Theo Calderara, for believing in this project and bringing life to our words, to Rachel Ruisard and Ganga Balaji for bringing our words to life, and to Lisa DeBoer for indexing them thoroughly and elegantly.

At various national conferences we observed, Sophie Bjork-James and Jon Burrow-Branine helped form an unofficial social scientists' affinity group. We were grateful for their collegiality and analyses, and to Jon in particular for sharing the notes he typed up from the back of the room when a speaker went off on a particularly relevant tangent that none of us could get all by hand, no matter how frantically we were scribbling.

A number of people we met in the course of our research provided insights, vital connections, and emotional support throughout this project. We are particularly grateful to Isaac Archuleta, Jason Bilbrey, Sharon Costanza, Michael Kimpan, Jennifer Ould, Kenji Kuramitsu, Justin Lee, Linda Robertson, Matthew Vines, and Paula Stone Williams for their insights, encouragement, suggestions, feedback, informal advice, and friendship. They may not agree with everything we write here, but their support and love have meant everything to us. As Dawne, the nonreligious one of us, once noted, when these folks talk about Jesus, he sounds like a *good* guy—which, sadly, is not the picture every believer paints of him.

Words can't express our overwhelming gratitude to Darren Calhoun for his openness and generosity with considerable time, analysis, insights, and love. And many thanks are due to Alicia T. Crosby-Mack for her work on this project (some of which is detailed in the methodological appendix). Her compassion, careful thought, critical eye, and intelligence infuse these pages. We hope that the finished product is worthy of the time and energy these two invested in it, and in us.

Most of all, we are grateful to everyone who shared their insights and experiences with us, including those who are quoted in these pages. Those who aren't quoted, please know that your contributions were valuable, and we have done our best to ensure that our arguments draw from what you shared with us as well, even though we know our analyses won't be in agreement with everyone. We are immensely grateful to everyone we interviewed; everyone who led workshops we attended; who spoke at or organized conferences and allowed us to attend; and showed us the love, care, and compassion they routinely strive to bring to the world and wish their churches had shown them. They are doing the work to make life more just and livable not just for LGBTQ+ conservative Christians, but for everyone whose life is affected by conservative Christians, which is pretty much all of us. Thanks for teaching us so much about love. We hope we have done everyone who helped us proud.

METHODS

A number of people have been surprised that as a sociologist and a philosopher, we could work together, but we have actually found it pretty easy to collaborate. Feminist and queer studies have always been interdisciplinary, so we were both trained in reading scholarship from a wide range of fields and are both critical of the conceits of our own disciplines and open to the insights of others. This project brought us together.[1] Dawne had already started work on the project in 2013, and when she received a call for grant proposals for interdisciplinary research from the Templeton Religion Trust's Self, Motivation, and Virtue Project (SMV), Theresa seemed the perfect person with whom to team up. Writing the grant proposal was a multi-stage process, and it gave us the opportunity to explore the overlap between Dawne's ethnographic studies of struggles over gender and sexuality and Theresa's philosophical explorations of spiritual violence—the ways people with religious power can use religious rituals and symbols to make people feel like God hates them or wants them to suffer.

We observed four main organizations. In Chicago, we participated in events held by The Marin Foundation, which fostered reconciliation and discussion between conservative heterosexual/cisgender Christians and LGBT people and apologized for harm caused by the church. After its biweekly meetings ended, a former staff member, Jason Bilbrey, collaborated with Alicia T. Crosby-Mack to establish the Center for Inclusivity,[2] an affirming organization founded to create "a place of peace at the intersection of faith and sexuality." We attended both groups' biweekly discussions, and their demonstrations of Christian love and acceptance at the annual Chicago Pride parade. Like several participants in these local groups, we also attended national/regional conferences of two main organizations. The Reformation Project (TRP) was founded in 2014 to equip conservative Christians to lead churches to affirm LGBT identities, same-sex marriage, and alternative gender expressions. The Gay Christian Network (GCN), founded in 2000, hosted online chats, local meetups, and an annual national conference to support LGBTQIA Christians. In 2017, it took the name Q Christian Fellowship (QCF), and as of this writing hosts events for various subgroups throughout the year in addition to their other work. With permission from each group's leadership, we conducted 540 hours of participant observation from 2013 to 2023.

Before we began working together, Dawne had already begun participant observation and qualitative interviews with The Marin Foundation in Chicago, and Theresa became an apprentice in these methods, first by doing them alongside Dawne, and then doing some on her own. In participant observation, a researcher participates in a group to learn about it at a deep level.[3] We participated in discussions as invited, contributing our own experiences, thoughts, and questions, and hand-jotting notes for later elaboration. Sometimes at national conferences we were asked to wear press badges, and at other times we weren't, but we identified ourselves in conversations and small workshops as researchers, and we were careful not to quote anyone unawares. We jotted quick notes during events when we could, and then fleshed out detailed narrative accounts immediately following the observation period.

The point of qualitative research is to learn from others by engaging with them, asking questions, and growing alongside them. We maintained a low profile to allow the event to flow as comfortably as it would in the absence of researchers, but we participated when remaining silent or too circumspect would have been creepy or otherwise aroused suspicion. Like a lot of participants, we were there to learn from others' experiences and expertise. We were who we were. Unlike most participants, though, as participant observers, we took notes and wrote up narratives, checked our interpretations with each other and other participants, and sought to produce as widely agreeable record of what happened as possible—even if participants might disagree with some (or all) of our analysis. We generally strove to focus on them, but as is always the case in qualitative research, we learned a great deal when those efforts failed. One time, when Dawne's partner had been threatened in an organized doxxing zap, Dawne's distress gave conference participants a chance to minister to her the way they ministered to each other in crisis, showing her a bit of what they meant by Christian love. Before publishing this book, we checked with people who might not have known we were there (such as speakers at conferences or blog authors) to see whether they would like to be quoted using their real name or a pseudonym, or not quoted at all. We removed passages that quoted those who wished not to be included.

Our purpose in this research was to see what we could learn from the people involved in the groups we observed. Because a lot of thoughts, feelings, and experiences go unsaid, even at events designed to create space for talking about the overlap of faith, gender, and sexuality, we used qualitative interviews to give participants space to share their stories and insights with us. Shared experiences also became interview topics, so that interviews flowed as organic conversations. As our goal was to learn from participants' perspectives, we did not have a rigid list of questions to shape the conversation. Interviews were intended to elicit participants' own stories to best capture their systems of meaning.[4] Participants began with a choice either to tell their story about faith, gender, and sexuality as it unfolded, or to share how they came to participate in whatever group(s) they did, or for their insight about a particular event both had witnessed. Follow-up questions were based on things the respondent had already said, so that we could be sure to understand their perspective as well as possible and to avoid as much as possible, allowing our preconceptions to shape their answers.[5] The two of us conducted seventy-seven interviews ourselves with sixty-four people, ranging from one to three-and-a-half hours and averaging ninety-three minutes.

This movement is predominantly white, and we are both white ourselves, but white people are often the least able to see how whiteness skews our perspectives. To learn the perspectives of more Christians of color than we could meet with in our observations, we hired Alicia T. Crosby-Mack, a queer, African American leader in this movement (a co-founder of the Center for Inclusivity), to conduct forty interviews with LGBTQ+

Christians of color. Alicia worked with a set list of questions but also felt free to engage in conversation and follow-up questions to fully understand her respondents' stories and perspectives, and she shared the recordings with us. Those interviews brought our total number to 117 interviews with 104 people. It is best when researchers transcribe their own interviews, but with this volume, that was not possible. Interviews, as well as some recorded speeches we heard, were transcribed either by us or by a professional trained in the protection of human subjects' rights and confidentiality, as were all of us. Our research protocol was approved by Marquette University's Internal Review Board.

We also read and coded things participants published themselves or mentioned finding helpful or noteworthy, including books, blogs, and articles.

We kept our fieldnotes, transcripts, and published articles and blogs in a database in Nvivo, which allowed us to search for key terms and make note of, or code, themes that emerged from the study—*Choosing Love*'s main themes of love, shame, humility, pride, and justice—but also other themes around Christianity, conflict, family, and the like. Our mode of analysis was based on the grounded theory method,[6] but rather than working purely inductively to produce theory, we allowed existing theories and concepts to enter into conversation with participants' own understandings, always mindful to respect our participants' realities.[7] As themes became apparent to us, we explored what writers in our own and other disciplines—including psychology, theology, literary criticism, and social justice organizing—had to say, to see how they helped us better understand what we were seeing, as well as how this very particular movement and the people in it helped to shed new light.[8] For instance, when it became apparent that shame seemed to have many of the characteristics attributed to sacraments in LGBTQ+ conservative Christians' lives, we asked participants what they thought about this, got suggestions for readings, and read or reread other scholarly readings about shame to refine our observations and arguments about it.

Philosophical ethics and feminist philosophy helped us assess the strengths of arguments or ideas people shared; to conceptualize, package, and derive implications from these ideas; and to consider moral dimensions of peoples' experiences and the emotions that shape the social contexts we observed and analyzed. For instance, we used philosophical concepts of personhood and Martin Buber's idea of *I–thou* connection to interrogate the experiences of harm LGBTQ+ Christians shared with us, and to illuminate moral tensions in Christians' claims to love LGBTQ+ people while treating them as a problem to be fixed. Along with sociological, psychological, and gender studies frameworks, philosophical frameworks helped us shape interview questions and analytical categories for observation. Feminist moral philosophy also provided frameworks for evaluating the data from a moral perspective, for instance not just describing peoples' experiences but also making moral arguments that some of those experiences are inconsistent with genuine love and constitute wrongful treatment. Sometimes empirical findings shed light on moral concepts, revealing them to be incomplete or overly simplified and helping us to refine or rework them to improve our moral understanding of the experiences of LGBTQ+ people, communities and groups in this movement.

As two white researchers who are concerned about how racism can shape interactions and institutions in subtle and unsubtle ways, who were studying a predominantly white movement, we noticed that the narratives that emerged at first tended to center the voices and experiences of white people. We know that what we can see about reality depends on the perspective we take in looking at it, so we rewrote each account, consciously working to center the experiences of Black people, Indigenous people, and other people of color to follow the intellectual pathways that opened up for us.[9] This made our analysis much more holistic, and, we hope, inspiring of a more sustainable and effective approach to understanding love's inextricable connection to justice.

We call this movement *conservative Christian* to indicate most participants experience a personal relationship with Jesus, hold a "high view" of Scripture, adhere to other characteristics of evangelicalism or fundamentalism, and identify with conservative Christian culture, including styles of prayer and music.[10] This label, along with *conservative Protestant*, encompasses most Black church traditions (which overlap with and differ from both liberal and evangelical predominantly white traditions) as well as churches that identify as evangelical or fundamentalist, whether members and leadership are predominantly white or of another racial group. We use the term "evangelical" as an abbreviation for the predominantly white category of "evangelical Protestant" in sociology's RELTRAD typology, which includes predominantly white evangelical denominations and theologically similar nondenominational churches.[11] Some Catholics, Orthodox, and liberal and fundamentalist Protestants participate, but the movement overwhelmingly consists of evangelical (and formerly evangelical) Protestants who themselves have highly diverse doctrines, politics, ethnicities, and racial and class backgrounds.

In line with much of the US evangelical culture, this movement grows by sharing its message and fostering leadership among members, so there is not a clear separation between the perspectives of "leaders" and "followers." For example, we witnessed newcomers grow to be workshop leaders, board members, and authors. The Reformation Project explicitly trained people to make the scriptural case for same-sex marriage in their daily lives, and GCN provided instructions for members to ask others for help reconciling faith and sexuality or navigating relationships with Christians who did not affirm them. We saw participants routinely refer each other to the books discussed here, referring even to national leaders by first name, as in, "I actually found Justin's book more helpful on this." We saw workshops led by relative newcomers, eager to share their stories and help others. We cite mostly published authors, workshop leaders, and keynote speakers because they stated most succinctly what other participants routinely relayed to us and each other. As such, we highlight the narrative revision occurring throughout the movement with examples that illustrate how participants usually framed things.

NOTES

PREFACE

1. "Jack" is a pseudonym. Public figures and some respondents have asked that we use their real names, which we denote by using first and last names. To protect confidentiality, we use made-up first names for most people we encountered.
2. Buber (1923/1970, 62–63).
3. Freire (2012, 89); see also Emerick (2016, 333).
4. The Center for Inclusivity was started by a previous employee of The Marin Foundation, and it picked up hosting The Marin Foundation's biweekly discussion groups. We conducted research there, and Dawne served on its board from 2015 to 2017.

INTRODUCTION

1. Here we draw from Martin Buber.
2. People with only a first name are referred to by pseudonyms; those listed with a surname are their real names, either at their request or because they are public figures making public comments. We then refer to participants, including leaders in the movement, by first name, following their custom.
3. By LGBTQ+ we mean lesbian, gay, bisexual, nonbinary, transgender, Same-Gender-Loving, Two-Spirit, same-sex attracted, questioning, queer, pansexual, ambisexual, asexual, aromantic, genderqueer, and other people who don't fully conform to the requirements of cisgender heterosexuality. We use bi+ to refer to bisexual, pansexual, ambisexual, and other categories, generally including people whose sexual orientation is defined by the binary construction of gender. We did encounter some asexual and polyamorous people in our research, but we did not find that many discussions included them, so they are not discussed here. Among conservative Christians, we observed many women referring to themselves as gay, rather than lesbian.
4. Wolkomir (2006); Barton (2012).

5. By LGBTQ+ conservative Christians, we are referring here mostly to evangelical and fundamentalist Protestants of all races, and many predominantly Black churches, which may not define themselves as Evangelical or fundamentalist.
6. The Pew Research Center's Religious Landscape Survey estimates that about 25 percent of Americans are "Evangelical Protestant" (the largest religious group in the United States) and another 6 percent are "Historically Black Protestant" (most, but not all, of those churches are conservative with regard to gender/sexuality) (https://www.pewresearch.org/religion/religious-landscape-study/). The 2022 Gallup Daily Tracking Survey estimated that 7.1 percent of Americans identify as LGBT, largely due to higher numbers among younger adults (https://williamsinstitute.law.ucla.edu/publications/adult-lgbt-pop-us/). Assuming those numbers map onto how many conservative Protestants would identify as LGBT if they could, we can make a rough estimate of 7.1 percent of 31 percent, or about 2.2 percent of the US population (or 7.3 million out of 332 million, which isn't inconsequential).
7. Hill Collins (2004); Crenshaw (1989); Moraga and Anzaldúa (1981/2015); Hull, Bell-Scott, and Smith (1982/2015).
8. Jasbir Puar (2007) has argued that more recent uses of the term *intersectionality* have distorted Black feminist thinkers' original purpose by focusing on lines of intersection as if they are separate in the first place, preferring the concept of "assemblage" to reflect life's actual messiness. Others have insisted on the term's enduring usefulness, calling attention to what was lost rather than dismissing the concept (Nash 2011; Seitz 2017).
9. Thanks to Raka Ray for this framing.
10. Orit Avishai (2020, 2023) discusses similar dynamics for Israeli orthodox LGBT people.
11. Hill Collins (2004); Brown Douglas (1999).
12. In *Taking America Back for God*, Andrew Whitehead and Samuel Perry (2020) analyzed robust national surveys and found that approximately 80 percent of white evangelical Christians supported the premises of White Christian Nationalism, which they measure using survey respondents' support for statements such as "The federal government should declare the United States a Christian nation" and "The success of the United States is part of God's plan." Support for these views corresponds strongly to views such as seeing immigration as an existential threat to the nation and homosexuality as always wrong.
13. Robertson (2016a).
14. Vines (2014); Lee (2012); Robertson (2016b); Garcia (2020); Hartke (2018); Baldock (2014); Martin (2016); VanderWal Gritter (2014); Conley (2017); Keen (2018); Gushee (2015); Marin (2009). The *Second Sunday* podcast highlights the testimonies of Black LGBTQ+ people of faith as well (secondsundaypod.com).
15. Some examples include McQueeney (2009); Bjork-James (2021); Barrett-Fox (2016); Burke (2015); Kobes Du Mez (2020); Diefendorf (2023); Barton (2010); Jordan (2011); Sumerau (2011, 2015); Sumerau and Schrock (2011); Sumerau, Padavic, and Schrock (2015); Whitehead (2014); Young (2022); White (2015); de Rogatis (2014). Regarding racism and sexual stigma see, for instance, Barnes (2013); Boykin (1997); Cohen (1999); Brown Douglas (1999); Hill Collins (2004); Lewin (2018); Snorton (2014); Higginbotham (1993); Young (2022, 2023).

NOTES 191

16. Some examples include Pitt (2010); Mahaffy (1996); Wilcox (2003, 2006, 2009); Yip (1997, 2010); Chu (2013); Creek (2013); Thomas and Olson (2012); O'Brien (2004); Thumma (2004); Wolkomir (2006); Rodriguez and Ouellette (2000); Dillon (1999); Kolyosh (2017); Woodell, Kazyak, and Compton (2015); Sumerau (2012); Sumerau, Padavic, and Schrock (2015); Gerber (2011, 2015); Erzen (2006); Wolkomir (2006); Stolakis (2021); Smid (2012); VanderWal Gritter (2014).
17. Fuist (2016); Gerber (2018); White (2015); Shipley and Page (2016); Yip (2010); Avishai (2020, 2022); Burrow-Branine (2021); Coley (2020); Golriz (2021); Petro (2015); Sumerau (2012); Sumerau and Shrock (2011); Wilcox (2003, 2009); Woodell, Kazyak, and Compton (2015); Lewin (2018); Stuart (2003).
18. Coley (2018, 2020); Burrow-Branine (2021); Lee (2016); Seitz (2017).
19. Bartky (1990); Scheff (2000); Moon (2004); Wolkomir (2006); Gould (2009); Shotwell (2011); Creek (2013); Ahmed (2015).
20. Lewis (1971); Scheff (2000); Velleman (2001); Sedgwick (2003); Calhoun (2004); Shotwell (2011); Ahmed (2015); Lehtinen (1998); Woodward (2000); Lewis (1992); Pattison (2000); Flanagan (2013); Manion (2002) Karlsson and Sojberg (2009); Tangney (2007); Taylor (1985); Thomason (2015); Tompkins (1995); Stein (2006); Deonna, Raffaele, and Teroni (2012); Bradshaw (1988); Burrus (2007).
21. Driver (2001); Taylor (1985); Snow (1995); Whitcomb et al. (2015); Thomason (2015); Roberts (2003); Roberts (2007).
22. See, for instance, hooks (2000); Hill Collins (2004); Lorde (2007); Nash (2011); Dixon (1970), Jordan (2003, cited in Nash 2011); King, Jr., (1963/1981, 1963/1986); Sales (2020); Kaur (2020); Seitz (2017); Ginwright (2022); Kim (2010); Brown (2010); Boggs (2012).

CHAPTER 1

1. Darren has shared his story in other places, including *People* magazine (Keating 2018) and the Second Sunday podcast (https://pod.link/1708662302).
2. Alicia later joined our team as a consultant, conducting forty interviews for this project with LGBTQ+ Christians of color who might not have felt comfortable speaking to us as white people.
3. Matthew 22:36–40; Mark 12:28–34; Luke 10:27–37.
4. Because a lot of conservative Christians don't distinguish among being gay, bi, or trans, for reasons we'll discuss in Chapter 2, trans people are also seen as disrupting the heterosexual mandate, even if they are heterosexual.
5. People who think about love a lot also often do not see these clear divisions. Martin Luther King Jr. defined *eros* as both romantic love and "the soul's yearning for the realm of the divine." From a secular perspective, Audre Lorde saw the erotic similarly as yearning for lifeforce, what drives human passion for life and the seat of joy (King [1963, 52]; Lorde [1984]). By these definitions, *eros* isn't just "sexual" love, as a lot of people tend to think of it. And *agape*, *storge*, and *philia* are also ways of connecting to the divine.
6. DeRogatis (2005); Burke (2014, 2015).
7. Buber (1923/1970).

8. Berger (1967).
9. One of the founders of contemporary sociology, Émile Durkheim (1912/1995), argued that human beings are inherently social creatures, and that being part of a society makes us who we are, our better selves. The ancient Greek philosopher Aristotle (1999) also believed human beings are social animals, that our capacities for moral growth and human thriving are developed in and through relationships with family, friends, and other members of our society.
10. We developed this definition drawing from Martin Buber, Barrett Emerick, and others cited in this chapter.
11. Nash (2011, 11).
12. Dixon (1970, quoted in Kaur [2020]).
13. Lorde (1984); Nash (2011); Baldwin (1963); King (1963/1981).
14. King (1963/1986).
15. King (1963/1981); Baldwin (1963).
16. Kaur (2020, 158–159).

CHAPTER 2

1. Many thanks for feedback on this and the next chapter are due to Kelsy Burke and Karl Britto.
2. Warren Blumenfeld, "God and Natural Disasters: It's the Gays' Fault?" *Huffpost*, November 5, 2012, https://www.huffpost.com/entry/god-and-natural-disasters-its-the-gays-fault_b_2068817; ABC News, "Falwell Suggests Gays to Blame for Attacks," September 14, 2001, https://abcnews.go.com/Politics/story?id=121322&page=1.
3. Patrick Strudwick, "Vicky Beeching, Christian Rock Star 'I'm Gay. God Loves Me Just the Way I Am,'" *Independent*, August 13, 2014, https://www.independent.co.uk/news/people/news/vicky-beeching-star-of-the-christian-rock-scene-im-gay-god-loves-me-just-the-way-i-am-9667566.html.
4. Pulliam Bailey (2014). See also Burk (2014, 2015).
5. Lee (2012). Medically, there is no such thing as "sex addiction," but many conservative Christians identify with the diagnosis.
6. See Tanis (2003).
7. Davis (2015); (https://isna.org/faq/frequency/).
8. Hartke (2018); DeFranza (2015); Hooker (2013).
9. Hamilton (2014); Mohler (2014, 18–19).
10. Burke (2015); DeRogatis (2005).
11. Rubin (1984/1993); Kobes Du Mez (2020); Graham and Dias (2022); Moslener (2015).
12. Alter (2004). The New International Version translates these phrases as "what is detestable" and "They must be put to death."
13. White (2015); Roggio (2022).
14. Church Clarity, www.churchclarity.org; Nick Duffy, "None of America's 100 Largest Churches Affirm Gay People," *Pink News*, January 1, 2018, http://www.pinknews.co.uk/2018/01/01/none-of-americas-100-largest-churches-affirm-lgbt-people/;

Amanda Casanova, "Church Sees Significant Decline in Membership Following Same-Sex Marriage Decision," *Christian Headlines*, November 14, 2017, https://www.christianheadlines.com/blog/church-sees-significant-decline-in-membership-following-same-sex-marriage-decision.html; Heidi Hall, "As One Evangelical Church 'Comes Out' for LGBT Rights, Others Cast a Wary Eye," *Religion News Service*, March 3, 2015, https://religionnews.com/2015/03/03/one-evangelical-church-comes-lgbt-rights-others-cast-wary-eye/?; Elizabeth Dias, "How Evangelicals Are Changing Their Minds on Gay Marriage," *TIME*, January 15, 2015, https://time.com/3669024/evangelicals-gay-marriage/.

15. Joseph Hartropp, "Megapastor John MacArthur Says 'No One Is Gay,' Compares Homosexuality to Adultery," *Christian Today*, June 29, 2017, https://www.christiantoday.com/article/megapastor-john-macarthur-says-no-one-is-gay-compares-homosexuality-to-adultery/110296.htm; J. D. Greear, "3 Misconceptions in the Church About Homosexuality," *Outreach Magazine*, September 17, 2019, https://outreachmagazine.com/features/discipleship/46770-3-misconceptions-in-the-church-about-homosexuality.html.
16. There are no solid answers as to what causes people to be LGBTQ+. There is not a lot of strong evidence that people are "born gay," but there is overwhelming evidence that sexual orientation and gender identity cannot be changed at will. The question of "cause" wouldn't be all that compelling if being LGBTQ+ weren't so heavily stigmatized.
17. Gagnon (2001, 254).
18. "Emergent" church leaders like Brian McLaren, whom many allies in particular found helpful (even though more than one said they threw one of his books across the room the first time they read it!), pointed out that church teachings today often seem to emphasize the institution's needs over Jesus's teachings. See McLaren (2010).
19. Lovejoy (1933/1976); Feagin (2013); Brown Douglas (1999); Schneider (2004).
20. Laqueur (1990); Fausto-Sterling (2000); InterAct Advocates (2021); DeFranza (2015); Preves (2002).
21. Fausto-Sterling (2000); Davis (2015).
22. Colson (1996), cited in DeFranza (2015).
23. DeFranza (2015); Van Ness (2019).
24. PBS, "A Map of Gender Diverse Cultures," *PBS*, August 11, 2015, http://www.pbs.org/independentlens/content/two-spirits_map-html/.
25. Gilley (2006); Smithers (2022); Brayboy (2016); Picq (2018).
26. Oyeronke (1997); Nzegwu (2006).
27. Baldwin (1986).
28. Goldberg (1992); Carby (1982); Patil (2018); Picq (2018); Schneider (2004); McClintock (1995).
29. Brayboy (2016); Smith (2004).
30. Snorton (2014) has argued that Black sexuality—including heterosexuality—can be characterized as in a "glass closet," often not spoken of but always visible and subject to shame and judgment.
31. Hill Collins (2004).

32. Snorton (2014, 94).
33. Pitt (2010). See also Lewin (2018).
34. The 2022 revelation that the Southern Baptist Convention enabled hundreds of sexual abusers and belittled their survivors over decades supports claims by Kristen Kobes du Mez (2020) and Andrew Whitehead and Sam Perry (2020) that conservative evangelical culture posits men's power and authority as part of God's sacred order.
35. Anderson (2015); Klein (2018).
36. Tisby (2019).
37. Whitehead and Perry (2020, 10) define White Christian Nationalism as tending to support six statements about the place of Christianity in American government, and they find strong correlations between this support and heightened (relative to others) levels of discomfort with interracial marriage and immigration as well as belief in the racial fairness of policing and Black tendencies to violence, and belief that traditional gender roles are God's plan.
38. Kobes du Mez (2020); Bjork-James (2021); Barrett-Fox and Yip (2021). The term *intersectionality* was coined by Kimberlé Crenshaw in her 1989 article, "Mapping the Margins" to explain how laws that protected white women and Black men from employment discrimination failed to protect Black women.
39. Whitehead and Perry (2020, 143, 145).
40. See, for instance, Rogers (2009); Vines (2014); Brownson (2013); Lee (2012); Gushee (2015); Scanzoni and Mollenkott (1978/1994); Keen (2018).
41. Gushee (2015).
42. Brownson (2013) argues that some use "complementarity" to mean reproductive capacity (though few conservative Protestant denominations have issues with birth control, much less infertile marriages), others the apparent fit of penis and vagina, and still others the notion that male and female are incomplete halves—none of which appears in the Bible. See also Hartke (2018); Keen (2018).
43. Hays and Hays (2024); Gagnon on X, https://twitter.com/RobertAJGagnon1/status/1776819109465817269.
44. Klein (2018); Anderson (2015); Harris (2003, 2023).
45. DeRogatis (2005).
46. Carter (2007) has an interesting analysis of how "normal" became synonymous with the white heterosexual "ideal" in the early twentieth century.

CHAPTER 3

1. Lewis (1992); Scheff (2000).
2. Moon (2014) citing the Church of the Nazarene.
3. Garcia (2020).
4. Archuleta (2016).
5. Garcia (2016).
6. Robinson (2015).
7. Keating (2018).
8. Belgau (ca. 2003).
9. Strudwick (2014).

NOTES 195

10. Barth (1936–1977); Deddo (1999).
11. Brown (2012). This distinction was made by Helen Block Lewis in her classic 1971 book, *Shame and Guilt in Neurosis*.
12. Whitcomb et al. (2005); Thomason (2015); Shotwell (2011); Flanagan (2013). Shame indicates both a desire to hide or withdraw and a yearning for recognition and belonging. See Lewis (1971); Scheff (2000); Velleman (2001); Sedgwick (2003); Calhoun (2004); Karlsson and Sjoberg (2009); Ahmed (2015).
13. Ahmed (2015); Shotwell (2011, 93–94).
14. Please be advised that we are using "fat" in the nonjudgmental terms of the fat acceptance movement. See, for instance, Gerber (2011). None of this is to say that white men aren't shamed too, sometimes, but that they aren't shamed, by those who have power over them precisely because they are white men. We suspect that many of our society's problems have to do with the way masculine ideals instill shame in men in exchange for a degree of power and authority. See Harris-Perry (2011); Halperin and Traub (2009); Smith (2004); King (1963/1986).
15. Burke (2014, 2015); Burke and Haltom (2020); DeRogatis (2005, 2015); Thomas (2016).
16. This fear is what Claude Steele (2010) calls "stereotype threat," which is the fear that one's own imperfections will serve as evidence supporting negative stereotypes of one's stigmatized group.
17. Truluck (2001); Tobin (2016, 2019); Panchuk (2018).
18. Barton (2010, 2012); Fanon (1967/1952).
19. MacArthur (2014); Ryan et al. (2009). As sociologist Brandon Andrew Robinson (2018) writes, "LGBTQ+ youth comprise approximately 5% to 8% of the U.S. youth population but comprise at least 40% of the population of youth experiencing homelessness."
20. Brown Douglas (1999); Schneider (2004); Moon and Tobin (2018).
21. Higginbotham (1993); Hill Collins (2004).
22. Hill Collins (2004); Brown Douglas (1999).
23. Robertson (2016a).
24. Conley (2016); Stolakis (2021).
25. Robertson and Robertson (2013).
26. Buber (1923/1970).
27. hooks (2000, 7–8).

CHAPTER 4

1. Hartke (2015).
2. Matthew Vines, Facebook post, March 30, 2016.
3. Here we build on the ideas of Whitcomb et al. (2005) and Thomason (2015).
4. The same humility applies in secular life as well; science works best when its practitioners are humbly open to new information so that their perspectives can grow and change.
5. Christians may note that the Bible does not always treat pride as sinful. In the New International Version, commonly used by people we heard from, the apostle Paul mentions non-sinful pride, for instance, in his letter to the Galatians (6:4), and

in his second letter to the church in Corinth at 7:4 and also 8:24, when he says "Therefore show these men the proof of your love and the reason for our pride in you, so that the churches can see it."
6. Roberts (2007); Austin (2024).
7. Brown Taylor (2009).
8. As time moved on, we saw "Side B" advocates for celibacy step back from contentious conversations with "Side A" advocates of same-sex marriage, many of whom saw the "Side B" view that God did, in fact, abhor any same-sex sex as judgmental and toxic as "welcoming but not affirming" churches. By the late 2010s, some "Side B" people who practiced celibacy began explicitly stating that they didn't judge *other* LGBTQ+ people or have any opinions of whether *others* should be celibate or not. Others retained the view that any same-sex sex was sinful.
9. Our examples of this seem to come particularly from African Americans, but this experience is not limited to people from the Black church tradition. Jon Burrow-Branine (2021, 125–140) shares similar stories from a number of people he met in his study of TRP, including Shae Washington.
10. Roberts (2009).
11. Hunter (1991); Kniss (1997); Fuist, Stoll, and Kniss (2012).
12. Sullivan-Blum (2006) found that people on different sides of the "homosexuality as sinful" question appeal to the same sources to come to their conclusions, which is what we find.
13. Edman (2016).
14. Edman (2016, 111, 113).
15. Edman (2016, 113).
16. Edman (2016, 115).
17. Garcia (2017).
18. Mills (2020).
19. Roberts (2009).
20. However, the framework of love that sustains these transitions reconfigures pride; this is not hubris, but it is also not conventional proper pride which both secular movements and Christians talk about it as a purely self-regarding emotion.
21. Lewin (2018) discusses TFAM's relationship to the historically Black church in depth.
22. Similarly, many anti-LGBTQ+ speakers have expressed their own disgust at thoughts of both trans people and same-sex sex. Supreme Court Justice Antonin Scalia famously declared in his decision authored in *Bowers v. Hardwick* (1987) that sex between men was "objectively disgusting," seeing his own feelings of disgust as signs both of God's disapproval and of the constitutionality of banning it by law. He did not consider in that decision that others might find contemplation of *his* sex life disgusting, nor whether that should be grounds for legally banning it. The twentieth-century anthropologist Mary Douglas (1978) defined dirt as "matter out of place" and argued that different things may disgust people from different cultures depending on what they see as "out of place."
23. Crenshaw (1989, 1992) coined the term "intersectionality" and provided a framework to analyze it; however, the concept was articulated much earlier in Black feminist thought. See also Cooper (1892).

24. Crenshaw (1992).
25. Buber (1923/1970, 62–63).

CHAPTER 5

1. Gushee (2015).
2. See, for instance, Barron (2016); Edwards (2008); Emerson and Smith (2000); Garces-Foley and Jeung (2013); Ince (2022); Martí (2005).
3. Edwards (2008).
4. Church Clarity, https://www.churchclarity.org/about.
5. See, for instance, Barrett-Fox and Yip (2021); Bjork-James (2021); Emerson and Smith (2000); Smith (1998); Diefendorf (2023).
6. Emerson and Smith (2000, 58).
7. Harvey (2014).
8. Diefendorf (2023).
9. Gerardo Marti (2012) has written about how multiracial churches (those with no more than 90 percent of one racial group) can intentionally work to preserve their multiracial character, including in their selection of music, but that this takes conscious work beyond the selection of music itself.
10. Harvey (2014); Feagin (2013); DiAngelo (2018).
11. Du Bois (1916); Butler (2021); Whitehead and Perry (2020); Mayrl (2023); Cone (1970/2010); King (1963/1986, 1963/1981); Tisby (2019).
12. Some might say that you can't be an ally if you believe same-sex sex is sinful, but our observations lead us to think that people's actions—how they treat others—are more important than their beliefs. As Andrew Marin has said, "It's not the job of Christians to convict the GLBT community. That's the Holy Spirit's job. It's not the job of Christians to judge the GLBT community. That's God's job. It's the job of Christians to love the GLBT community in a way that is tangible, measurable, and unconditional—whether we see our version of 'change' happening or not!" (2009, 108).
13. VanderWal Gritter (2014, 13–14).
14. Gushee (2015).
15. Gushee (2014).
16. Marin (2009, 85).
17. Gushee (2015).
18. Gushee (2014).
19. Luke 10:25–37 recounts when Jesus was asked how to achieve eternal life. Jesus asked this expert on the law what the law said, and his response was that it was to love God and love your neighbor as yourself. The questioner asked, "And who is my neighbor?" and Jesus replied with a story: A traveler was lying on the side of the road between Jerusalem and Jericho having been beaten and robbed. A priest and a Levite each gave the man wide berth and went along their way. A Samaritan, an outsider of low status, bound up his wounds and carried him to an inn, took care of him, and paid the innkeeper to care for him and to let him stay and heal. Jesus instructed his questioner to be a neighbor like the Samaritan.
20. Gushee (2003).

CHAPTER 6

1. Marin (2009, 108).
2. As a result of conducting this research, Dawne served on the board of CFI for two years.
3. Fish (1997).
4. Reagon (1983).
5. King (1963/1986, 295).
6. Bebbington (1989, 1–19).
7. Whitehead and Perry (2020, 10); see also Gorski and Perry (2022).
8. Wolfe (1999) found the same thing in the 1990s—that the "culture wars" was an overblown way of understanding American civic life—except around homosexuality, which really did polarize the country.
9. Lee (2016).
10. Robinson (2015).
11. https://www.qchristian.org/about.
12. Burk (2017a, 2017b, 2018); Barrett-Fox and Yip (2021).
13. Vines (2014).
14. See, for instance, https://www.lgbtmap.org/policy-and-issue-analysis/LGBTQ-people-of-color.
15. Reformation Project, "Our Values" https://reformationproject.org/values/.
16. Crenshaw (1989) coined the term to talk about a concept that nonacademic Black and Third World feminist thinkers had been developing for over a century (see, e.g., Cooper 1892; Nash 2011).
17. Kelly (2019, 293–327); Harvey (2014); Cone (1970/2010); Emerson and Smith (2000).
18. Whitehead and Perry (2020); Kobes du Mez (2020); Bjork-James (2021); Butler (2021); Martí (2020).
19. Diefendorf (2023); Bjork-James (2021).
20. Bjork-James (2021).
21. See Barton (2012); Diefendorf (2023).
22. Garcia (2016).
23. King (1963/1986, 291).
24. Dobson (2001); Moslener (2015).
25. King (1963/1986, 291).
26. This phrase comes from Barrett Emerick's and Scott Wisor's co-edited special issue of *Feminist Philosophy Quarterly* 5, no. 2 (2019) honoring the work of feminist philosopher Alison M. Jaggar.
27. Seitz (2017, 1–2).
28. Seitz (2017); Berlant (1997).

CHAPTER 7

1. hooks (2000, xix).
2. Hill Collins (2004, 250).
3. Nash (2011, 11); Dixon (1970, quoted in Kaur 2020).
4. Bjork-James (2021).
5. Ahmed (2015, 122–143).
6. King (1963/1981).
7. Kaur (2020, 107).
8. King (1963/1981).
9. Kaur (2020).
10. Kaur (2020, 140).
11. Sales (2020).
12. Kaur (2020, 139–140).
13. Kaur (2020, xvi).
14. Kaur (2020, 140).
15. Brown (2010).
16. Moslener (2015); Bivins (2008).
17. Kim (2010, 39–40).
18. Kaur (2020, xvi).
19. Táíwò, quoted in Emerick and Yap (2023). Baldwin (1963) and Kaur (2020) have expressed a similar link between patience and hope.
20. Harvey (2014); Spade (2015).
21. Ginwright (2022).

METHODS

1. We are grateful to Jodi Melamed for first introducing us, and to Nancy Snow and Darcia Narvaez for directing the program that made us a team.
2. As a result of this research, Moon served on the Center for Inclusivity's board from 2015 to 2017.
3. Emerson, Fretz, and Shaw (1995); Lofland et al. (2006).
4. Emerson, Fretz, and Shaw (1995).
5. Lofland et al. (2006).
6. Charmaz (2006); Glaser and Strauss (1967); LaRossa (2005); Morse et al. (2009); Strauss and Corbin (1998).
7. Wilcox (2009); Burawoy (1998); Holstein and Gubrium (2008).
8. We talk more about how these themes developed in Tobin and Moon (2019).
9. Collins (1986, 2000); Smith (1989).
10. Moon and Tobin (2018).
11. Steensland et al. (2000).

REFERENCES

ABC News. 2001. "Falwell Suggests Gays to Blame for Attacks." *ABC News*, September 14. https://abcnews.go.com/Politics/story?id=121322&page=1.

Ahmed, Sara. 2015. *The Cultural Politics of Emotion*. 2nd ed. New York: Routledge.

Alter, Robert. 2004. *The Five Books of Moses: A Translation with Commentary*. New York: W. W. Norton and Co.

Anderson, Diana E. 2015. *Damaged Goods: New Perspectives on Christian Purity*. New York: Jericho Books.

Archuleta, Isaac. 2016. "Open Letter to My Conservative Christian Family: A Response to the Orlando Shooting." *Huffpost*, June 21. https://www.huffpost.com/entry/an-open-letter-to-my-conservative-christian-family_b_10511618.

Aristotle. 1999. *Nicomachean Ethics*. Translated by Terence Irwin. New York: Hachette.

Austin, Michael W. 2024. *Humility: Rediscovering the Way of Love and Life in Christ*. Grand Rapids, MI: Eerdmans.

Avishai, Orit. 2020. "Religious Queer People Beyond Identity Conflict: Lessons from Orthodox LGBT Jews in Israel." *Journal for the Scientific Study of Religion* 59, no. 2: 360–378.

Avishai, Orit. 2023. *Queer Judaism: LGBT Activism and the Remaking of Jewish Orthodoxy in Israel*. New York: NYU Press.

Baldock, Kathy. 2014. *Walking the Bridgeless Canyon: Repairing the Breach the Church and the LGBT Community*. Reno, NV: Canyonwalker Press.

Baldwin, James. 1963. *The Fire Next Time*. New York: Dial Press.

Baldwin, James. 1980. "Dark Days." *Esquire*, October, 42–46.

Barnes, Sandra L. 2013. "To Welcome or Affirm: Black Clergy Views about Homosexuality, Inclusivity, and Church Leadership." *Journal of Homosexuality* 60, no. 10: 1409–1433.

Barrett-Fox, Rebecca. 2016. *God Hates: Westboro Baptist Church, American Nationalism, and the Religious Right*. Lawrence: University Press of Kansas.

Barrett-Fox, Rebecca, and Andrew Kam-Tuk Yip. 2021. "Crosses and Crossroads: American Conservative Christianity's Anti-Intersectionality Discourse and the Erasure of LGBTQ+ Believers." In *Intersecting Religion and Sexuality: Sociological Perspectives*, edited by Sarah-Jane Page and Andrew Kam-Tuck Yip, 212–227. Boston: Brill.

Barron, Jessica. 2016. "Managed Diversity: Race, Place, and an Urban Church." *Sociology of Religion* 77, no. 1: 18–36.

Barth, Karl. 1936–1977. *Church Dogmatics*. Translated by G. T. Thomson. Edinburgh: T&T Clark.

Bartkowski, John P. 2001. *Remaking the Godly Marriage: Gender Negotiation in Evangelical Families*. New Brunswick, NJ: Rutgers University Press.

Bartky, Sandra. 1990. *Femininity and Domination: Studies in the Phenomenology of Oppression*. New York: Routledge Press.

Barton, Bernadette. 2010. "'Abomination': Life as a Bible Belt Gay." *Journal of Homosexuality* 57: 465–484.

Barton, Bernadette. 2012. *Pray the Gay Away: The Extraordinary Lives of Bible Belt Gays*. New York: NYU Press.

Bebbington, D. W. 1989. *Evangelicalism in Modern Britain: A History from the 1730s to the 1980s*. New York: Routledge.

Belgau, Ron. 2003. "The Great Debate: Ron's View." https://ronbelgau.com/great-debate/.

Berger, Peter L. 1967. *The Sacred Canopy: Elements of a Sociological Theory of Religion*. New York: Anchor.

Berlant, Lauren. 1997. *The Queen of America Goes to Washington City: Essays on Sex and Citizenship*. Durham, NC: Duke University Press.

Bivins, Jason. 2008. *Religion of Fear: The Politics of Horror in Conservative Evangelicalism*. New York: Oxford University Press.

Bjork-James, Sophie. 2021. *The Divine Institution: White Evangelicalism's Politics of the Family*. New Brunswick, NJ: Rutgers University Press.

Blumenfeld, Warren. 2012. "God and Natural Disasters: It's the Gays' Fault?" *Huffpost*, November 5. https://www.huffpost.com/entry/god-and-natural-disasters-its-the-gays-fault_b_2068817.

Boggs, Grace Lee, with Scott Kurashige. 2012. *The Next American Revolution: Sustainable Activism for the Twenty-First Century*. Berkeley: University of California Press.

Boykin, Keith. 1997. *One More River to Cross: Black and Gay in America*. New York: Anchor.

Bradshaw, John. 1988. *Healing the Shame that Binds You*. Deerfield Beach, FL: Health Communications Inc.

Brayboy, Duane. 2016. "Two Spirits, One Heart, Five Genders." *Indian Country Today*, January 23. https://indiancountrytoday.com/archive/two-spirits-one-heart-five-genders-9UH_xnbfVEWQHWkjNn0rQQ.

Brown, Adrienne Maree. 2010. "By Any Means Necessary." May 19. https://adriennemareebrown.net/2010/05/19/by-any-means-necessary/.

Brown, Brené. 2012. "Listening to Shame." *TED Talks*. March. https://www.ted.com/talks/brene_brown_listening_to_shame?language=en&subtitle=en.

Brown Douglas, Kelly. 1999. *Sexuality and the Black Church: A Womanist Perspective*. Maryknoll, NY: Orbis.

Brown Taylor, Barbara. 2009. *Leaving Church: A Memoir of Faith*. New York: HarperOne.

Brownson, James V. 2013. *Bible, Gender, Sexuality: Reframing the Church's Debate on Same-Sex Relationships*. Grand Rapids, MI: Eerdmans.

Buber, Martin. 1923/1970. *I and Thou*. Translated by Walter Kaufman. New York: Simon & Schuster.

Burawoy, Michael. 1998. "The Extended Case Method." *Sociological Theory* 16, no. 1 (March): 4–33.

Burk, Denny. 2014. "Suppressing the Truth in Unrighteousness: Matthew Vines Takes on the New Testament." In *God and the Gay Christian? A Response to Matthew Vines*, edited by R. Albert Mohler, Jr., 43–58. Louisville, KY: SBTS Press.

Burk, Denny. 2015. "Is Homosexual Orientation Sinful?" *Journal of the Evangelical Theological Society* 58, no. 1: 95–115.

Burk, Denny. 2017a. "The Intersectional Case for Teenage Sodomy." July 17. http://www.dennyburk.com/the-intersectional-case-for-teenage-sodomy/.

Burk, Denny. 2017b. "Two Ways in Which Intersectionality Is at Odds with the Gospel." July 19. http://www.dennyburk.com/why-intersectionality-may-be-at-odds-with-the-gospel/.

Burk, Denny. 2018. "Intersectionality as Religion . . . It's Infecting Evangelicals Too." March 6. http://www.dennyburk.com/intersectionality-as-religion-its-infecting-evangelicals-too.

Burke, Kelsy. 2014. "What Makes a Man: Gender and Sexual Boundaries on Evangelical Christian Sexuality Websites." *Sexualities* 17, no. 1/2: 3–22.

Burke, Kelsy. 2015. *Christians Under Covers: Evangelicals and Sexual Pleasure on the Internet*. Berkeley: University of California Press.

Burke, Kelsy, and Trenton M. Haltom. 2020. "Created by God and Wired to Porn." *Gender & Society* 34, no. 2: 233–258.

Burrow-Branine, Jon. 2021. *Come Now, Let Us Argue It Out: Counter-Conduct and LGBTQ Evangelical Activism*. Lincoln: University of Nebraska Press.

Burrus, Virginia. 2007. *Saving Shame: Martyrs, Saints, and Other Abject Subjects*. Philadelphia: University of Pennsylvania Press.

Butler, Anthea. 2021. *White Evangelical Racism: The Politics of Morality in America*. Chapel Hill: University of North Carolina Press.

Calhoun, Cheshire. 2004. "An Apology for Moral Shame." *Journal of Political Philosophy* 12, no. 2: 127–146.

Carby, Hazel V. 1982. "White Woman, Listen! Black Feminism and the Boundaries of Sisterhood." In *The Empire Strikes Back: Race and Racism in 70s Britain*, edited by The Centre for Contemporary Cultural Studies, 212–235. London: Hutchinson.

Carter, Julian B. 2007. *The Heart of Whiteness: Normal Sexuality and Race in America, 1880–1940*. Durham, NC: Duke University Press.

Casanova, Amanda. 2017. "Church Sees Significant Decline in Membership Following Same-Sex Marriage Decision." *Christian Headlines*, November 14. https://www.christianheadlines.com/blog/church-sees-significant-decline-in-membership-following-same-sex-marriage-decision.html.

Charmaz, Kathy. 2006. *Constructing Grounded Theory: A Practical Guide Through Qualitative Analysis*. Thousand Oaks, CA: SAGE.

Chu, Jeff. 2013. *Does Jesus Really Love Me? A Gay Christian's Pilgrimage in Search of God in America*. New York: Perennial.

Church Clarity. n.d. https://www.churchclarity.org/.

Cohen, Cathy. 1999. *The Boundaries of Blackness: AIDS and the Breakdown of Black Politics*. Chicago: University of Chicago Press.

Coley, Jonathan S. 2018. *Gay on God's Campus: Mobilizing for LGBT Equality at Christian Colleges and Universities*. Chapel Hill: University of North Carolina Press.

Coley, Jonathan S. 2020. "Reframing, Reconciling, and Individualizing: How LGBTQ Activist Groups Shape Approaches to Religion and Sexuality." *Sociology of Religion* 81, no. 1: 45–67. https://doi.org/10.1093/socrel/srz023.

Colson, Charles. 1996. "Blurred Biology: How Many Sexes Are There?" *BreakPoint*, October 16. http://www.colsoncenter.org/commentaries/5213-blurred-biology.

Cone, James H. 1970/2010. *A Black Theology of Liberation*. 40th anniversary ed. Maryknoll, NY: Orbis Books.

Conley, Garrard. 2016. *Boy Erased: A Memoir*. New York: Riverhead Books.

Cooper, Anna Julia. 1892. *A Voice from the South*. Chapel Hill: University of North Carolina Press.

Creek, S. J. 2013. "'Not Getting Any Because of Jesus': The Centrality of Desire Management to the Identity Work of Gay, Celibate Christians." *Symbolic Interaction* 36, no. 2: 119–136.

Crenshaw, Kimberlé. 1989. "Demarginalizing the Intersection of Race and Sex: A Black Feminist Critique of Antidiscrimination Doctrine, Feminist Theory, and Antiracist Politics." *University of Chicago Legal Forum* 1989, no. 1: 139–167.

Crenshaw, Kimberlé. 1991. "Mapping the Margins: Intersectionality, Identity Politics, and Violence Against Women of Color." *Stanford Law Review* 43: 1241–1299.

Crenshaw, Kimberlé. 1992. "Whose Story Is It, Anyway? Feminist and Anti-Racist Appropriations of Anita Hill." In *Race-ing Justice, En-gender-ing Power*, edited by Toni Morrison, 402–440. New York: Pantheon Books.

Davis, Georgiann. 2015. *Contesting Intersex: The Dubious Diagnosis*. New York: New York University Press.

Deddo, Gary W. 1999. *Karl Barth's Theology of Relations: Trinitarian, Christological, and Human: Towards an Ethic of the Family*. New York: P. Lang.

DeFranza, Megan. 2015. *Sex Difference in Christian Theology: Male, Female, and Intersex in the Image of God*. Grand Rapids, MI: William B. Eerdmans.

Deonna Julien A., Raffaele Rodogno, and Fabrice Terroni. 2012. *In Defense of Shame: The Faces of an Emotion*. New York: Oxford University Press.

DeRogatis, Amy. 2005. "What Would Jesus Do? Sexuality and Salvation in Protestant Evangelical Sex Manuals, 1950s to the Present." *Church History* 74, no. 1: 97–137.

DeRogatis, Amy. 2015. *Saving Sex: Sexuality and Salvation in American Evangelicalism*. New York: Oxford University Press.

DiAngelo, Robin. 2018. *White Fragility: Why It's So Hard for White People to Talk About Racism*. Boston: Beacon Press.

Dias, Elizabeth. 2015. "How Evangelicals Are Changing Their Minds on Gay Marriage." *TIME*, January 15. https://time.com/3669024/evangelicals-gay-marriage/.

Diefendorf, Sarah. 2023. *The Holy Vote: Inequality and Anxiety Among White Evangelicals*. Berkeley: University of California Press.

Dillon, Michele. 1999. *Catholic Identity: Balancing Reason, Faith, and Power*. New York: Cambridge University Press.

Dixon, Terence, dir. 1970. *Meeting The Man: James Baldwin in Paris*. https://www.youtube.com/watch?v=6xpE2-IGPy8 Excerpt.
Dobson, James. 2001. *Bringing Up Boys: Practical Advice and Encouragement for Those Shaping the Next Generation of Men*. Wheaton, IL: Tyndale House Publishers.
Douglas, Mary. 1978. *Purity and Danger: An Analysis of the Concepts of Pollution and Taboo*. New York: Routledge & Kegan Paul.
Driver, Julia. 2001. *Uneasy Virtue*. Cambridge: Cambridge University Press.
Du Bois, W. E. B. 1916. "The White Church." *The Crisis* 11, no. 6: 302.
Duffy, Nick. 2018. "None of America's 100 Largest Churches Affirm Gay People." *Pink News*, January 1. http://www.pinknews.co.uk/2018/01/01/none-of-americas-100-largest-churches-affirm-lgbt-people/.
Durkheim, Émile. 1912/1995. *The Elementary Forms of the Religious Life*. New York: Free Press.
Edman, Elizabeth. 2016. *Queer Virtue: What LGBTQ People Know about Life and Love and How It Can Revitalize Christianity*. Boston: Beacon Press.
Edwards, Korie L. 2008. *The Elusive Dream: The Power of Race in Interracial Churches*. New York: Oxford University Press.
Emerick, Barrett. 2016. "Love and Resistance: Moral Solidarity in the Face of Perceptual Failure." *Feminist Philosophy Quarterly* 2, no. 2: 1–21.
Emerick, Barrett, and Scott Wisor. 2019. "Introduction to the Special Issue: In the Unjust Meantime." *Feminist Philosophy Quarterly* 5, no. 2: 1–4.
Emerick, Barrett, and Audrey Yap. 2023. *Not Giving Up on People: A Feminist Case for Prison Abolition*. Lanham, MD: Rowman and Littlefield.
Emerson, Michael O., and Christian Smith. 2000. *Divided by Faith: Evangelicals Religion and the Problem of Race in America*. New York: Oxford University Press.
Emerson, Robert M., Rachel I. Fretz, and Linda Shaw. 1995. *Writing Ethnographic Fieldnotes*. Chicago: University of Chicago Press.
Erzen, Tanya. 2006. *Straight to Jesus: Sexual and Christian Conversions in the Ex-Gay Movement*. Berkeley: University of California Press.
Fanon, Franz. 1967/1952. *Black Skin, White Masks*. New York: Grove Press.
Fausto-Sterling, Anne. 2000. *Sexing the Body: Gender Politics and the Construction of Sexuality*. New York: Basic Books.
Feagin, Joe. 2013. *The White Racial Frame: Centuries of Racial Framing and Counter-Framing*. 2nd ed. New York: Routledge.
Fish, Stanley. 1997. "Boutique Multiculturalism: Or, Why Liberals Are Incapable of Thinking about Hate Speech." *Critical Inquiry* 23, no. 2: 378–395.
Flanagan, Owen. 2013. "The Shame of Addiction." *Frontiers in Psychiatry* 4: 1–11.
Fuist, Todd Nicholas. 2016. "'It Just Always Seemed Like It Wasn't a Big Deal, Yet I Know for Some People They Really Struggle with It': LGBT Religious Identities in Context." *Journal for the Scientific Study of Religion* 55, no. 4: 770–786.
Fuist, Todd Nicholas, Laurie Cooper Stoll, and Fred Kniss. 2012. "Beyond the Liberal–Conservative Divide: Assessing the Relationship Between Religious Denominations and Their Associated LGBT Organizations." *Qualitative Sociology* 35: 65–87.
Gagnon, Robert A. J. 2001. *The Bible and Homosexual Practice: Texts and Hermeneutics*. Nashville, TN: Abingdon Press.

Gallagher, Sally K. 2003. *Evangelical Identity and Gendered Family Life*. New Brunswick, NJ: Rutgers University Press.

Gallagher, Sally K. 2004a. "The Marginalization of Evangelical Feminism." *Sociology of Religion* 65, no. 3: 215–237.

Gallagher, Sally K. 2004b. "Where Are the Antifeminist Evangelicals? Evangelical Identity, Subcultural Location, and Attitudes Towards Feminism." *Gender & Society* 18, no. 4: 451–472.

Garces-Foley, Kathleen, and Russell Jeung. 2013. "Asian American Evangelicals in Multiracial Church Ministry." *Religions* 4, no. 2: 190–208.

Garcia, Kevin Miguel. 2016. "I Tried to Pray the Gay Away and It Nearly Killed Me." *TheKevinGarcia.com*, January 19. http://www.thekevingarcia.com/.

Garcia, Kevin Miguel. 2017. "This Is When I Figured Out What #PRIDE Meant." *TheKevinGarcia.com*, June 7. http://www.thekevingarcia.com/.

Garcia, Kevin Miguel. 2020. *Bad Theology Kills: Undoing Toxic Beliefs and Reclaiming Your Spiritual Authority*. Monee, IL: Kevin Garcia. www.thekevingarcia.com

Gerber, Lynne. 2011. *Seeking the Straight and Narrow: Weight Loss and Sexual Reorientation in Evangelical America*. Chicago: University of Chicago Press.

Gerber, Lynne. 2015. "Grit, Guts, and Vanilla Beans: Godly Masculinity in the Ex-Gay Movement." *Gender & Society* 29, no. 1: 26–50.

Gerber, Lynne. 2018. "We Who Must Die Demand a Miracle: Christmas 1989 at the Metropolitan Community Church of San Francisco." In *Devotions and Desiresa: Histories of Sexuality and Religion in the Twentieth-Century United States*, edited by Gillian A. Frank, Bethany Moreton, and Heather R. White, 253–276. Chapel Hill: University of North Carolina Press.

Gilley, Brian Joseph. 2006. *Becoming Two Spirit: Gay Identity and Social Acceptance in Indian Country*. Lincoln: University of Nebraska Press.

Ginwright, Shawn. 2022. *The Four Pivots: Reimaging Justice, Reimagining Ourselves*. Berkeley, CA: North Atlantic Books.

Glaser, Barney G., and Anselm L. Strauss. 1967. *The Discovery of Grounded Theory: Strategies for Qualitative Research*. New York: Aldine de Gruyter.

Goldberg, Jonathan. 1992. *Sodometries: Renaissance Texts, Modern Sexualities*. New York: Fordham University Press.

Golriz, Golshan. 2021. "'I Am Enough': Why LGBTQ Muslim Groups Resist Mainstreaming." *Sexuality & Culture* 25: 355–376.

Gorski, Philip S., and Samuel L. Perry. 2022. *The Flag and the Cross: White Christian Nationalism and the Threat to American Democracy*. New York: Oxford University Press.

Gould, Deborah B. 2009. *Moving Politics: Emotion and ACT UP's Fight Against AIDS*. Chicago: University of Chicago Press.

Graham, Ruth, and Elizabeth Dias. 2022. "Southern Baptist Sex Abuse Report Stuns, From the Pulpits to the Pews." *New York Times*, May 23. https://www.nytimes.com/2022/05/23/us/southern-baptist-sex-abuse-report.html.

Greear, J. D. 2019. "3 Misconceptions in the Church About Homosexuality." *Outreach Magazine*, September 17. https://outreachmagazine.com/features/discipleship/46770-3-misconceptions-in-the-church-about-homosexuality.html.

Gushee, David P. 2003. *Righteous Gentiles of the Holocaust: Genocide and Moral Obligation*. 2nd rev. ed. St. Paul, MN: Paragon House.

Gushee, David P. 2014. "I'm an Evangelical Minister. I Now Support the LGBT Community—and the Church Should, Too." *Washington Post*, November 4. https://www.washingtonpost.com/posteverything/wp/2014/11/04/im-an-evangelical-minister-i-now-support-the-lgbt-community-and-the-church-should-too/?noredirect=on&utm_term=.6ae926795921.

Gushee, David P. 2015. *Changing Our Mind*. 2nd ed. Canton, MI: Read the Spirit Books.

Hall, Heidi. 2015. "As One Evangelical Church 'Comes Out' for LGBT Rights, Others Cast a Wary Eye." *Religion News Service*, March 3. https://religionnews.com/2015/03/03/one-evangelical-church-comes-lgbt-rights-others-cast-wary-eye.

Halperin, David M., and Valerie Traub. 2009. *Gay Shame*. Chicago: University of Chicago Press.

Hamilton, James M., Jr. 2014. "How to Condone What the Bible Condemns: Matthew Vines Takes on the Old Testament." In *God and the Gay Christian? A Response to Matthew Vines*, edited by R. Albert Mohler, Jr., 25–42. Louisville, KY: SBTS Press.

Hartke, Austen. 2015. "Androgyny, Loneliness, and Genesis 2." *Transgender and Christian*. https://www.youtube.com/watch?v=jwlLSR578_4.

Hartke, Austen 2018. *Transforming: The Bible and the Lives of Transgender Christians*. Louisville, KY: Westminster John Knox Press.

Harris, Joshua. 2003. *I Kissed Dating Goodbye: A New Attitude Toward Romance and Relationships*. Colorado Springs, CO: Multnomah Books.

Harris, Joshua. 2023. "Statement on *I Kissed Dating Goodbye*." July 11. https://joshharris.com/a-statement-on/.

Harris-Perry, Melissa. 2011. *Sister Citizen: Shame, Stereotypes, and Black Women in America*. New Haven, CT: Yale University Press.

Hartropp, Joseph. 2017. "Megapastor John MacArthur Says 'No One Is Gay,' Compares Homosexuality to Adultery." *Christian Today*, 29 June. https://www.christiantoday.com/article/megapastor-john-macarthur-says-no-one-is-gay-compares-homosexuality-to-adultery/110296.htm.

Harvey, Jennifer. 2014. *Dear White Christians: For Those Still Longing for Racial Reconciliation*. Grand Rapids, MI: William B. Eerdmans.

Hays, Richard, and Christopher Hays. 2024. *The Widening of God's Mercy: Sexuality Within the Biblical Story*. New Haven, CT: Yale University Press.

Higginbotham, Evelyn Brooks. 1993. *Righteous Discontent: The Women's Movement in the Black Baptist Church, 1880–1920*. Cambridge, MA: Harvard University Press.

Hill Collins, Patricia. 1986. "Learning from the Outsider Within: The Significance of Black Feminist Thought." *Social Problems* 33, no. 6: S14–S32.

Hill Collins, Patricia. 2000. *Black Feminist Thought: Knowledge, Consciousness, and the Politics of Empowerment*. 2nd ed. New York: Routledge.

Hill Collins, Patricia. 2004. *Black Sexual Politics: African Americans, Gender, and the New Racism*. New York: Routledge.

Holstein, James A., and Jaber F. Gubrium 2008. *Handbook of Constructionist Research*. New York: Guilford.

Hooker, Alan. 2013. "Queer Creation: Queering the Image of God." *Alan Hooker: Hebrew Bible, Theology, Religion, LGBTQ*. https://awhooker.wordpress.com/2013/10/01/queer-creation-queering-the-image-of-god/.

hooks, bell. 2000. *All About Love: New Visions*. New York: Harper Collins.

Hull, Akasha (Gloria T), Patricia Bell-Scott, and Barbara Smith (1982/2015). *All the Women Are White, All the Blacks Are Men, but Some of Us Are Brave*. New York: Feminist Press at CUNY.

Hunter, James D. 1991. *Culture Wars: The Struggle to Define America*. New York: Basic Books.

Ince, Jeylani. 2022. "'Saved' by Interaction, Living by Race: The Diversity Demeanor in an Organizational Space." *Social Psychology Quarterly* 85, no. 3: 259–278.

Independent Lens. 2015. Map of Gender Diverse Cultures. *PBS.org*. https://www.pbs.org/independentlens/content/two-spirits_map-html/.

InterAct Advocates for Intersex Youth. 2021. "How Common Is Intersex?" https://interactadvocates.org/faq/#howcommon.

Jordan, June. 2003. *Some of Us Did Not Die*. New York: Basic Books.

Jordan, Mark D. 2011. *Recruiting Young Love: How Christians Talk about Homosexuality*. Chicago: University of Chicago Press.

Karlsson, G., and L. G. Sjoberg. 2009. "The Experiences of Guilt and Shame: A Phenomenological-Psychological Study." *Humanistic Studies* 32: 335–355.

Kaur, Valarie. 2020. *See No Stranger: A Memoir and Manifesto of Revolutionary Love*. New York: One World.

Keating, Caitlin. 2018. "Conversion Therapy Survivor Recalls Surrendering His Life to His Pastor for Two Years." *People*, November 12. https://people.com/human-interest/darren-calhoun-gay-conversion-therapy/.

Keen, Karen R. 2018. *Scripture, Ethics, and the Possibility of Same-Sex Relationships*. Grand Rapids, MI: Eerdmans.

Kelly, Conor M. 2019. "The Nature and Operation of Structural Sin: Additional Insights from Theology and Moral Psychology." *Theological Studies* 80, no. 2 (June 1): 293–327.

Kelly, Kimberly. 2012. "In the Name of the Mother: Renegotiating Conservative Women's Authority in the Crisis Pregnancy Center Movement." *Signs: Journal of Women in Culture and Society* 38, no. 1: 203–230.

Kim, David Kyumon. 2010. "The Public Life of Love." *The Good Society* 19, no. 2: 37–43.

King Jr., Martin Luther. 1963/1981. *Strength to Love*. Philadelphia: Fortress Press.

King Jr., Martin Luther. 1963/1986. "Letter from Birmingham City Jail." In *A Testament of Hope: The Essential Writings of Martin Luther King, Jr.*, edited by James M. Washington, 289–302. New York: HarperOne.

Klein, Linda Kay. 2018. *Pure: Inside the Evangelical Movement That Shamed a Generation of Young Women and How I Broke Free*. New York: Atria.

Kniss, Fred. 1997. "Culture Wars(?): Remapping the Battleground." In *Cultural Wars in American Politics: Critical Reviews of a Popular Myth*, edited by Rhys H. Williams, 259–280. New York: Aldine de Gruyter.

Kobes Du Mez, Kristen. 2020. *Jesus and John Wayne: How White Evangelicals Corrupted a Faith and Fractured a Nation*. New York: Liveright.

Kolyosh, Simone. 2017. "Straight Gods, White Devils: Exploring Paths to Non-Religion in the Lives of Black LGBTQ People." *Secularism and Nonreligion* 6, no. 2: 1–13.

Laqueur, Thomas. 1990. *Making Sex: Body and Gender from the Greeks to Freud.* Cambridge, MA: Harvard University Press.

LaRossa, Ralph. 2005. "Grounded Theory Methods and Qualitative Family Research." *Journal of Marriage and Family* 69: 845–862.

Lee, Deborah Jian. 2016. *Rescuing Jesus: How People of Color, Women, and Queer Christians Are Reclaiming Evangelicalism.* Boston: Beacon Press.

Lee, Justin. 2012. *Torn: Rescuing the Gospel from the Gays-vs.-Christians Debate.* New York: Jericho Books.

Lehtinen, Ullaliina. 1998. "How Does One Know What Shame Is? Epistemology, Emotions, and Forms of Life in Juxtaposition." *Hypatia* 13, no. 1: 56–77.

Lewin, Ellen. 2018. *Filled with the Spirit: Sexuality, Gender and Radical Inclusivity in a Black Pentecostal Church Coalition.* Chicago: University of Chicago Press.

Lewis, Helen. 1971. *Shame and Guilt in Neurosis.* New York: International Universities Press.

Lewis, Michael. 1992. *Shame: The Exposed Self.* New York: Free Press.

Lofland, John, David Snow, Leon Anderson, and Lyn H. Lofland. 2006. *Analyzing Social Settings: A Guide to Qualitative Observation and Analysis.* 4th ed. Belmont, CA: Wadsworth/Thomson Learning.

Lorde, Audre. 1984. *Sister Outsider: Essays and Speeches by Audre Lorde.* Berkeley, CA: The Crossing Press Feminist Series.

Lovejoy, Arthur C. 1933/1976. *The Great Chain of Being.* Cambridge, MA: Harvard University Press.

MacArthur, John. 2014. "Grace to You: John MacArthur on How to Respond to a Homosexual Child (Selected Scriptures)." *YouTube.* https://www.youtube.com/watch?v=tWYAwknMlH4&feature=emb_title.

McClintock, Anne. 1995. *Imperial Leather: Race, Gender and Sexuality in the Colonial Contest.* New York: Routledge.

Mahaffy, Kimberly A. 1996. "Cognitive Dissonance and Its Resolution: A Study of Lesbian Christians." *Journal for the Scientific Study of Religion* 35: 392–402.

Manion, J. C. 2002. "The Moral Relevance of Shame." *American Philosophical Quarterly* 39, no. 1: 73–90.

Marin, Andrew. 2009. *Love is an Orientation: Elevating the Conversation with the Gay Community.* Downers Grove, IL: InterVarsity Press.

Martí, Gerardo. 2005. *A Mosaic of Believers: Diversity and Innovation in a Multiethnic Church.* Bloomington: Indiana University Press.

Martí, Gerardo. 2012. *Worship Across the Racial Divide: Religious Music and the Multiracial Congregation.* New York: Oxford University Press.

Martí, Gerardo. 2020. *American Blindspot: Race, Class, Religion, and the Trump Presidency.* New York: Rowman and Littlefield.

Martin, Colby. 2016. *Unclobber: Rethinking our Misuse of the Bible on Homosexuality.* Louisville, KY: Westminster John Knox Press.

Mayrl, Damon. 2023. "The Funk of White Souls: Toward a Du Boisian Theory of the White Church." *Sociology of Religion* 84, no. 1: 16–41.

McLaren, Brian. 2010. *A New Kind of Christianity: Ten Questions That Are Transforming the Faith.* New York: HarperOne.

McQueeney, Krista. 2009. "'We Are God's Children, Y'All': Race, Gender, and Sexuality in Lesbian- and Gay-Affirming Congregations." *Social Problems* 56, no. 1: 151–173.

Mills, Claudia. 2020. "Pride: The Complexities of Virtue and Vice." In *Philosophy for Girls*, edited by Melissa Shew and Kim Garcher, 39–50. Oxford: Oxford University Press.

Mohler, R. Albert, Jr. 2014. "God, the Gospel, and the Gay Challenge: A Response to Matthew Vines." In *God and the Gay Christian? A Response to Matthew Vines*, edited by R. Albert Mohler, Jr., 9–24. Louisville, KY: SBTS Press.

Moon, Dawne. 2004. *God, Sex and Politics: Homosexuality and Everyday Theologies*. Chicago: University of Chicago Press.

Moon, Dawne. 2014. "Beyond the Dichotomy: Six Religious Views of Homosexuality." *Journal of Homosexuality* 61, no. 9: 1215–1241.

Moon, Dawne, and Theresa W. Tobin. 2018. "Sunsets and Solidarity: Overcoming Sacramental Shame in Conservative Christian Churches to Forge a Queer Vision of Love and Justice." *Hypatia* 33, no. 3: 451–468.

Moraga, Cherríe, and Gloria Anzaldúa. 1981/2015. *This Bridge Called My Back: Writings by Radical Women of Color*. New York: State University of New York Press.

Morse, Janice M., Phyllis Noerager Stern, Juliet Corbin, Barbara Bowers, Adele E. Clarke, and Kathy Charmaz. 2009. *Developing Grounded Theory: The Second Generation*. New York: Aldine de Gruyter.

Moselener, Sara. 2015. *Virgin Nation: Sexual Purity and American Adolescence*. New York: Oxford University Press.

Movement Advancement Project. 2024. "LGBTQ People of Color." https://www.lgbtmap.org/policy-and-issue-analysis/LGBTQ-people-of-color.

Nash, Jennifer. 2011. "Practicing Love: Black Feminism, Love Politics, and Post-Intersectionality." *Meridians* 11, no. 2: 1–24.

Nzegwu, Nkiru. 2006. *Family Matters: Feminist Concepts in African Philosophy of Culture*. New York: SUNY Press.

O'Brien, Jodi. 2004. "Wrestling the Angel of Contradiction: Queer Christian Identities." *Culture and Religion* 5, no. 2: 179–202.

Oyěwùmí, Oyèrónké. 1997. *The Invention of Women: Making an African Sense of Western Gender Discourses*. Minneapolis: University of Minnesota Press.

Panchuk, Michelle. 2018. "The Shattered Spiritual Self: A Philosophical Exploration of Religious Trauma." *Res Philosophical* 95, no. 3: 505–530.

Patil, Vrushali. 2018. "The Heterosexual Matrix as Imperial Effect." *Sociological Theory* 36, no. 1: 1–26.

Pattison, Stephen. 2000. *Shame: Theory, Therapy, Theology*. Cambridge: Cambridge University Press.

Petro, Anthony. 2015. *After the Wrath of God: AIDS, Sexuality, and American Religion*. New York: Oxford University Press.

Picq, Manuela. 2018. "Decolonizing Indigenous Sexualities: Between Erasure and Resurgence." In *The Oxford Handbook of Global LGBT and Sexual Diversity Politics*, edited by Michael Bosia, Sandra McEvoy, and Momin Rahman, 168–184. New York: Oxford University Press.

Pitt, Richard N. 2010. "'Still Looking For My Jonathan': Gay Black Men's Management of Religious and Sexual Identity Conflicts." *Journal of Homosexuality* 57: 39–53.

Preves, Sharon E. 2002. "Sexing the Intersexed: An Analysis of Sociocultural Responses to Intersexuality." *Signs* 27, no. 2: 523–556.

Puar, Jasbir. 2007. *Terrorist Assemblages: Homonationalism in Queer Times*. Durham, NC: Duke University Press.

Pulliam Bailey, Sarah. 2014. "Gay, Christian and . . . Celibate: The Changing Face of the Homosexuality Debate." *Religion News Service*, August 4. https://religionnews.com/2014/08/04/gay-christian-celibate-changing-face-homosexuality-debate/.

Q Christian Fellowship. n.d. "About Us." https://www.qchristian.org/about.

Reagon, Bernice Johnson. 1983. "Coalition Politics: Turning the Century." In *Home Girls: A Black Feminist Anthology*, edited by Barbara Smith, 356–368. New York: Kitchen Table: Women of Color Press.

Reformation Project. 2019. "Our Values." https://reformationproject.org/values.

Roberts, Robert C. 2007. "Humility as a Moral Project." In *Spiritual Emotions: A Psychology of Christian Virtues*, 78–93. Grand Rapids, MI: Eerdmans.

Roberts, Robert C. 2009. "The Vice of Pride." *Faith and Philosophy* 26, no. 2: 119–133.

Roberts, Robert C., and W. Jay Woods. 2003. "Humility and Epistemic Goods." In *Intellectual Virtue: Perspectives from Ethics and Epistemology*, edited by Michael DePaul and Linda Zagzebski, 257–279. Oxford: Oxford University Press.

Robertson, Brandan. 2016a. "Dear Church (A Frank Letter from a Queer Christian)." *Patheos: Hosting the Conversation on Faith* (weblog), May 26. http://www.patheos.com/blogs/revangelical/2016/05/26/dear-church-a-frank-letter-from-a-queer-christian.html.

Robertson, Brandan. 2016b. *Nomad: A Spirituality for Traveling Light*. Minneapolis: Augsburg Books.

Robertson, Rob, and Linda Robertson. 2013. "Just Because He Breathes: Learning to Truly Love our Gay Son." Justbecasehebreathes.com.

Robinson, Allyson Dylan. 2015. "The Grace of a Bloodied Nose." *Medium*, June 13.

Robinson, Brandon Andrew. 2018. "Conditional Families and Lesbian, Gay, Bisexual, Transgender, and Queer Youth Homelessness." *Journal of Marriage and Family* 80: 383–396.

Rodriguez, Eric M., and Suzanne C. Ouellette. 2000. "Gay and Lesbian Christians: Homosexual and Religious Identity Integration in the Members and Participants of a Gay-Positive Church." *Journal for the Scientific Study of Religion* 39, no. 3: 333–347.

Rogers, Jack. 2009. *Jesus, the Bible, and Homosexuality: Explode the Myths, Heal the Church*. Rev. and exp. ed. Louisville, KY: Westminster John Knox Press.

Roggio, Sharon, dir. 2022. "Rocky." In *1946: The Mistranslation That Shifted Culture*. Minneapolis, MN: Acowsay Film Co. [video].

Rubin, Gayle. 1993/1984. "Thinking Sex: Notes for a Radical Theory of the Politics of Sexuality." In *The Lesbian and Gay Studies Reader*, edited by Henry Abelove, Michèle Aina Barale, and David M. Halperin, 3–44. New York: Routledge.

Ryan, Caitlin, David Huebner, Rafael M. Diaz, and Jorge Sanchez. 2009. "Family Rejection as a Predictor of Negative Health Outcomes in White and Latino Lesbian, Gay, and Bisexual Young Adults." *Pediatrics* 123: 346–352.

Ryan, Caitlin, Russell B. Toomey, Rafael M. Diaz, and Stephen T. Russell. 2018. "Parent-Initiated Sexual Orientation Change Efforts with LGBT Adolescents: Implications for Young Adult Mental Health and Adjustment." *Journal of Homosexuality* 67, no. 2: 159–173. https://doi.org/10.1080/00918369.2018.1538407.

Sales, Ruby. 2020. "'On Being' with Krista Tippett." *National Public Radio*, January 16.

Scanzoni, Letha Dawson, and Virginia Ramey Mollenkott. 1978/1994. *Is the Homosexual My Neighbor? A Positive Christian Response*. San Francisco: Harper.

Scheff, Thomas J. 2000. "Shame and the Social Bond: A Sociological Theory." *Sociological Theory* 18, no. 1: 84–99.

Schneider, Laurel. 2004. "What Race is Your Sex?" In *Disrupting White Supremacy from Within*, edited by Jennifer Harvey, Karen A. Case, and Robin Hawley Gorsline, 142–162. Cleveland, OH: Pilgrim Press.

Scholz, Susanne. 2005. "The Christian Right's Discourse on Gender and the Bible." *Journal of Feminist Studies in Religion* 21, no. 1: 81–100.

Sedgwick, Eve Kosofsky. 2003. *Touching Feeling: Affect, Pedagogy, Performativity*. Durham, NC: Duke University Press.

Seitz, David. 2017, *A House of Prayer for All People: Contesting Citizenship in a Queer Church*. Minneapolis: University of Minnesota Press.

Shipley, Heather, and S. J. Page. 2016. "Sexuality." In *Handbook of Religion and Society*, edited by David Yamane, 395–419. New York: Springer.

Shotwell, Alexis. 2011. *Knowing Otherwise: Race, Gender, and Implicit Understanding*. University Park: Pennsylvania State University.

Smid, John J. 2012. *Ex'd Out: How I Fired the Shame Committee*. Memphis, TN: John J. Smid.

Smith, Andrea. 2004. "Rape and the War Against Native Women." In *Reading Native American Women*, edited by Inés Hernandez-Avila, 63–76. Walnut Creek, CA: Alta Mira Press.

Smith, Christian. 1998. *American Evangelicalism: Embattled and Thriving*. Chicago: University of Chicago Press.

Smith, Dorothy E. 1989. *The Everyday World as Problematic: A Feminist Sociology*. Boston: Northeastern University Press.

Smithers, Gregory D. 2022. *Reclaiming Two-Spirits: Sexuality, Spiritual Renewal, and Sovereignty in Native America*. Boston: Beacon Press.

Snorton, C. Riley. 2014. *Nobody is Supposed to Know: Black Sexuality on the Down Low*. Minneapolis: University of Minnesota Press.

Snow, Nancy. 1995. "Humility." *Journal of Value Inquiry* 29: 203–216.

Spade, Dean. 2015. *Normal Life: Administrative Violence, Critical Trans Politics, and the Limits of Law*. Durham, NC: Duke University Press.

Steele, Claude. 2010. *Whistling Vivaldi*. New York: Norton and Co.

Steensland, B., J. Z. Park, M. D. Regnerus, L. D Robinson, W. B. Wilcox, and R. D. Woodberry. 2000. "The Measure of American Religion: Improving the State of the Art." *Social Forces* 79, no. 1: 291–318.

Stolakis, Kristine, dir. 2021. *Pray Away*. Netflix.

Strauss, Anselm C., and Juliet M. Corbin. 1998. *Basics of Qualitative Research: Techniques and Procedures for Developing Grounded Theory*. 2nd ed. Thousand Oaks, CA: SAGE.

Strudwick, Patrick. 2014. "Vicky Beeching, Christian Rock Star: 'I'm Gay. God Loves Me Just the Way I Am.'" *Independent*, August 13. https://www.independent.co.uk/news/people/news/vicky-beeching-star-of-the-christian-rock-scene-im-gay-god-loves-me-just-the-way-i-am-9667566.html.

Stuart, Elizabeth. 2003. *Gay and Lesbian Theologies: Repetitions with Critical Difference*. Burlington, VT: Ashgate.

Stein, Arlene. 2006. *Shame/less: Sexual Dissidence in American Culture*. New York: New York University Press.

Sullivan-Blum, Constance R. 2006. "'The Natural Order of Creation': Naturalizing Discourses in the Christian Same-Sex Marriage Debate." *Anthropologica* 48, no. 2: 203–215.

Sumerau, J. Edward. 2012. "'That's What a Man Is Supposed to Do': Compensatory Manhood Acts in an LGBT Christian Church." *Gender & Society* 26, no. 3: 461–487.

Sumerau, J. Edward, and Douglas P. Schrock. 2011. "'It's Important to Show Your Colors': Counter-Heteronormativity in a Metropolitan Community Church." In *Embodied Resistance: Challenging the Norms, Breaking the Rules*, edited by Samantha Kwan and Chris Bobel, 99–110. Nashville, TN: Vanderbilt University Press.

Sumerau, J. Edward, Irene Padavic, and Douglas P. Schrock. 2015. "'Little Girls Unwilling to Do What's Best for Them': Resurrecting Patriarchy in an LGBT Christian Church." *Journal of Contemporary Ethnography* 44, no. 3: 306–344.

Tangney, June Price. 2007. Self-relevant Emotions. In *Handbook of Self and Identity*, edited by M. R. Leary and J. P. Tangney, 384–400. New York: Guilford Press.

Tanis, Justin. 2003. *Trans-Gendered: Theology, Ministry, and Communities of Faith*. Cleveland, OH: Pilgrim Press.

Taylor, Gabriele. 1985. *Pride, Shame and Guilt*. Oxford: Oxford University Press.

Thomas, Jeremy. 2016. "The Development and Deployment of the Idea of Pornography Addiction Within American Evangelicalism." *Sexual Addiction and Compulsivity* 23, no. 2–3: 182–195.

Thomas, Jeremy N., and Daniel V. A. Olson. 2012. "Evangelical Elites' Changing Responses to Homosexuality 1960–2009." *Sociology of Religion* 73, no. 3: 239–272.

Thomason, Krista K. 2015. "Shame, Violence, and Morality." *Philosophy and Phenomenological Research* 91, no. 1: 1–24.

Thumma, Scott, and Edward Gray, eds. 2004. *Gay Religion*. New York: Alta Mira Press.

Tisby, Jemar. 2019. *The Color of Compromise: The Truth About the American Church's Complicity in Racism*. Grand Rapids, MI: Zondervan Academic.

Tobin, Theresa. 2016. "Spiritual Violence, Gender, and Sexuality: Implications for Seeking and Dwelling Among Some Catholic Women and LGBT Catholics." In *Seekers and Dwellers: Plurality and Wholeness in a Time of Secularity*, edited by Philip J. Rossi, 133–167. Washington, DC: The Council for Research in Values and Philosophy.

Tobin, Theresa. 2019. "Religious Faith in the Unjust Meantime." *Feminist Philosophy Quarterly* 5, no. 2: 1–30.

Tobin, Theresa W., and Dawne Moon. 2019. "Reflections on our Sociological-Philosophical Study of the Self, Motivation, and Virtue among LGBTI Conservative Christians and Their Allies." In *Self, Motivation, and Virtue: Innovative Interdisciplinary Research*, edited by Darcia Narvaez and Nancy Snow, 147–166. New York: Routledge.

Tomkins, Silvan. 1995. *Shame and Its Sisters: A Silvan Tomkins Reader*. Edited by E. K. Sedgwick and A. Frank. Durham, NC: Duke University Press.

Truluck, Rembert S. 2001. "Spiritual Abuse: How to Recognize It and One Way to Overcome It." *Whosoever*, May 1. http://www.whosoever.org/v5i6/violence.html.

Van Ness, Paul, dir. 2019. *Stories of Intersex and Faith*. Intersex and Faith [video].

VanderWal Gritter, Wendy. 2014. *Generous Spaciousness: Responding to Gay Christians in the Church*. Grand Rapids, MI: Brazos Press.

Velleman, David. 2001. "On the Genesis of Shame." *Philosophy and Public Affairs* 30, no. 1: 27–52.

Vines, Matthew. 2014. *God and the Gay Christian: The Biblical Case in Support of Same-Sex Relationships*. New York: Convergent.

Vines, Matthew. 2012. *The Gay Debate: The Bible and Homosexuality*. YouTube. https://www.youtube.com/watch?v=ezQjNJUSraY.

Vines, Matthew. 2016. Facebook post. March 30.

Whitcomb, Dennis, Heather Battaly, Jason Baehr, and Daniel Howard-Snyder. 2005. "Intellectual Humility: Owning Our Limitations." *Philosophy and Phenomenological Research* 91, no. 1: 509–539.

White, Byron Raymond, and Supreme Court of The United States. 1985. U.S. Reports: *Bowers v. Hardwick*, 478 U.S. 186.

White, Heather. 2015. *Reforming Sodom: Protestants and the Rise of Gay Rights*. Chapel Hill: University of North Carolina Press.

Whitehead, Andrew. 2014. "Politics, Religion, Attribution Theory, and Attitudes Toward Same-Sex Unions." *Social Science Quarterly* 95, no. 3: 701–718.

Whitehead, Andrew L., and Samuel L. Perry. 2020. *Taking America Back for God: Christian Nationalism in the United States*. New York: Oxford.

Wilcox, Melissa. 2003. *Coming Out in Christianity: Religion, Identity, and Community*. Bloomington: Indiana University Press.

Wilcox, Melissa. 2009. *Queer Women and Religious Individualism*. Bloomington: Indiana University Press.

Wolfe, Alan. 1999. *One Nation, After All: What Americans Really Think About God, Country, Family, Racism, Welfare, Immigration, Homosexuality, Work, the Right, the Left and Each Other*. New York: Penguin.

Wolkomir, Melissa. 2006. *Be Not Deceived: The Sacred and Sexual Struggles of Gay and Ex-Gay Christian Men*. New Brunswick, NJ: Rutgers University Press.

Woodell, Brandi, Emily Kazyak, and D'Lane Compton. 2015. "Reconciling LGB and Christian Identities in the Rural South." *Social Sciences* 4: 859–878.

Woodward, Kathleen. 2000. "Traumatic Shame, Televisual Culture, and the Cultural Politics of Emotion." *Cultural Critique* 46: 201–240.

Yip, Andrew K. T. 1997. "Dare to Differ: Gay and Lesbian Catholics' Assessment of Official Catholic Positions on Sexuality." *Sociology of Religion* 58, no. 2: 165–180.

Yip, Andrew K. T. 2010. "Coming Home from the Wilderness: An Overview of Recent Scholarly Research on LGBTQI Religiosity/Spirituality in the West." In *Queer Spiritual Spaces: Sexuality and Sacred Places*, edited by Kath Browne, Sally Munt, and Andrew K. T. Yip, 35–50. Burlington, VT: Ashgate.

Young, Luther, Jr. 2022. "To Condemn or Not to Condemn: Perceived Climates Concerning Sexual Orientation in Black Churches." *Sociology of Religion* 83, no. 2: 169–193.

Young, Luther, Jr. 2023. "'Ye Double-Minded': Black Parishioners' Attitudes toward Nonaffirming Church Climates." *Journal for the Scientific Study of Religion* 62, no. 1: 108–125.

INDEX

For the benefit of digital users, indexed terms that span two pages (e.g., 52–53) may, on occasion, appear on only one of those pages.

abstinence until marriage, 44–45, 148–49. *See also* purity culture
abuse. *See* violence and abuse
acceptance, 90, 141, 183–84. *See also* self-acceptance
accountability, 1, 41, 44–45, 64, 67–68, 99–100, 137–38, 158, 168
Adam, creation of, 48, 84–85, 86
addiction, 31, 59, 67, 77, 79–80, 118, 163
affirming and inclusive churches, 12, 15–16, 35, 76–77, 98–99, 105–6, 125–26, 149–50
affirming organizations, 1, 2–4, 145–46, 153
agape, 20–21, 24
allies, xii–xiii, 3–4, 111–36, 164–65, 197n.12
    Biblical interpretation and, 121–26, 127–28
    humility and, 86, 111–16, 117–32, 160, 164–66
    love and, 135–36
    marginalization and, 132–34
    power and, 112, 115–16
    race and, 112–15
    relationships and, 111–12, 116–17, 119–28, 138
    shame and, 163–65
    systemic oppression and, 111–15
ambisexual people, 5–6
Anderson, Carmarion D., 105–6, 107, 155–56
Anderson, Dianna, 49
anti-LGBTQ+ attitudes, 150–51, 163–65, 196n.22
    among conservative Christians, 1–3, 7–9, 10–11, 17, 20–22, 28–36, 51–53, 57–58, 60–61, 69, 93, 136, 150–51, 153–54
    in Black churches, 27, 29–30, 42, 66, 68–70, 72–73, 75–76
    physical violence, 70–72
    See also complementarity doctrine; "love the sinner, hate the sin"; reparative therapies
antiracism, 17, 139–40, 144–45, 150–52, 158, 170–71
Arab Americans, 126
Archuleta, Isaac, 58
Aristotle, 192n.9
arrogance, 86, 95–96, 97, 100–1, 106, 107–8, 109–10, 116, 117–18, 128–32, 166, 167–68

Assemblies of God, 40–41
authority, viii, 24, 122, 131
    allyship and, 112, 115
    arrogance and, 166
    of the Bible, 142
    of God, 99–100, 167
    masculine, 36, 46–47, 153–54, 194n.34
    spiritual violence and, 70

Baldock, Kathy, 123–24
Baldwin, James, xi, 13–14, 22–23, 24–25, 38–39, 162–63, 168, 199n.19
banishment, 71–72
Baptists, xi, 28, 60, 68, 94. *See also* Southern Baptists
Barth, Karl, 63
Barton, Bernadette, 71
Bebbington, David, 142
Beeching, Vicky, 62–63
Belgau, Ron, 61–62
belonging, 14–15, 59, 65, 149, 155, 168, 195n.12
bestiality, 19, 52
Bible
    1 Corinthians, 119, 131–32
    2 Corinthians, 195–96n.5
    Ezekiel, 116
    Galatians, 154–55, 195–96n.5
    Genesis, 33, 34–35, 48, 50, 84–85, 86
    Gospel of John, 105–6
    Gospel of Luke, 132
    Gospel of Matthew, 52–53, 67
    Gospels, 27–28, 99–100, 154–56
    Isaiah, 159–60
    Leviticus, 20, 34–35, 47–48, 116
    Romans, 34–35, 47–48
Biblical interpretation, 52–53, 166
    conservative, 147, 148–49
    on gender and sexuality, 9, 15–16, 19–20, 34–35, 37, 47–48, 61–62, 84–85, 116–17, 121–26, 127–28
    humility and, 15–16, 89–90, 95–100, 131
    on non-sinful pride, 195–96n.5
    social hierarchies and, 45–46
Bilbrey, Jason, 139–40, 154–55, 183–84

binaries, 33, 48. *See also* complementarity doctrine
BIPOC. *See* Black people, Indigenous people, and people of color (BIPOC)
bisexual people, 5–6, 33, 72, 97–99
Bjork-James, Sophie, 46–47
Black church communities, 11–12, 17, 19, 187–88, 190n.5, 196n.9
    anti-LGBTQ+ attitudes in, 27, 29–30, 42, 66, 68–70, 72–73, 75–76
    gender expression and, 27, 40–41
    LGBTQ+-affirming, 105–6
    love ethic, 172–73
    respectability politics, 41–44, 73
Black feminism, 4–5, 22–23, 196n.23, 198n.16
Black Lives Matter, 107–8, 114. *See also* Movement for Black Lives
Black people, Indigenous people, and people of color (BIPOC)
    colonization and, 5, 39, 98
    feminists of color, 5 (*see also* Black feminism)
    Hawai'ian third gender, 38, 54–55
    shame and, 58
    social justice movements, 3–4, 5, 13–14, 142, 168, 172–73
    See also Black church communities; racism
Boggs, Grace Lee, 13–14, 168
Bowers v. Hardwick (1987), 196n.22
Brown, Brené, 64
Brownson, James, 48, 50, 194n.42
Buber, Martin, viii–xi, 80–81, 107–8, 115–16, 186–87, 192n.10
Burk, Denny, 30, 46–47, 48, 127–28
Burke, Kelsy, 66
Burrow-Branine, Jon, 12, 196n.9
Butterfield, Rosaria, 30

Calhoun, Darren, 17–19, 30–31, 42–44, 60–61, 75–76, 92–94, 145–46, 151–52, 170–71, 177–78
"calling in," 170–71
cancel culture, 170
Canyonwalkers, 2–3

INDEX

Catholic Church, xii–xiii, 38–39
celibacy, 17, 30–31, 49–50, 51–52, 54–55, 62–63, 74, 75–76, 93–95, 116, 123–25, 140, 143
Center for Inclusivity (CFI), 10, 19, 139–40, 183–84, 185–86, 189n.4, 199n.2
CenterPeace, 2–3, 152, 166
certainty, viii, 56
    arrogance and, 108, 129 (*see also* arrogance)
    "certainty walls," xii, 171
    humility and, 98, 109–10, 112, 121–22, 129, 134–35
    prioritized over relationships, 12–13, 111–12, 136
Chambers, Alan, 77
Christian love, 166–67
    centrality of, 27–28
    definitions of, vii–viii, 13–14
    demonstrations of, vii, 17–19, 183–85
    failures of, 1–3, 7, 8, 21–22, 52–53, 54–56, 77, 132, 159
    justice and, 9–10
Christians, conservative. *See* conservative Christians; LGBTQ+ conservative Christians
Chu, Jeff, 166–67, 175
ChurchClarity.org, 112–13
cisgender identity, 71, 73
City of Refuge Church, 76
civil rights movement, 5, 13–14, 142, 168, 172–73
Coley, Jonathan, 12
Collins, Patricia Hill, 5, 13–14, 41
colonization, 5, 39, 98
Columbus, Christopher, 39
commandments, 33, 144–45, 167–68. *See also* Ten Commandments
compartmentalization, 43, 64–65, 76, 105, 159
compassion, xii, 25–26, 107, 118–19, 144
complementarity doctrine, 14–15, 27–53, 57–58, 66, 82, 115–16, 129, 143, 153, 156–57, 173, 194n.42

creation stories and, 48, 84–85
    debates on, 47–48
    purity culture and, 44–45, 49–50
    race and, 38–44, 45–47, 58, 73
    shame and, 67–68, 75, 77
conditional love, x, 14, 67–68, 73–75, 78, 159, 167
Conley, Garrard, 77
connection, 3–4, 6, 162–63
    learning and growing through, 14, 21, 22–23, 67–68, 82–83, 115–16
    See also *I-thou* connection; relationships
conservative Christians
    identities and definitions of, 2, 16, 99–100, 142–43, 153–54, 187–88
    See also LGBTQ+ conservative Christians
conservative Protestants, 187–88. *See also* white evangelical Protestants
control, 23, 57–58, 67–68, 112, 128–30, 158, 167–68
Crenshaw, Kimberlé, 5, 194n.38, 196n.23, 198n.16
Crosby-Mack, Alicia T., 10, 19–20, 117, 139–40, 165, 177, 183–84, 185–86
culture wars, xi, 7–8, 29, 161–62, 198n.8
"cures" for LGBTQ+ people. *See* exorcism; reparative therapies

DeFranza, Megan, 37–38
dehumanization, xii–xiii, 10, 13–14, 21, 24–26, 115–16, 161, 169
dialogue, 113–14
Diefendorf, Sarah, 114
disability, 5–6, 96–97, 164–65
discrimination, 2, 5, 24, 128, 164–65, 194n.38
disgust, 196n.22
divorce, 29, 51, 65–66
Dobson, James, 156–57
domination, xi, 23, 168–69
Douglas, Mary, 196n.22
drug use, 79–80
Durkheim, Émile, 192n.9

219

Edman, Elizabeth, 100–1, 107, 108–9
Edwards, Korie, 112–13
Emerick, Barrett, 192n.10, 198n.26
Emerson, Michael, 113–14
emotions
    liberation and, 3–4
    as social experiences, 12–13
    See also humility; love; pride; shame
empathy, 21, 25–26, 132–34
Episcopal church, 100–1
equality, 107–8, 176–77
    as equilibrium state, 156–58
    See also inequalities
eros, 20–21
ethics, 22–23, 37–38
evangelicalism, 147–48, 187–88
    definitions of, 142–43
    "Evangelical bubble," 155–58
    See also conservative Christians
evangelism, x
Eve, creation of, 48
ex-gay ministry. *See* reparative therapies
Exodus (organization), 77
exorcism, 17, 31–32, 51–52, 59–60, 70–71, 72

faith, vii, 3, 58, 80, 129, 157–58, 167–68
false prophets, fruits as tool for determining, 52–53, 67, 88, 93, 124–25
Falwell, Jerry, 29
Family Acceptance Project, 72
Fanon, Franz, 71
Fausto-Sterling, Anne, 37
fear, ix, 20, 56, 80, 82, 91, 117, 128–29, 131–32, 135, 173–74. *See also* shame
Fellowship of Affirming Ministries, The (TFAM), 105–6
femininity, 33–34, 102–3. *See also* gender
feminist philosophy, 186–87
feminists of color, 5. *See also* Black feminism
feminist studies, 183
forgiveness, 25–26, 36, 56, 79–80, 169, 172, 175–76, 177

Freire, Paolo, ix
friendships, 61–62. *See also* relationships
fundamentalism, 46, 74, 147–48, 187–88. *See also* conservative Christians

Gagnon, Robert, 36, 48, 127–28
Garcia, Kevin, 57–58, 59, 103–5, 155–56, 171
Gay Christian Network (GCN), 2–3, 10, 31, 70–71, 85, 123, 171, 183–84
    conferences, xi–xiii
    founding of, 58, 143
    leadership in, 188
    tensions in social justice organizing, 144–47, 150–51
    See also Q Christian Fellowship (QCF)
gender, 27–53
    "common sense" ideas on, 28, 36
    conservative Christian ideas on (*see* complementarity doctrine)
    pronouns and, 38
    race and, 27, 38–44
    religion and, 1–2
    as social/cultural construct, 36–43
    as a spectrum, 36–38
gender studies, 186–87
Ginwright, Shawn, 177
God's love, 28, 56, 67, 68–70
Golden Rule, 168
Good Samaritan, parable of, 132–33, 144–45, 158, 167–68, 197n.19
grace, 169
graciousness, 176–77
Graham, Billy, 137
Greear, J. D., 35, 64
Grindr, 50
grounded theory method, 186
Gushee, David, 48, 111, 127–28, 132, 135–36

Hagee, John, 29
Hamilton, James, 33–34
Harris, Joshua, 49
Hartke, Austen, 84–85
Harvey, Jennifer, 113–14, 175–77
Hays, Christopher, 48

INDEX

Hays, Richard, 48
healing, 1, 65, 82–83, 177
  humility and, 89–90
  from toxic shame, 87–95, 100–9, 155–56
  See also pride
heterosexuality
  gender hierarchy and, 46
  as mandatory, 20–21
  as natural and normal, 38–39, 51–52, 66, 71
  race and, 193n.30
homelessness, 70–71, 72
homophobia. *See* anti-LGBTQ+ attitudes
honesty, 95, 103, 109
Hooker, Alan, 33
hooks, bell, 13–14, 81, 168
hubris, 86, 100–1, 107, 108, 196n.20
humility, 3–4, 10–11, 86–110, 161–63, 165–66
  allyship and, 86, 111–16, 117–32, 160, 164–66
  Biblical interpretation and, 15–16, 89–90, 95–100, 131
  definitions of, 12–13, 86–87
  love and, 22–23, 86, 109, 112, 131–32, 170
  openness to new information, ix–xii, 88–93, 98, 109–10, 134, 160, 177–78, 195n.4
  personal limitations and, 12–13, 86, 91, 93–94, 98, 100–1, 104, 109, 165
  pride and, 3–4, 86–87, 104
  public displays of, 138–39
  relationships and, 15–16, 108–10, 119, 166
  shame and, 86, 170–71
  vulnerability and, 129, 170
  See also listening to others

I-thou connection, viii–xi, 80–82, 186–87
idolatry, 36, 47–48
indifference, 23–26, 168–69
Indigenous people. *See* Black people, Indigenous people, and people of color (BIPOC)
individualism, 113, 164
inequalities, 38–39, 107–8. *See also* oppression

intersectionality, 4–7, 46–47, 107–8, 115, 148, 149, 152, 190n.8
intersex people, 2, 5–6, 32, 37–38, 84
InterVarsity Christian Fellowship, 94–95, 98
intimacy, 81
  shame and, 60–61
  systemic oppression and, 3–4
  See also relationships; sexuality
isolation, 6, 60–61, 62–63, 94, 108–9

Jackson, Mahalia, 42–43
Jaggar, Alison M., 198n.26
Jesus, 18, 27–28, 36, 52–53, 87, 89–90, 155–56
Jews, 130–31, 135–36
Jordan, June, 13–14, 168
joy, 45, 52, 81, 87, 93, 100–1, 103–5, 132, 173, 175, 191n.5
judgment, 42, 50, 57, 62, 91, 106, 119–20, 137, 160, 197n.12
justice. *See* social justice

Kaur, Valarie, 168–69, 171–73, 175, 199n.19
Keen, Karen, 48
Kim, David Kyuman, 175
King, Martin Luther, Jr., ix, 13–14, 24–25, 141–42, 156–58, 167–69, 175–76, 191n.5
Klein, Linda Kay, 49
Kobes du Mez, Kristen, 46–47, 194n.34
Korean American Christian Reform church, 40

Landis-Aina, Bukola, 146–47
Lee, Deborah Jian, 12
Lee, Justin, 31, 58, 132–34, 135–36, 143–45, 158, 172
LGBTQ+ conservative Christians
  families of, 136, 137–38
  groups supporting, 2–3
  identities and definitions of, 2–9, 155–56, 190n.5
  individual efforts to change sexual orientation or gender identity, 59–60, 75–76 (*see also* reparative therapies)

LGBTQ+ conservative Christians (*cont.*)
  leaving the church, viii, 2
  negative attitudes towards
    (*see* anti-LGBTQ+ attitudes)
  numbers of, 4
  perspectives and insights of, 4–7
  scholarship on, 11–14
  "Side A" (proponents of same-sex
    marriage), 49, 196n.8
  "Side B" (proponents of celibacy), 49,
    123–25, 143, 196n.8
  social movements and, 16 (*see also*
    social justice)
LGBTQ+ conservative Christians of color,
  1–2, 174–75
  identities, 107–8
  in predominantly white or mixed
    congregations, 112–14
  productive tension and, 159–60
  shame and, 54–56
  silencing and invisibility of, 72–73
  social justice and, 148–53
  See also Black church communities;
    multiracial evangelical churches
LGBTQ+ identities
  causes of, 35, 57–58, 86, 193n.16
  Christian identity and, 95
  definitions of labels, 51–52, 189n.3
  pride celebrations and, 85–86, 101, 108,
    138–39, 183–84
LGBTQ+ youth, 72
liberals and progressives, 99–100, 110, 141,
  146, 152, 163–64, 168–69
Lighthouse Church of Chicago, 76
listening to others, vii, 4–10, 57, 82–83,
  93–94, 112–15, 124, 132, 137–38, 144,
  157–59, 161–62, 164–65, 170–73, 177–
  78. *See also* humility; relationships
Lorde, Audre, 13–14, 24, 168, 191n.5
love, vii–xiii, 3–4, 17–26
  allyship and, 135–36
  Black church and, 172–73
  capacity to, 20–22, 58, 61, 86
  definitions of, 13–14, 22–26, 81
  humility and, 22–23, 86, 109, 112, 131–32, 170
  as idealistic cliché, 169–70, 175

  intersectional perspectives on, 6–7
  kinds of, 20–21
  labor of, 173
  misuses of, viii–xi, 10–11, 23, 67–68,
    75–82, 130, 157, 167–68 (*see also*
    control; "love the sinner, hate the
    sin"; manipulation; shame)
  openness to new information and, 157,
    158–59
  privilege and, 168–69
  social justice movements and, 13–14
  transformative power of, viii–xi, 10–11
  See also Christian love; conditional
    love; connection; God's love;
    intimacy; relationships; sexuality;
    unconditional love
Love Boldly, 2–3
"love the sinner, hate the sin," 57, 67–68,
  75–82
"love your enemies," xii–xiii, 13–14, 25, 168,
  175–76

MacArthur, John, 35, 64, 72
manipulation, x–xi, 167–68
marginalized groups, 5, 132–34, 144, 146–
  50, 164–65
Marin, Andrew, 130, 137–40, 197n.12
Marin Foundation, The (TMF), 2–3, 10, 17,
  44–45, 72, 82–83, 183–84
  founding of, 137–38
  "Living in the Tension" discussion
    group, vii, 138–41
  participant observation at, 184
  tensions in social justice organizing,
    138–41, 150–51
marriage
  abstinence until, 44–45, 148–49 (*see also*
    purity culture)
  abuse within, 34
  as ideal, 21, 30–31, 48, 67–68 (*see also*
    complementarity doctrine)
  See also same-sex marriage
Marti, Gerardo, 197n.9
masculinity, 33–34. *See also* gender
McLaren, Brian, 193n.18
methods, research, vii–xiii

INDEX

Metropolitan Community Church (MCC), 98–99, 159–60
Mills, Claudia, 105
mixed-race people, 5–6
Mohler, Albert, 33–34, 46–47
moral arguments, 14–15, 186–87
Morrison, Toni, 168, 172
Mott, Stephanie, 78
Movement for Black Lives, 135–36, 145. *See also* Black Lives Matter
multiracial evangelical churches, 113–15, 197n.9

Nash, Jennifer, 22–23, 162–63
Native Americans, 97–99
neglect, 23–24, 148
New Testament, 27–28, 34–35, 47–48, 61–62, 89
nonbinary people, 5–6

Obama administration, 145
Obergefell v. Hodges (2015), xi, 29. *See also* same-sex marriage
objects or problems, treating others as, viii–xi, 10–11, 23, 67–68, 75–82, 130, 157
oppression, 24–25, 107–8, 161
  allyship and, 111–15
  intersectionality and, 5
  intimate relationships and, 3–4
  productive tension and, 156–60 (*see also* social justice)
  shame and, 164–65
  See also anti-LGBTQ+ attitudes; dehumanization; racism

pansexual people, 5–6
participant observation, 184–86
patience, 175–77
Paul (apostle), 34–35, 47–48, 49–50, 61–62, 116, 131–32, 195–96n.5
Pentecostal church, 60, 68, 99–100
people of color. *See* Black people, Indigenous people, and people of color (BIPOC)
Perry, Samuel, 45–46, 47, 142, 190n.12, 194n.34
personhood, 73, 100–1, 186–87

philia, 20–21
philosophical frameworks, ix–x, 183, 186–87
poverty, 173–74
power, 158
  allyship and, 112, 115–16
  empathy and, 134
  intersections of identities and, 4–7
  love and, 168–69
  See also social hierarchies
pride, 10–11, 85–110, 161–62
  conventional, 196n.20
  definitions of, 12–13, 85–86
  humility and, 3–4, 86–87, 104
  LGBTQ+ pride, celebration of, 85–86, 101, 108, 138–39, 183–84
  relational, 15–16, 100–9
  shame and, 85–86
  virtuous, 104–5
  worthiness and, 100–9
Primitive Baptist church, 94
privilege, 113, 115–16, 134–35, 152–54, 158, 164–65, 168–69, 170
progressives. *See* liberals and progressives
promiscuity, 49–50
pronouns, gender in, 38, 54–55
Protestants, conservative, 187–88. *See also* white evangelical Protestants
psychological frameworks, 186–87
Puar, Jasbir, 190n.8
public policy, 176–78
Puerto Rico, 33, 39
purity culture, xii–xiii, 44–45, 49–50, 148–49, 152

Q Christian Fellowship (QCF), 2–3, 58, 66, 146–47, 170–71. *See also* Gay Christian Network (GCN)
qualitative interviews, 184–86
queer studies, 183
queer theorists of color, 5

race. *See* Black church communities; Black people, Indigenous people, and people of color (BIPOC); multiracial evangelical churches; White Christian Nationalism; whiteness

racism, 1, 5, 135–36, 156, 187
    color-blind responses to, 133–34, 158
    in predominantly white churches, 7, 76–77, 93–94, 112–14
    sexual stigmatization, 39–44, 49–50, 66, 72–73, 193n.30
    shame and, 66
    social justice organizing and, 148–53 (*see also* antiracism)
    See also white supremacy
Reagon, Bernice Johnson, 141
reconciliation, 113–15
recovery, 163, 177. *See also* healing
Reformation Project, The (TRP), viii, 2–3, 12, 65, 97, 129, 135, 183–84
    Academy for Racial Justice, 17–18, 148
    community in, 91–93
    founder of, 85
    Leadership Development Cohort, 1, 9
    leadership in, 188
    on same-sex marriage, 49–51
    tensions in social justice organizing, 147–54
relationships, 17–26
    broken, 14–16, 57, 64–75, 80–82, 106, 163 (*see also* shame)
    definition of, 14
    emotions and, 12–13 (*see also* humility; love; pride; shame)
    facilitated by healthy pride, 104
    fear of, 54–56, 61–63, 103
    importance of, vii–xiii, 4, 14, 21–22, 63–64, 158–59, 162–63, 168, 174–75
    intersectional perspectives on, 6–7
    prioritizing of, 12–13, 14–15, 67–68, 111–12, 136, 166, 170
    relational love *(I-thou)*, viii–xi, 80–82, 186–87
    types of, viii–xi
    violations of, 63–64 (*see also* violence and abuse)
    See also connection; listening to others; love
Religious Right, 29, 57

reparative therapies, 2, 7, 11–12, 17, 31–33, 51–52, 70–71, 77–78, 94–95, 134–35
    toxic shame and, 64, 75–82
repentance, 131, 132
respectability politics, 41–44, 73
Restored Hope Network, 77
Roberts, Bob, 91, 105
Robertson, Brandan, 8, 74–75
Robertson, Linda, 78–82, 128–29, 170–71, 173
Robertson, Pat, 29
Robertson, Rob, 78–82, 128–29
Robertson, Ryan, 78–82, 128–29
Robinson, Allyson, xi–xiii, 60, 145
Robinson, Brandon Andrew, 195n.19
Robinson, Harold, 29–30, 117–18, 125

sacramental shame, 54–82
    broken relationships and, 67–75 (*see also* relationships)
    complementarity doctrine and, 67–68, 75, 77
    definition of, 57
    fear of relationships, 54–56, 61–63, 103
    "loving" forms of ("love the sinner, hate the sin"), 57, 67–68, 75–82
    toxic dynamics of, 3–4, 14–15, 64, 70–72, 75–82, 87, 158–59, 161–62, 163–64 (*see also* self-harm; self-hatred)
    worthiness and, 56, 58, 61, 64–67, 163, 173–74
Sales, Ruby, 172–73
same-sex marriage
    celibacy and, 30–31
    conservative Christian debates on, 49–51, 196n.8
    culture wars and, xi, 29
    legalization of, xi, 29, 145
Scalia, Antonin, 196n.22
secrecy, 31–32, 62, 72
Seitz, David, 12, 159–60
self-acceptance, 100–9
self-harm, 87, 90, 163. *See also* addiction; suicide

INDEX

self-hatred, 54–55, 58–61, 62–63, 95, 100–1, 104–5
Seventh-Day Adventists, 33
sexism, 21–22, 49, 108, 110, 111, 148–49, 163–65
sexual abuse, 25–26, 34, 44–45, 194n.34
  by clergy, xii–xiii, 70
sexuality
  conservative Christian ideas on, 14–15, 27–36 (*see also* complementarity doctrine)
  pleasure and, 34, 51, 66
  racist stereotypes, 39–44, 49–50, 66, 72–73, 193n.30
  stigmatizing women, 44–45
sexual orientation. *See* LGBTQ+ identities
shame, 54–82
  allies and, 163–65
  compared to guilt, 64
  definitions of, 12–13
  gender-based, xii–xiii (*see also* purity culture)
  humility and, 86, 170–71
  intimacy and, 60–61
  love and, 58
  oppression and, 164–65
  pride and, 85–86
  public shaming rituals, 57, 103–4, 163–64
  race and, 54–56, 58
  as social emotion, 56
  social hierarchies and, 64–65
  social justice movements and, 82–83
  See also sacramental shame
Simon, Lianne, 37–38
sin, 7–9, 14–15
  hierarchy of, 29–30, 32–33, 36, 117–18, 130
  homosexuality and trans expression as, 20–21, 29–36, 42–43, 77, 85
  "love the sinner, hate the sin," 57, 67–68, 75–82 (*see also* shame)
  sexual, xii–xiii, 50, 65–66
slavery, 39–40

Smedes, Lewis, 172
Smith, Christian, 113–14
Snorton, C. Riley, 41, 193n.30
social hierarchies, 38–39, 45–47, 153–54
  allyship and, 112
  challenges to, 97–98
  gendered, 36, 45–47, 153–54, 156–57, 194n.34 (*see also* complementarity doctrine)
  as God's will, 156–58, 164, 167
  shame and, 64–65
  See also white supremacy
social justice, 3–4, 113–15, 133, 135–36, 137–60, 186
  conservative approach to, 153–60
  radical politics of love, xi–xiii, 6, 9–11, 13–14, 21, 24–26, 161–63, 174–78
  The Reformation Project and, 148–53
  restorative, 176
  shame and, 82–83
  tensions in organizing, 138–42, 144–54
sociological frameworks, ix–x, 183–87
Sodom, 34–35
solidarity, 135–36, 160. *See also* allies; social justice
Southern Baptists, 31, 33–34, 46–47, 94, 97–98, 99, 100–1, 194n.34
Spade, Dean, 176–77
spiritual trauma, 166
spiritual violence, 52–53, 65, 70–71, 135
Steele, Claude, 195n.16
stereotype threat, 195n.16
storge, 20–21
stress, 62–63
suffering, 54–56, 70–75, 157, 167–68
suicide, 59–60, 62–63, 65, 70, 88
Sullivan-Blum, Constance R., 196n.12
Supreme Court, xi, 29, 145, 196n.22

Taino, 39
Táíwò, Olúfémi, 175–76
Taylor, Barbara Brown, 91
Templeton Religion Trust, 183
Ten Commandments, 33, 36, 48, 63

tension
    productive, 156–60
    in social justice organizing, 138–42, 144–54
theological frameworks, 47–48, 186–87
third gender, 38, 54–55, 97–99
TMF. *See* Marin Foundation, The (TMF)
trans people, 5–6, 10–11, 85, 191n.4
transphobia, 9, 136, 148, 150–51, 163–65. *See also* anti-LGBTQ+ attitudes
trauma, 8, 75, 169
    spiritual, 166
TRP. *See* Reformation Project, The (TRP)
Trump, Donald, 145–46, 153–54, 171
twelve-step groups, 163

uncertainty, 67–68, 98. *See also* humility
unconditional love, 56, 67, 78, 87
unworthiness. *See* worthiness

Vines, Matthew, 50–51, 85, 121–23, 147–53
Vines, Monte, 121–23, 129
violence and abuse, 2, 23, 25–26, 70–72, 75, 163, 167–73, 175–76. *See also* sexual abuse; spiritual violence
virtuous pride, 104–5
vulnerability, 23, 67–68, 100–1, 104, 109, 129, 135, 158–59, 162–63, 170

Washington, Booker T., 172–73
Washington, Shae, 97, 105, 196n.9
wealth, 173–74

"welcoming but not affirming" churches, 30–31, 54–55, 57, 58, 61, 75–76, 93–94, 138–40, 196n.8
Westboro Baptist Church, 28
White Christian Nationalism, 7–8, 45–47, 142, 190n.12, 194n.37
white evangelical Protestants, 187–88
    allyship and race, 112–15
    attitudes on sexual pleasure, 34
    gender and sexual hierarchy and, 45–47
Whitehead, Andrew, 45–46, 47, 142, 190n.12, 194n.34
whiteness, 139, 173–74, 185–86
    centering of, 38–39, 112–15
    decentering of, 187 (*see also* antiracism)
    privilege and, 134–35, 152–54
white supremacy, 38–39, 41, 45–46, 71, 113–14, 152–54, 158, 164–65. *See also* racism
wholeness, 1, 91–93, 104, 107–8, 109, 159, 177
Wisor, Scott, 198n.26
Wolfe, Alan, 198n.8
worthiness
    humility and, 86–88, 90, 91–93, 100–1, 109, 135
    pride and, 100–9
    of relationships and love, 21–22, 64, 91, 158–59, 161–62, 177
    shame and, 56, 58, 61, 64–67, 163, 173–74
    violation and, 63–64